AF737138

Child Justice Administration in Africa

Mariam Adepeju Abdulraheem-Mustapha

Child Justice Administration in Africa

palgrave
macmillan

Mariam Adepeju Abdulraheem-Mustapha
Department of Public Law
Faculty of Law
University of Ilorin
Ilorin, Kwara State, Nigeria

ISBN 978-3-030-19014-9 ISBN 978-3-030-19015-6 (eBook)
https://doi.org/10.1007/978-3-030-19015-6

© The Editor(s) (if applicable) and The Author(s), under exclusive license to Springer Nature Switzerland AG 2020
This work is subject to copyright. All rights are solely and exclusively licensed by the Publisher, whether the whole or part of the material is concerned, specifically the rights of translation, reprinting, reuse of illustrations, recitation, broadcasting, reproduction on microfilms or in any other physical way, and transmission or information storage and retrieval, electronic adaptation, computer software, or by similar or dissimilar methodology now known or hereafter developed.
The use of general descriptive names, registered names, trademarks, service marks, etc. in this publication does not imply, even in the absence of a specific statement, that such names are exempt from the relevant protective laws and regulations and therefore free for general use.
The publisher, the authors and the editors are safe to assume that the advice and information in this book are believed to be true and accurate at the date of publication. Neither the publisher nor the authors or the editors give a warranty, expressed or implied, with respect to the material contained herein or for any errors or omissions that may have been made. The publisher remains neutral with regard to jurisdictional claims in published maps and institutional affiliations.

This Palgrave Macmillan imprint is published by the registered company Springer Nature Switzerland AG
The registered company address is: Gewerbestrasse 11, 6330 Cham, Switzerland

Preface

The motivation for this book arose out of the author's personal experiences in courts and correctional homes where there is an increasing number of child offenders in the Nigerian custodial institutions. The author became very interested with the intricacies of African child justice system in general and the Nigerian child justice system in particular especially the ways it addresses the procedural process of child offenders in the family courts and the inadequacies in the protection of children generally. Indeed, as will be shown in the remaining parts of the book, child justice administration entails much more than scholars acknowledged. This is especially true for the African continent. While quite a lot has been done in this regard in other climes, Africa has unfortunately taken a back seat. All this makes this book not only timely but very significant.

The book comprises seven incisive chapters. The first chapter contains an introduction. This chapter sets the scene for the book in that it contains a brief description of the background, methodology and limitation of the chapter. The next chapter, Chapter 2, considers the concept of child delinquency in the administration of child justice (in Africa). Here, the concept of childhood is analysed before an analysis is carried out of the theories of child delinquency. The chapter focuses on the naturalism, demonology, classical/free-will, biological, psychological and sociological theories. These theories represent the major theories explaining the causes of child delinquency in majority of the literature. Among all these theories, the sociological theory seems to be a recurring explanation. This is the reason why the book focuses on this theory specifically with an explanation of the major causes under the theory. Chapter 2 also considers various preventive mechanisms for child delinquency available. Chapter 3 addresses the nature of child justice administration specifically. The central thesis of the chapter is that a child who has violated criminal laws must undergo a special kind of justice system which fosters the best interest of such a child. In this regard, the history of child justice administration is outlined before the theories of child justice administration are examined. The uniqueness of the child justice administration is discussed from the point of view of the procedural process when a child comes into conflict with the law. The next chapter, Chapter 4, considers the international and regional legal framework of the administration of child justice. In this chapter, the major international instruments on child justice administration are reviewed from an African perspective. Still in the chapter, some analyses are carried out of the African regional instrument. Chapters 5 and 6 analyses the legal and institutional frameworks in child justice administration in Nigeria and South Africa, respectively. From the discussion in the two chapters, a set of themes are put forth in Chapter 7 for reforming the child justice system in Africa and the chapter draws the conclusion of the book and the way forward.

Ilorin, Kwara State, Nigeria — Mariam Adepeju Abdulraheem-Mustapha
2019

Acknowledgements

Let me start by giving special thanks and gratitude to Allah, the Lord of the heavens and the earth and all that is between them, the All-Mighty, the Oft-Forgiving, who gave me the strength, the wisdom and the direction to write this book which has been tasking and energy sapping. All praises and adorations are due to Him. I am indebted to a lot of people in the process leading up to the production of this book. I must commend the spirit of Dr. Ibrahim Imam, Dr. Lukman Abdulrauf and Dr. Azizat O. Amoloye-Adebayo who encouraged me in times of despair. They painstakingly and dexterously proofread the entire manuscripts and, in the process, gave me useful tips. They have been my greatest inspiration, and they kept on telling me that all is not over until it is all over. Thank you for your encouragements and for being there for me. I must also commend the efforts of Dr. Durosinmi, O. Muhideen from Department of English Language, Faculty of Arts, University of Ilorin, Nigeria for painstakingly agreed to read and comment on the entire manuscripts. It was an exciting experience to interact with so many stakeholders of child justice administration during my fieldwork at different parts of Nigeria and South Africa. In the light of experience gathered, I say thank you for your support. I must not forget to express gratitude to the Association of African Universities and the American Council of Learned Society for their awards which have sustained the writing of this book and extending it beyond. I am also indebted to the reviewers for the time and efforts they put into the review process, and also the copy editors and the entire Palgrave Macmillan community especially,

Alina Yurova, my editor and Mary Fata, my editorial assistant who without their support, this book could not have been out within the record time. My family has always been an unshakeable pillar of strength and support throughout the book writing process. To my wonderful son, (Mustapha Bolaji Mustapha), who has always played his supportive role as my child and friend, I pray for his continued spiritual and intellectual growth. Thank you. Finally, my warm and affectionate appreciation goes to my darling husband, Dr. Abdulrafiu Mustapha. Alhamdulillah for bringing us together and for using you as a solid source of my spiritual and intellectual growth.

Contents

Abbreviations

AC	Appeal Cases
ACJA	Administration of Criminal Justice Act
ACRWC	African Charter on the Rights and Welfare of the Child
AMR	All Monthly Report
CCA	Criminal Code Act
CLR	Criminal Law Report
COP	Commissioner of Police
CRA	Child Rights Act
CRC	Convention on the Rights of the Child
CRP	Constitutional Rights Project
CYPA	Children and Young Persons Act
DPP	Director of Public Prosecution
FIR	First Information Report
FSC	Federal Supreme Court
JDLS	United Nations Rules for the Protection of Juveniles Deprived of their Liberty (The United Rules)
LFN	Laws of Federation of Nigeria
NGOs	Non-Governmental Organisations
NHRC	National Human Rights Commission
NMLR	Nigeria Monthly Law Report
NWLR	Nigeria Weekly Law Report
PCA	Penal Code Act
PRI	Penal Reform International
SACSSP	South Africa Council for Social Services Professions
SAIRR	South Africa Institute of Race Relations
SAP	Structural Adjustment Programme

SC	Supreme Court Judgment
SCC	Supreme Court Cases
SPCL	Shariah Penal Code Law
StatsSA	Statistics South Africa
UNBR	United Nations Standard Minimum Rules for the Administration of Juvenile Justice (Beijing Rules)
UNCRC	United Nations Convention on the Rights of the Child
UNRG	United Nations Guidelines for the Prevention of Juvenile Delinquency (The Riyadh Guidelines)
USA	United States of America

Table of Cases

R v. Bangaza 1960 (5) FSC
S v. Mahlangu & Ors CC 70/2010
Arnit Das v. State of Bihar (2000) 5 SCC 488; 2000 SCC (Cri) 962; AIR 2000 SC 2264; 2000 Cri LJ 2971 (SC)
Pratap Singh v. State of Jharkhand
Rajinder Chandra v. State of Chhattisgarh
Umesh Chandra v. State of Rajasthan (1982) 2 SCC 202; 1982 SCC (Cri) 396; AIR 1982 Sc 1057; 1982 Cri LJ 994 (SC)
Gopinath Ghosh v. State of West Bengal (1984) Supp SCC 228; 1984 SCC (Cri) 478; AIR 1984 SC 237; 1984 Cri LJ 168 (SC)
Bhola Bhagat v. State of Bihar (1997) 8 SCC 720, AIR 1998 SC 236
R v. Oladimeji (1984) NMLR (pt. 30) at 17
Modupe v. The State (1988) 4 NWLR (pt. 130) 124
R v. Machambere & Another 1950 (1) SA 315 (SR)
S v. Mavhungu 1988 (3) SA 67 (V)
Joseph Uwa v. The State (1965) I ANLR, 356
S v. M 1967 (1) SA 70 (N) at 71
S v. Reynders 1972 (1) SA 570 (C)
S v. Dial 2006 (1) SACR 395 (E)
S v. Ngoma 1984 (3) SA 666 (A)
S v. Tsankobeb 1981 (4) SA 614 (A)
S v. Swartz 1970 (2) SA 240 (NC)
Jaya Mala v. Home Secretary, Govt. of J & K (1982) 2 SCC 538; 1982 SCC (Cri) 333; AIR 1982 SC 1297; 1982 Cri LJ 1777 (SC)

Bhoop Ram v. State of U.P. (1989) 3 SCC1; 1989 SCC (Cri) 486; AIR 1989 SC 1329; (1989) 2 Crimes 294
SMT. Kamiesh & Anor. v. State of U.P. (2002) Cri LJ 3680 (Allahabad)
Grootboom v. Oostenberg Municipality 2000 (3) BCLR 277(C)
Du Toit v. Minister of Welfare and Population Development (Lesbian and Gay Equality Project as Amicus Curiae) 2003 (2) SA 198 (CC)
South African Human Rights Commission v. President of the Republic of South Africa 2005 (1) SA 580 (CC)
AD v. DW (Centre for Child Law as Amicus Curiae) 2008 (3) SA 183 (CC); *Director of Public Prosecutions, Transvaal v. Minister of Justice and Constitutional Development and Others* 2009 (4) SA 222 (CC)
Governing Body of the Juma Musjid Primary School and Others v. Essay NO and Others (Centre for Child Law and Another as Amicus Curiae) 2011 (8) BCLR 761 (CC) *(hereafter Juma Musjid)*
C and Others v. Department of Health and Social Development, Gauteng, and Others 2012 (2) SA 208 (CC)
Ex parte Crouse 4 Wharton, Pa., 9 (1838)
State v. Pendergrass (1837)
In Re Gault 387 U.S. 1, 42 (1967)
Centre for Child Law v. Minister of Social Development and others. 2011a. (North Gauteng High Court) Case number 21726/11. Order of 10 May 2011, unreported
Centre for Child Law v. Minister of Social Development and others. 2011b. (North Gauteng High Court) Case number 21726/11. Order of 08 June 2011, unreported
In Applications of *Johnnie J.Billie and Leroy Jewelryman*, 429 P.2d699 (Ariz. 1967)
Haley v. Ohio 332 U.S. 596, 599–600 (1948)
In re Winship 397 U.S. 358 (1970)
Roper v. Simmons 543 U.S. 551 (2005)
Johnson v. Zerbst, 304 U.S. 458 (1938)
Carnley v. Cochran, 369 U.S. 506 (1962)
United States ex rel. Brown v. Fay, 242 F. Supp. 273 (D.C.S.D.N.Y.1965)
State ex rel. Juvenile Dept. Linn County v. Anzaldua, 109 Or App 617 (1991)
State v. Twitty, 85 Or App 98, 102 (1987). The Supreme Court held in *U.S. v. Padilla*, 819 F. 2d 952, 956 (10th Cir. 1987)
Von Moltke v. Gillies, 332 U.S. 708, 723–24 (1948)

S v. Gumede (unreported, ECG Case No. CA&R181/2011, 17 November 2011)
Mpofu v. Minister for Justice and Constitutional Development 2013 (2) SACR 407 (CC)
S v. Swato 1977 (3) SA 992 (O)
R v. Machambere & Another 1950 (1) SA 315 (SR)
R v. Botha & Another 1947 (2) SA 1281 (C); *S v. M* 1967 (1) SA 70 (N)
S v. Dumba 2011 (2) SACR 5 (NCK) at 4
S v. Nyathi 1978 (2) SA 20 (B)
R v. Hadebe & Another 1960 (1) SA 488 (T)
R v. Hlongwane 1960 (1) SA 309 (T)
R v. Fana 1960 (4) SA 277 (T)
S v. Sibiya 1964 (2) SA 379 (N)
S v. Butelezi 1964 (3) SA 519 (N)
S v. Manyololo 1969 (4) SA 356 (E)
S v. Tango 1969 (2) SA 648 (C)
S v. Mavundla & Another; S v. Sibisi 1976 (2) SA 162 (N)
S v. Mavhungu 1988 (2) SA 67 (V)
S v. Kumalo 1991 (2) SACR 694 (W); *S v. Dumba* 2011 (2) SACR 5 (NCK)
S v. Thomas 1961 (4) SA 850 (C)
S v. Skenjane 1965 (2) SA 86 (O)
R v. Ndhlovu 1948 (1) SA 289 (O)
R v. Kuwuseb 1949 (1) SA 651 (SWA)
S v. Chiloane; S v. Masango; S v. Mabusa 1977 (4) SA 69 (T)
R v. Kaplan 1942 OPD 232; R v. C 1955 (1) SA 380 (C)
S v. Mbelo 2003 (1) SACR 84 (NC)
S v. EA 2014 (1) SACR 183 (NCK) at 13–14, 16, 19
National Directorate of Public Prosecution v. Puma 2009 (1) SACR 361 (SCA) at 39, 80
S v. Fortuin Unreported NCK Case No. 38/2011, at 13, 64
S v. FM 2013 (1) SACR 57 (GNP)
S v. CS 2012 (1) SACR 595 (ECP) at 13 and 26
S v. LM (Faculty of Law, University of the Western Cape: Children Rights Project of the Community Law Centre & Others as Amici Curiae) 2013 (1) SACR 188 (WCC)
S v. Sekoere 2013 (2) SACR 426 (FB) at 28.2, 30
S v. Z & 23 Similar Cases 2004 (1) 400 (E) 1 at 403f-h

S v. Myaka & Others (unreported, GSJ Case No. A5040/2011, 215/2005, 21 September 2012) at 4
New Clicks South Africa (Pty) Ltd. v. Minister of Health & Another 2005 (3) SA 238 (SCA) at 4–6
S v. Maredi 2000 (1) SACR 611 (T)
S v. Jackson & Others 2008 (2) SACR 274 (C)
Sanderson v. Attorney-General, Eastern Cape 1998 (1) SACR 227 (CC), 1997 (12) BCLR 1075 (CC)
Barker v. Wingo 407 US 514 (1972)
S v. Ndibe (unreported, WCC Case No. 14/544/2010, 14 December 2013) at 6
Director of Public Prosecutions North Gauteng v. Makhubela (unreported, GNP Case No. A91/2014, 6 August 2014) at 19
S v. Khalema and Five Similar Cases 2008 (1) SACR 165 (C) at 26–30
S v. Thenga 2012 (2) SACR 628 (NCK)
S v. Mahlangu & Another GSJ Case No. CC70/2010, 22 May 2012 (unreported)
S v. Ndwandwe KZP Case R 99/12, 6 August 2012 (unreported)
S v. Mgcina 2007 (1) SACR 82 (T)
S v. Bekisi 1992 (1) SACR 39 N (C)
S v. Manuel & Others 1997 (2) SACR 505 (C)
S v. M (Centre for Child Law as Amicus Curiae) 2008 (3) SA 232 (CC) para 25 at 249D
Van Deiji v. Van Deiji 1966 (4) SA 260 (R) at 261H
French v. French 1971 (4) SA 298 (W) 298H
Martens v. Martens 1991 (4) SA 287 (T)
McCall v. MacCall 1994 (3) SA 201(C) 205 B-G
Legal Aid Board in re Four Children (unreported, 512/10 (2011) ZASCA 39, 29 March 2011) para 11
Phillip v. Commissioner of Child Welfare, Bellville 1956 (2) SA 330 (C)
AD and Another v. DW and Others (Centre for Child Las as Amicus Curiae; Department for Social Development as Intervening Party) 2008 (3) SA 183 (CC)
De Gree and Another v. Webb and Others (Centre for Child Law, University of Pretoria as Amicus Curiae) 2006 (6) SA 51 (W)
De Gree and Another v. Webb and Others (Centre for Child Law, University of Pretoria as Amicus Curiae) 2007 (5) SA 185 (SCA)

SS v. Presiding Officer of the Children's Court, Krugersdrop and Another Unreported GSJ Case No. A3056/11, 29 August 2012 para 19
Elizabeth Municipality v. Various Occupiers 2005 (1) SA 217 (CC)
S v. M (Centre for Child Law as Amicus Curiae) 2008 (3) SA 232 (CC)
Dikoko v. Mokhatla 2006 (6) SA 235 (CC)
Case of *Centre for Child Law v. Minister for Social Development and Others* (unreported, GNP Case No. 21726/11)
Johncom Media Investments Ltd. v. M and Others (Media Monitoring Project as Amicus Curiae) 2009 (4) (CC)
S v. Motsasi 1998 (2) SACR 35 (W)
Motsasi en andere 2000 (1) SACR 574 (W)

List of Statutes

African Charter on the Rights and Welfare of the Child (ACRWC) 1990
Borstal Institutions and Remand Centre Act
Child Rights Act (CRA), 2003
Child Justice Act 78 of 2008
Children's Act 35 of 2005
Children and Young Persons Act (CYPA), 1958
Constitution of the Federal Republic of Nigeria 1999
Constitution of the Republic of South Africa 200 of 1993
Constitution of the Republic of South Africa 1996
Criminal Code Act (CCA), 1965
Egyptian Childhood Law 1996
Egyptian Childhood (amendment) Law 2008
Hague Convention
Juvenile Justice Act 2000
Kenyan Children's Act
Kenyan Constitution 2010
Masters and Servants Act 1856
National Integrated Child Rights Policy
Penal Code Act (PCA), 1960
Police Act
Reformatory Institution Act 1879
Rules of Professional Conduct and Legal Practitioners Act
Shariah Penal Code Law, 1999
South Africa Abduction Act 72 of 1996

South Africa Criminal Procedure Act 51 of 1977
South Africa Deserted Wives and Children's Protection Act 7 of 1895
South Africa Cruelty to Animals Act 13 of 1895
South Africa Care of Neglected Children's Act 24 of 1895
South Africa Child Protection Act 38 of 1901
South Africa Natal Act 1901
South Africa Children's Care and Protection Act 25 of 1913
South Africa Children's Charter 1913
South Africa Children's Act 31 of 1937
South Africa Children's Act 33 of 1960
South Africa Child Care Act 74 of 1983
South Africa Magistrates' Act 32 of 1944
South Africa Rules Board for Courts of Law Act 107 of 1985
Ugandan Constitution
Ugandan Children (amendment) Act 2016
United Nations Convention on the Rights of the Child (UNCRC) 1989
United Nations Guidelines for the Prevention of Juvenile Delinquency (The Riyadh Guidelines) 1990
United Nations Rules for the Protection of Juveniles Deprived of their Liberty (United Nations Rules) 1990
United Nations Standard Minimum Rules for the Administration of Juvenile Justice (The Beijing Rules) 1985

CHAPTER 1

Introduction

1 Background

Child justice is a critical aspect of administration of justice in any country. This is no surprise considering the special place of children in a given community. Their vulnerable and special position means that they must be protected by an organised and coherent legal regime. This is true for a child who must come in contact with the administration of justice for a crime in which he or she has committed or participated in. The general philosophy behind child justice administration is that, children being vulnerable persons must undergo a special process when they come into contact with the criminal justice system. Without a doubt, the child justice system in other jurisdictions like Europe and North America has far advanced. The importance of a sui generis child justice administration is only recently being realised in African countries. This is one of the inspirations behind this book. As rightly noted by Odongo that, "The history of child justice systems in Africa is more recent compared to other contexts such as Europe and the USA".[1] It is important to state at the outset that the terms "child", "juvenile" and "young offenders" are interchangeably used in this book to refer to the subject of concern

[1] Godfrey O. Odongo, "Introduction: The History of Juvenile Justice Systems in Africa", in S. H. Decker and N. Marteache (eds.), *International Handbook of Juvenile Justice* (Switzerland: Springer, 2017), 2.

© The Author(s) 2020
M. A. Abdulraheem-Mustapha,
Child Justice Administration in Africa,
https://doi.org/10.1007/978-3-030-19015-6_1

which is children who are "in conflict with the law" or "children that are in need of care and protection" or "children that are beyond parental control".[2]

A child is viewed as a dependent and valuable being that deserves special care.[3] This proposition remains sacrosanct regardless of whether the child is beyond parental control or is in conflict with the law or in need of care and protection. Generally, child justice administration has evolved based on this proposition, hence the noticeable difference in the treatment of child and adult offenders. A global conceptualisation of child was proposed in this book. This was done by investigating the historical evolution of child justice administration and its theoretical perspectives based on the international and regional legal instruments on the protection of the children's rights. It further investigated the pre-colonial era in Nigeria and South Africa which were incidentally colonised by the British. The disposition of the colonialist to the fundamental rights of children which later served as the foundation for all other developmental steps taken towards creating safe and proactive environment for equitable justice is explored. On the other hand, it also argued that particularly in the Nigerian case in its Northern region, the continued effects of colonialism are insurgencies such as the *Boko Haram* against Western influence and ideologies.

One of the uniqueness of this book is the inclusion of a discussion on certain key post-colonial factors/events in the child justice system of African countries. These post-colonial factors are not necessarily positive development. For example, Nigeria's long years of military dictatorship and *Boko Haram* insurgency have some form of impact on the child justice system of the country even today. With regard to South Africa, the long apartheid rule and incessant xenophobic attacks significantly impacted on the child justice system.

[2] Roy, N., Justice Denied: The Treatment of Children in Conflict with the Law (Final Report, Save the Children UK Juvenile Justice Global Review, 2001). Available at http://www.crin.org/docs/save/jjmodern_concepts.pdf-similar. Accessed 14 February 2011.

[3] This assertion has been affirmed by The World Declaration on the Survival and Development of Children thus: "Children of the world are innocent, vulnerable and dependent. They are also curious, active and full of hope. Their time should be one of joy and peace, of playing, learning and growing. Their future should be shaped in harmony and cooperation. Their lives should mature as they broaden their perspectives and gain new experiences".

Comparatively, the book identifies; analyses and assesses the legal and institutional regimes for child justice administration and the dispositions for handling child delinquents generally and within Nigeria and South Africa as case studies respectively of a developing and a transitioning context in Africa. The book evaluates the extent to which the child justice administration in the two countries complies with the international standards. It further analyses the inherent problems and challenges associated with children in the process of criminal justice system. This book takes care of the dearth of materials in these areas of study. Hence, this book shows that children are not only neglected, scholars and practitioners also have no access to materials to use in this area of the law in Africa.

It is pertinent to note that very few studies have been conducted in the area of child offenders although much have been written about victim children and children in need of care and protection. The State machinery keeps this class of offenders in institutions such as prison, Borstal institutions, Government-Approved Schools and Remand homes where outsiders are not allowed to tread, abandon them without adequate attention being paid to their well-being and rehabilitation. Children in these institutions are eventually released to the society ill-equipped to handle challenges of life upon completion of their terms of confinement. It is important to note that this treatment meted out to child offenders is most deplorable, especially when children legislations recognise that children alleged to have committed an offence require special care and protection. The system of child justice has been based on a balance between the need to punish or control young offenders and to encourage them to be accountable for their actions. The system also employs strategies which take account of many problems which may have led to the involvement of children and young persons in crime (otherwise known as welfare-based approach). It also carries out intensive monitoring as an effort to control and limit the opportunities for criminal activity.

Child justice system has evolved over the years from the assumption that children that violated criminal laws should be treated distinctly from adults.[4] However, the major challenges that have continued to besiege

[4]Roberts, Cynthia H., Juvenile Delinquency: Causes and Effect (Yale-Haven Teachers Institute, 1986). Available at http://www.yale.edu/yhnt/curriculum. Accessed 2 May 2012.

the entire criminal justice system are lack of separate and adequate custodial facilities for child offenders in Nigeria[5] unlike South Africa.[6] In addition, the system contends with the serious challenges of poor child justice administration, with a large number of child offenders incarcerated in grimy prison yards and mostly deprived of the salutary impact of reformative and rehabilitative custodial environments.

An examination of the existing materials on child justice administration shows that the sector of child justice has remained a weak area without much priority within the adjudicatory system. Also, lack of separate and specific courts dedicated to child justice in Africa and poor legal representation during prosecution of child offenders most often results in many of them being incarcerated with adults.

Implementation of the existing laws in the child justice system is also another problem. This manifests in the absence of support services to weak families which becomes a major factor in turning their children into delinquency. For example, greater emphasis was laid on institutional organisations as compared to non-institutional services in the Nigerian Children and Young Persons Act 1958.[7] The study has shown that the facilities and services in these institutions in different States of the federation of Nigeria are found to possess no yardstick for standardisation.[8] There is also a dearth of services and programmes for children of special needs. Furthermore, there is no form of measurement of index of performance of institutions in the area of child justice. Therefore, there is no means of ascertaining the quality of performance of these segments of child justice in Nigeria.

Although there are few research materials that establish and provide lines of argument on the legal and institutional frameworks for child justice administration, there are substantial provisions of law (and other strategic initiatives) both at the national and international levels that adequately address the issues across Africa. For example, in Uganda, the Bill of Rights in the Ugandan Constitution makes

[5] See Chapter 5 and field work carried out by the author in this book for detail analysis. See also, Alemika, E. E. O., and Chukwuma, I. C., *Juvenile Justice Administration in Nigeria: Philosophy and Practice* (Lagos: Centre for Law Enforcement Education, 2001), 15.

[6] See Chapter 6 and field work carried out by the author in this book for detail analysis.

[7] See Chapter 5 of this book for detail analysis.

[8] Alemika, E. E. O., and Chukwuma, I. C., *Juvenile Justice Administration in Nigeria: Philosophy and Practice* (Lagos: Centre for Law Enforcement Education, 2001), 16.

unique provision for children's right. Apart from the general rights in the Constitution, there are also specific rights for children. The Ugandan Children (amendment) Act 2016 also reforms child justice administration generally. The Rwandan government has also demonstrated strong commitment towards children's right. Apart from it being a signatory to numerous international conventions with support of its Constitution and other legislation, the government of Rwanda has developed a National Integrated Child Rights Policy. Egypt has also made significant strides in this regard being a signatory to human rights conventions. In addition, Egypt has hosted quite a number of human rights-related dialogues. With regard to domestic legislation, Egypt has enacted a comprehensive Childhood Law in 1996 which was further strengthened by amendments in 2008. For Kenya, the 2010 Constitution of Kenya[9] (Article 53) recognises the need for all children to be protected from abuse, neglect, harmful cultural practices, all forms of violence, inhumane treatment and punishment, and hazardous or exploitative labour.[10] Kenya being a signatory to many conventions on the protection of the right of children, enacted the Children's Act[11] in compliance with international best practices.

In similar manner in Nigeria, efforts have been made to reform laws on the rights of the child in order to comply with the principles contained in the United Nations Convention on the Rights of the Child (CRC) which the country has ratified. But despite the domestication of CRC, the enactment of the Child Rights Act 2003, the Children and Young Persons Act (CYPA) just like the South African Child Justice Act and Children's Act, remain the most important legislations in the countries dealing with the treatment of child offenders. Nigeria is therefore, one of the countries that have opted to include both protection and child justice measures in a single Act, as opposed to the approaches taken in South Africa and other countries.[12] It is instructive to note that child

[9] Article 53.

[10] Chapter Five (5) of the Constitution contains the Bill of Rights, which offers protection for the safeguards of the individual rights and freedoms for every Kenyan. These include the right to association, movement, secure protection of the law, religion and conscience, and the right to life.

[11] Cap 586 Laws of Kenya.

[12] Alemika, E. E. O., and Chukwuma, I. C., *Juvenile Justice Administration in Nigeria: Philosophy and Practice* (Lagos: Centre for Law Enforcement Education, 2001).

justice administration in South Africa has been argued to be the best practice in the world.[13]

Despite years of the enactment of specific laws aimed at dealing with child delinquency in Africa, the situation on the ground has not changed much. Child justice system therefore, calls for a complete overhaul to tackle the sluggish pace of adjudicatory processes and lack of adequate care at custodial institutions. There is clearly a need for greater concern about, and discussion of, the current orientation toward delinquent behaviours, and how it can be ameliorated. There is also the need to empirically examine different options currently in use both in the child and adults' justice system for those described as young adults. It is hoped that this book would be recommended for various child institutions across Africa and will be a beginning of an era of improvement in child justice administration in order to enable Africa, particularly Nigeria and South Africa catch up with the developments in the rest of the world in the field of study.

In summary, as international attention continues to focus on this area, there is a need for countries like Nigeria to conform with the international standards in regard to child justice system and ensure that children are adequately protected.

The distinctive feature of this book is that it represents the first major attempt at making a comparative analysis on child justice administration in Nigeria and South Africa in an empirical way. In particular, most of the materials available in Nigeria were essentially doctrinal in methodology and thus, this effort provides opportunity to have primary access to the challenges confronting the child justice system in Nigeria.

The key findings of this book are that:

i. child justice administration in Africa, Nigeria and South Africa in particular, is not performing creditably well;
ii. existing laws and policies on child custodial institutions in Nigeria are inadequate to engender efficient child justice administration compare to South Africa;

[13]See Hema, Hargovan, 'Child Justice in Practice: The Diversion of Young Offenders'. Available at https://www.researchgate.net. Accessed 22 December 2018. See also, Ngatsha Kankasa, Sindiso, *The Child Justice System and the Rights of the Child in Conflict with the Law: A Case Study of Zambia* (Master of Programme in International Human Rights Law, Faculty of Law, Lund University, Sweden, 2006).

iii. the risk factor of child delinquency is premised on dysfunctional family, low socio-economic background, media violence, drug abuse and peer group pressure;
iv. the rights of a child offender to separate court and trial in privacy are not substantially and adequately observed under the Nigerian child justice administration compared with what is obtainable in South Africa;
v. institutional mechanism for children welfare should be strengthened; and
vi. there is insufficient budgetary allocations for the child justice administration in Africa.

It was concluded in this book that child justice administration is facing serious challenges. The book therefore, recommends the need for the enlightenment of parents and guardians on the dangers inherent in child delinquency and proposed re-orientation of the law enforcement agencies on matters affecting child offenders. In compliance with the Child Rights Act 2003, child/juvenile special units and separate courts should be established in the Police force and judiciary. The book further recommends the amendment of the Child Rights Act and the need to apply it in all States of the federation for effective protection of child offenders. This is important in view of the South African child justice regime which represents a universal application. Establishment of more Borstal training institutions, rehabilitation of government-approved schools and remand homes were all recommended. Also, punishment of child offenders should focus attention on rehabilitation and reformation objectives by committing them to children corrective institutions. Finally, government should provide adequate fund to achieve effective child justice administration in Nigeria.

The book contributes to knowledge in the following areas:

i. First, the findings have shown that; child justice administration is not performing creditably well to address child delinquency in most parts of Africa. This has been the existing situation which had hardly changed especially in Nigeria.
ii. Second, the book makes a significant contribution to the area of legal history and methodology of its research on the issue of child justice administration. Traditionally in Nigeria, legal research is conducted by examining provisions of the law contained in the legal

sources in an attempt to understand the inadequacies in the law. This is done without examining the socio-legal effects of such laws on affected individuals. This book therefore, constitutes a departure and as such enriched legal literature by contributing to socio-legal studies in Nigeria on the subject of child offenders generally.

iii. Finally, the book further contributes to existing knowledge by emphasising the imperativeness of the adoption of empirical research methodology in the study of legal problems.

2 Methodology

Two major methods of legal research are basically adopted for the purpose of this book. These are the doctrinal and non-doctrinal methods of research.

2.1 The Doctrinal Method

The doctrinal method is also qualitative in nature, and this involved the reliance on materials in the libraries and other existing databases. These materials comprise primary and secondary sources of information. With regard to the primary sources, these include; international instruments on child justice such as United Nations Convention on the Right of the Child, the Beijing Rules and Riyadh Guidelines. Also relevant to this book is the provisions of the African Charter on the Rights and Welfare of the Child. The book therefore, makes use of domestic instruments as part of the primary sources. In this regard, the legislation on child justice in certain African countries especially Nigeria and South Africa was consulted. The legislation, for Nigeria, includes the Constitution of the Federal Republic of Nigeria, 1999; the Nigerian Children and Young Persons Act, 1958; and the Child Rights Act, 2003, the Police Act, Prison Act, Penal and Criminal Codes, 2004; Criminal Procedure Code, 2004 and the Criminal Procedure Act, 2004. For South Africa, the 1996 Constitution, the Child Justice Act 75 of 2008 and the Children's Act 35 of 2005 have been very useful primary sources. In both countries, judicial decisions were very critical primary sources for the analysis in this book. For example, the Nigerian and South African cases of *R v. Bangaza*[14] and *S v. Mahlangu & Ors*[15] respectively, form an interesting

[14] 1960 (5) FSC.
[15] CC 70/2010.

focus point on the debate with regard to the age of a child for the purpose of this book.

Secondary sources were also widely used in this book as part of the doctrinal research. Indeed, this is obvious considering the fact that there is a lot of scholarship on various aspects of child justice. Secondary sources also present the current state of the primary sources and the legal regime in general. From this perspective, text books and journal articles from African authors were heavily relied upon. This is also true for reports manuals, documents obtained from seminars, training workshops, conferences and materials downloaded from the internet. Others were case laws, law reports, research reports, theses, dissertations, reports of judicial and investigative panels, reports by human rights and other Non-Governmental Organisations. Also, newspapers and magazines, and other internet-based resources were sourced and studied for review and critical analyses in addressing the focus of this book.

As much as the book adopts a doctrinal method, it is analytical in form. A careful analysis is carried out of the extant legal regime on child justice. This is done so as to bring out the flaws of the regime in order to make appropriate reforms. The book is therefore, not merely descriptive but critically analytical in form and content.

2.2 The Non-doctrinal Method

The non-doctrinal method on the other hand, is generally used among social scientists to conduct researches using empirical techniques like interviews, questionnaires, observation, experimental designs and statistical analysis.[16] The non-doctrinal method adopted in this book was a descriptive survey[17] through quantitative and qualitative methods to collect data directly from the Police and Prisons, Judiciary, Welfare officers, remand homes, Legislatures, Legal Practitioners, Parents, Non-Governmental Organisations and Community leaders in Nigeria.[18] The cities in which the sampling was drawn in Nigeria include Bauchi, Enugu, Ilorin, Kaduna, Lagos and Port Harcourt. The criterion for the selection was based on the six geopolitical zones of the country excluding Federal Capital Territory,

[16] Alemika, E. I., *Law and the Rights of Suspects in Nigeria*. Unpublished (Ph.D. Law and Diplomacy University of Jos, Jos Nigeria, 2010).

[17] See Appendix B for the research survey.

[18] These are the target population from Nigerian perspective.

Abuja, and the states were selected due to the fact that they were cosmopolitan and industrial cities compared to other states in each of the zones. Significantly, the rate of child delinquency in these cities is likely to be higher within the geographical zones. The selection of the sample from which the data of this book were drawn was through multi-stage purposive sampling techniques. Purposive sampling technique was adopted primarily because of the non-availability of a sampling frame for the target population. The target population was randomly selected, and a total of 1500 respondents (250 in each of the cities) were selected from the above listed target population. All the agencies dealing with child justice system were chosen because the author wanted representation from all the stakeholders in order to increase the authenticity of the study. Thus, since the child justice administration forms a species of the criminal justice and relatively small, simple random sampling was employed (200 respondents at the average of 40 for each agency of the police, prison, judiciary, delinquents' officer and legal practitioners). In the realm of other stakeholders which comprises of NGOs, community leaders and parents, a total number of 50 respondents were sampled from each city of the geographical zones.

In the process of analysis, 242 respondents did not return their questionnaires, leaving the study with 1258 respondents. Information derived through the questionnaires and interview was analysed to determine the adequacy or inadequacy of the framework for child justice administration in Nigeria.

For South Africa, the empirical method was in the form of interview to specific class of persons. A structured interview was carried out on relevant stakeholders in the bench and bar. These include magistrates, correctional service officers, attorneys, scholars and some NGOs. The interview was carried out by the author in 2014 and 2015 at Pretoria in the Gauteng Province, Cape Town, Western Cape Province and Grahamstown in the Eastern Province. These areas appear to cover the major part of South Africa. To support the findings of the interviews, the reports from the Statistics South Africa (StatsSA) and the Department, Justice and Constitutional Development in South Africa were relied upon.

3 Limitation

The concept of criminal justice administration is very wide in scope such that it is not possible to address issues, problems and challenges associated with it in a single book like this. The book also acknowledges the complexity of child justice administration which cannot be limited to situations where conflict with the criminal law has arisen. Due to this vacuum, this book focuses on child justice in Africa. Even in this respect, two African countries are selected and used as case studies. They are Nigeria and South Africa. A number of reasons influence the choice of both countries chiefly among which is the level of accessibility to the research. With regard to Nigeria, being a Nigerian citizen who lives in Nigeria, obtaining resources by the author was made easy. With regard to South Africa, the author was able to access funds which enabled a research visit and a consequent field research in South Africa. Other reasons behind the selection of both countries are the argument that they are former colonies of Britain and members of the Commonwealth of Nations and their criminal justice systems have been deeply influenced by the British colonialism and its legacies. More importantly, the two countries' systems of child justice represent two of the most prominent and politically important nations in Africa.

The book relies on information from the stakeholders on child justice administration through questionnaire[19] and direct interview methods. The scope of this book is limited to the sampled cities of Bauchi in the North-East, Enugu in the South-East, Ilorin in the North-Central, Kaduna in the North-West, Lagos in the South-West and Port Harcourt in the South-South geo-political zones of Nigeria. An interview was carried out by the author in South Africa in 2014 and 2015 at Pretoria in the Gauteng Province, Cape Town in the Western Cape Province and Grahamstown in the Eastern Province.

In order to attain the cardinal goal, some selected destinations in both Nigeria and South Africa were used as the study areas. These include the police, prisons, judiciary, delinquent homes, legal practitioners, and State Houses of Assembly. The choice of these areas in the metropolis was based on the consideration that they are the stakeholders that are required in the administration of child justice. First, the child may be arrested or summoned by police or welfare/social officers. Second, a child offender may be taken to court for prosecution depending on the nature of the offence committed; third, a child may be committed to prison or remand homes or Borstal institutions or alternative care or community service; fourth, it is trite for the child to be legally represented in court in any proceeding; fifth, Child Rights Laws were legislated by the State Houses of Assembly or parliament; and sixth, parents, NGOs and community leaders participate in solving child delinquency.

[19] See Appendix B of this book.

The book analysed child justice administration primarily from the South African and Nigerian perspectives in order to identify the problems and challenges of child justice system in Nigeria and South Africa. A preference could have been to cover other cities in the Federation of Nigeria and South Africa; this however, could not be done due to finance and time limitations. Particularly, reference was made to the international child justice system and the historical antecedent of child justice administration which is mostly from a foreign perspective. This is to enable the book to juxtapose the two worlds of juveniles without jeopardising the primary focus of the book.

References

Alemika, E. E. O., and Chukwuma, I. C., *Juvenile Justice Administration in Nigeria: Philosophy and Practice* (Centre for Law Enforcement Education, Lagos, 2001), 15.

Alemika, E. I., *Law and the Rights of Suspects in Nigeria*. (Unpublished, Ph.D. Law and Diplomacy University of Jos, Jos Nigeria, 2010).

Godfrey O. Odongo, "Introduction: The History of Juvenile Justice Systems in Africa," in S. H. Decker and N. Marteache (eds.), *International Handbook of Juvenile Justice* (Springer, Switzerland, 2017), 2.

Hema, Hargovan, Child Justice in Practice: The Diversion of Young Offenders. Available at https://www.researchgate.net. Accessed 22 December 2018.

Ngatsha Kankasa, Sindiso, *The Child Justice System and the Rights of the Child in Conflict with the Law: A Case Study of Zambia*. (Unpublished, Master of Programme in International Human Rights Law, Faculty of Law, Lund University, Sweden, 2006).

Roberts, Cynthia H., *Juvenile Delinquency: Causes and Effect* (Yale-Haven Teachers Institute, 1986).

Roy, N., Justice Denied: The Treatment of Children in Conflict with the Law (Final Report, Save the Children UK Juvenile Justice Global Review, 2001). Available at http://www.crin.org/docs/save/jjmodern_concepts.pdf-similar. Accessed 14 February 2011.

CHAPTER 2

Understanding the Concept of Child Delinquency in the Administration of Child Justice

1 Introduction

Children, due to mental immaturity, emotional instability, tender and vulnerable age, weak physique, proneness to vices and violence and inability to look after themselves, require special care, protection, treatment and kind handling geared to shape their personalities into socially—acceptable persons. The rights of children demand well-oriented and guarded protection exploitation that may occur through moral and material abandonment. Parents, society and the State are bound to ensure observance of the rights of all children. Child justice administration in the modern context organises efforts to prevent and treat child social maladjustment in keeping with the interests and rights of children. This book argues that child justice administration covers not only the children coming in conflict with the law but also those likely to drift into criminogenic culture because of various situational compulsions. Child justice administration as an important component of social and distributive justice has concern itself with the well-being and welfare of all children including those that are beyond parental control or in need of care and protection.

Importantly in some cases, a child may engage in serious crime, such as robbery, murder, housebreaking, drug trafficking and rape. However, because of the special procedure for the treatment of children, laws

© The Author(s) 2020
M. A. Abdulraheem-Mustapha,
Child Justice Administration in Africa,
https://doi.org/10.1007/978-3-030-19015-6_2

dealing with this class of offender are somewhat problematic.[1] It is therefore observed that exposure of children to formal criminal processes especially in the case of capital offences may have a negative effect on subsequent attempts at their reformation, rehabilitation and reintegration into the society.

More importantly, a child under the age of eighteen years who gets himself or herself into trouble with the law may ordinarily have his/her case heard in the children's court, but this is not always the case. It is important to note that the idea of child justice system is as old as antiquity.[2] Therefore, when considering the problem of youth crime in the early twentieth century, one is met with discourse of "clamping down" on young persons' crime, of "Zero tolerance", and of "anti–social behaviour". Yet, criminologists and advocates within child justice administration have attacked this punitive philosophy.[3]

This chapter seeks to examine the theoretical underpinnings of the concept of child justice in Africa. After the introduction, the next part starts with an analysis of the concept of childhood. It looks at the age of a child that falls within the child justice system for responsibility. It also examines the procedure in determining the age of the child. The third section looks at the causes of child delinquency and the preventive mechanisms for child delinquency. The fourth part considers different theories on child delinquency with more examination on the causes of child delinquency and the sociological theory in the fifth part. The chapter posits that sociological theory is usually applied so as to substantiate the restoration view of justice.[4] Therefore, if environment and relationship

[1] Ordinarily, in Nigeria and South Africa, courts are prohibited from trying child offenders in public or open court with the public in attendance irrespective of the crime allegedly committed. But on the contrary, a child offender who committed a crime with an adult is usually tried in the public.

[2] Alemika, E. E. O., and Chukwuma, I. C., *Juvenile Justice Administration in Nigeria: Philosophy and Practice*, 15.

[3] See Goldson, B., *The New Youth Justice* (Lyme Regis, 2000), 309; Goldson, B., and Muncie J., *Youth, Crime and Justice: Critical Issues* (London, 2006), 202; and Garlard, D., *The Culture of Control: Crime and Social Order in Contemporary Society* (London: Oxford, 2002) in Bradley, Kate, *Juvenile Delinquency and the Evolution of the British Juvenile Courts, c. 1900–1950*. Available at http://www.history.ac.uk/ihr/Focus/welfare/articles/bradleyk.html. Accessed on 30 May 2011.

[4] Adolphe Quetelet and Andre Michel Guerry were among the first scholars to repudiate the classical free-will doctrine from their working independently on the relation of

between individuals control people's behaviours then, it follows that improvement of the quality of their social environment will change their behaviours in a positive way.

2 The Concept of Childhood

The most important criterion in any discussion on child justice administration is the question of when a person can be properly called a child/juvenile and when that child status terminates. However, there is no universally acceptable definition of a child or juvenile, because the meaning of a child depends on the respective legal system and based on the social, economic, political and cultural setting of the respective country. This assertion is evidenced from the laws of different nations where different age brackets are stipulated to describe a child/juvenile. Besides, the concept of a child is sometimes used interchangeably with other concepts like a "minor", "adolescent" and "youth". The local legislations of all nations lay down minimum age for which a person is exempted from prosecution and punishment. The reason behind such exemption is the absence of *mens rea*, that is, "not to criminalise the acts of those who at the time of commission of the crime did not know the right from the wrong".[5] The basis for this proposition is that "persons below the age of criminal responsibility may not realise nor intend the consequences of their acts". For instance, Article 40(3)(a) of CRC provides that:

> State Parties shall seek to promote the establishment of laws, procedures, authorities and institutions specifically applicable to children alleged as, accused of, or recognised as having infringed the penal law, and in particular:
> (a) The establishment of a minimum age below which children shall be presumed not to have the capacity to infringe the penal law.

crime statistics to such factors as poverty, sex, race, age and climate to mention just but few, concluded that society and not the decisions of individual offenders were responsible for criminal behaviour. See Quetelet, *A Treatise on Man*, 103. See also, Cheatwood, Derral, 'Is There a Season for Homicide?' (1988), *Criminology*, 26, 287–306. Quoted in Freda, Adler, Gerhard, O. W. Mueller, and Williams, S. Laufer, *Criminology and the Criminal Justice System*. Ibid.

[5] Doherty, O., *Criminal Procedure in Nigeria* (Lagos: Blackstone Press, 1990), 57. See also Smith, J. C., and Hogan, B., *Criminal Law* (London: Butterworth, 1983), 98.

However, pursuance to CRC's provision advising States parties to adopt minimum age for determination of child culpability, the argument is that, before the review of the provisions of CRC, there is no clear international standard[6] regarding the minimum age at which criminal responsibility can be imputed on a child. Consequently to the review and in compliance with international standard, South Africa cabinet met on "17th February, 2016" and approved the report submitted to the house on the increase of the minimum age for child criminal liability to 12 years and putting in place some form of special protection measures for children under the age of 13 and 14 years.[7] In Nigeria however, there is no uniform minimum age as the country still maintains its staggering age limit for child criminal culpability. For instance, under the Nigerian law, a child is either a person "under fourteen years of age or who falls within fourteen and seventeen years of age".[8] A juvenile/child is also by inference described as "a person not having attained the age of eighteen years".[9] Under the Shari'ah (Islamic) legal system, the age of criminal responsibility is normally established either by "puberty" or if the "person has reached the age of eighteen years", except in the "adultery" or "fornication" (*Zina*) where the age of criminal responsibility is "fifteen years".[10] The position of the majority of the Islamic jurists[11] on legal capacity is that it is dependent on the "capacity of the human being

[6] See Appendix A to this study.

[7] See South African Press Report dated 22 February 2016.

[8] See Section 2 of Children and Young Persons Law, Cap C10 Laws of Lagos State 2004. Section 2(k) of the Juvenile Justice Act 2000 defined a juvenile or child to mean a person who has not completed the eighteenth year of age. A boy or girl under 18 years of age is a juvenile or child. In the United Nations Standard Minimum Rules for the Administration of Juvenile Justice (The Beijing Rules), the age definition of a juvenile is made dependent on each respective legal system so as to accommodate the different economic, social, political, cultural and legal systems of member states. See Appendix A, Beijing Rules 2.2(a).

[9] Section 35(1)(d) 1999 Constitution.

[10] See Sections 5(b) and 7(1) of Shari'ah Court Laws of Zamfara State which provides that the Courts shall have jurisdiction in criminal proceedings under Islamic law involving or relating to any offence, penalty or forfeiture, punishment or other liability in respect of an offence committed by any person. See Integrated Regional Information Networks (IRIN), Nigeria: Focus on the Administration of Juvenile Justice, 26 August 2002. Available at http://www.irinnews.org/report.asp?ReportID=29531. Accessed on 7 February 2010.

[11] See Imran, *Islamic Jurisprudence*, 111.

to issue statements and perform acts to which the Lawgiver has assigned certain effects".[12] They opined that the basis of the capacity for execution is "*aql*"[13] (intellect) and, the Lawgiver has associated it with "puberty".[14] Therefore, a child does not possess a complete capacity for execution until he or she attains the age of "legal puberty", and he or she cannot be held "criminally liable" but he or she may be "subjected to discipline".[15]

Determining the true age of an arrested suspect is always a challenge for law enforcement agents whenever there is controversy as to whether he/she is an adult or a child. The material factor to be taken into consideration is the age of the child in order to be availed of the benefit of the provision of the law. As such, the question often arises as to the reckoning of age of the child. Some of the courts have held that the reckoning date of a child offender is the "date of production before the court" while others held that it is the "date of an offence".[16] But this controversy has been resolved in *Pratap Singh v. State of Jharkhand*,[17] where it was held that, "the reckoning date for the determination of the age of the child is the date of an offence and not the date when he is produced

[12] Sadr al-Shari'ah, Al-Tawdih, Vol. 2, p. 755, cited in Imran, *Islamic Jurisprudence*, 111.

[13] Aql implies the full development of the mental faculty.

[14] In the view of the Islamic jurists, puberty is associated with the external standard of puberty, that is, the physical signs indicating the attainment of puberty are the commencement of ejaculation in a male and menstruation in a female. And in the absence of these signs, puberty is presumed at the age of fifteen in both males and females. But according to minority jurists like Abu Hanifah, puberty is presumed at the age of eighteen for males and seventeen for females. See Imran, *Islamic Jurisprudence*, 113.

[15] Ibid.

[16] For example, in *R v. Bangaza* (1960) 5 F.S.C., the then Federal Supreme Court was faced with the problem of interpreting the provisions of Section 319(2) of the Criminal Code, 1954 wherein the Court applied the literal rule of interpretation to the extreme by interpreting the provisions to mean that age of liability is the age of conviction and not the age of commission. In this case, the accused person who was charged for murder was given capital punishment even though the accused person committed the crime before he attained the age of majority.

[17] AIR 2005 Sc 2731 (2005) 1 Crimes 286 (SC), 2005 All MR (Cri) 2258 (SC); 2005 Cr LJ 3091; 2005 AIR SCW 3088. The above case was differentiated from *Arnit Das v. State of Bihar* (2000) 5 SCC 488; 2000 SCC (Cri) 962; AIR 2000 SC 2264; 2000 Cri LJ 2971 (SC) where the Supreme Court observed that: "the relevant date at which juvenility was to be determined was the date on which the juvenile was produced before the competent authority". However, the Supreme Court hold in the case of Umesh Chandra v. State of Rajasthan (1982) 2 SCC 202; 1982 SCC (Cri) 396; AIR 1982 Sc 1057; 1982 Cri LJ

before the authority or in court". Also, in *Rajinder Chandra v. State of Chhattisgarh*,[18] the court held that, "where two views are possible about the age in borderline cases, a view which is in favour of holding the accused to be juvenile should be adopted and hyper-technical approach should be avoided". From the Nigerian perspective, the problem of determining the age of a child is also addressed under the "Children and Young Persons' Law of Lagos State"[19] that, "where the age of a suspect is in issue, he is to be taken to court" for inquiry, and the court may take such "evidence as may be forthcoming including the production of birth certificate" or a "certificate signed by a government medical officer". Any determination of age thereafter shall be deemed to be the true age

994 (SC) that: "As regards the general applicability of the act, we are clearly of the view that the relevant date is the date on which the offence takes place". The rationale for the enactment of the Children Act was "to protect young children from the consequences of their criminal acts on the footing that their mind at that age could not be said to be mature for imputing *mens rea* as in the case of an adult". The intendment of this Act shows that a clear finding must be recorded with regard to the relevant date for applicability of the Act to be "the date on which the offence takes place…" we are clearly of the view that the relevant date for applicability of the Act so far as age of the accused, who claims to be a child, is concerned, is "the date of the occurrence and not the date of the trial".

[18]2002 All MR (Cri) 713 (SC), AIR 2002 SC 748, 2002 Cr LJ 1014, 2002 AIR SCW 385.

[19]See Section 32, Children and Young Persons Law, Cap C10 Laws of Lagos State 2004. In *Gopinath Ghosh v. State of West Bengal* (1984) Supp SCC 228; 1984 SCC (Cri) 478; AIR 1984 SC 237; 1984 Cri LJ 168 (SC), the Apex Court "instructed Magistrates to conduct an inquiry about age when it appeared that the accused was under 21 years of age". The court holds that: "it is the responsibility of the Magistrate Court "to take measures to determine the age of the accused". The Criminal Manual A. K. Gupte and S. D. Dighe Hind Law House, 2001 is in tandem with the decision of the Apex Court. For instance, page 149 in Chapter VI of the Fifth edition issued by the High Court of Judicature (Appellate Side) Bombay for the guidance of the criminal courts, and their subordinate officers states that: "All Courts should, whenever a youthful offender or a party is produced before them, take steps to ascertain his age. If the age given by the police does not appear to be correct from the appearance of the offender or party, and if the police cannot produce satisfactory evidence regarding the age, the court should consider the desirability of sending the offender or party to the Medical Officer for the verification of his age before proceeding with the case…". It was stated further that "at the time of the examination of the accused, the Sessions Judge or Magistrate should therefore, specifically ask such accused person his or her age for the purpose of recording it…". "If the Session Judge or Magistrate suspects that the age stated by the accused, having regard to his or her general appearance or some other reason, has not been correctly stated then, the Session Judge or Magistrate should make a note of his estimate". In the same vein, "the Court may also, when it so deems fit

of the person. The Supreme Court underscored the importance of age in the criminal justice system in the case of *R v. Oladimeji*[20] *and* similar position was upheld in *Modupe v. The State*[21] when the court said that:

> the provisions of Section 368(3) of the Criminal Procedure Act indicate that, if the evidence on record points to the fact that at the time the offence was committed, an accused who is charged with capital offence has not attained the age of 17 years, it will be erroneous of the judge to sentence him to death, not even to talk of pronouncing such sentence. If the trial judge felt that the accused reduce his age rather low, the Supreme Court further held that the trial court is free to adjourn the matter and call for a medical witness to give a testimony as to the exact age of the accused.[22]

Instead of adopting a unified age for criminal liability, various age brackets have been adopted in Nigeria which liability may or may not be assigned depending on the circumstances of the offence. Thus, in Nigeria, there are four main classifications of people as follows: "infants", "children", "young person" and "adults".[23] A child who is lower than 7 years of age is not responsible criminally for any wrong.[24] A child who

or proper, order a medical examination of the accused for the purpose of ascertaining his correct age and if any documentary evidence on the point of age is readily available, the prosecution may be ask to produce it". Quoted from Adenwalla, Ms. Maharukh, 'Child Protection and Juvenile Justice System: For Juvenile in Conflict with the Law'. Available at www.childlineindia.org.in/pdf/cp-JJ-JCL.pdf-similar. Accessed on 22 February 2011. See also, *Bhola Bhagat v. State of Bihar* (1997) 8 SCC 720, AIR 1998 SC 236.

[20](1984) NMLR (pt. 30) at 17.

[21](1988) 4 NWLR (pt. 130) 124.

[22]Morenike, Francis, 'Juvenile Justice in Nigeria: Dilemma of a Criminal Justice System'. Available at https://www.jjn/html. Accessed on 25 November 2008.

[23]See Section 2 of the Criminal Procedure Act Cap C41 Laws of the Federation, 2004 and Section 30 of the Criminal Code, Cap C38 Laws of the Federation, 2004. See Section 2 of the Criminal Procedure Act and Section 2 of the Children and Young Persons Act. See generally Section 29 of Juveniles Act which provides thus: (1) it shall be conclusively presumed that no child under the age of ten years can be guilty of any offence; (2) a person of or over the age of ten and under the age of twelve years is not criminally responsible for an act or omission, unless it is proved that at the time of doing the act or making the omission he had capacity to know that he ought not to do the act or make the omission; and (3) a male person under the age of twelve years is presumed to be incapable of having carnal knowledge.

[24]Ibid.

falls between the ages of 7–12 years will not be ordinarily held responsible for his or her actions unless it can "be proved that at the time of committing the offence, he or she had the capacity to know that he or she ought not to do it".[25] A male child below 12 years of age cannot have sexual intercourse and therefore cannot be held responsible for any offence in that regard.[26] A child who is "above 12 years of age is criminally liable for his actions; however such a child remains subject to criminal proceedings in a Juvenile/Family court until he/she attains eighteen years".

The problem with the age-based definition is that it is always arbitrarily applied and indeed it risks the possibility of being rendered obsolete by modern perceptions and findings on children as a study has shown.[27] The study shows that:

> 48.2% of parents questioned responded that any person under 20 years of age is a child, while a significant 14.3% felt that anyone under 30 years of age is a child. But 63.1% of parents felt that anyone who is dependent on parents or cannot care for himself or herself remains a child, irrespective of the age.

The above findings show that the perception of the people is at variance with the age-based definition of the Children and Young Persons Act.[28] Besides, there is a peculiar problem in the determination of age in a predominantly illiterate community. For instance, the Supreme Court in *Joseph Uwa v. The State*[29] took into consideration the fact that "when an Ibo villager says that he is thirteen years old, it does not necessarily mean that he is thirteen years old as one would expect". The court accepted

[25] Ibid.

[26] See generally Section 29 of Juveniles Act which provides thus: (1) it shall be conclusively presumed that no child under the age of ten years can be guilty of any offence; (2) a person of or over the age of ten and under the age of twelve years is not criminally responsible for an act or omission, unless it is proved that at the time of doing the act or making the omission he had capacity to know that he ought not to do the act or make the omission; and (3) a male person under the age of twelve years is presumed to be incapable of having carnal knowledge.

[27] See generally, Ayua, A. A., and Okagbue, I. E, *The Rights of the Child in Nigeria* (Lagos: Nigerian Institute of Advanced Legal Studies, 1996), 15.

[28] Ibid., at 31.

[29] (1965) I ANLR, 356.

the fact that "200 villagers reckon their ages by certain festivals and that the result may well be that an Ibo boy who says he is thirteen may only actually be twelve".[30]

A similar controversy over the issue of age for criminal responsibility arose in the celebrated case of the 12 children sentenced to death for armed robbery by the Robbery and Firearms Tribunal headed by Justice Moshood Olugbani in 1988.[31] Although the prosecution insisted that all the suspects except one were above seventeen, the suspects maintained that they were below the age of seventeen years. Their families also asserted the point. At any rate, even the suspect whom the prosecution conceded was not up to 17 years of age at the time of the alleged offence was given death penalty along with the rest convicts, thus lending credence to the view that the prosecution had arbitrarily assigned ages to the suspects in order to facilitate their prosecution.[32] The Children and Young Persons Law also provides that "a court's judgment shall not be negated by any subsequent proof that the age as presumed or declared by the court was not the correct age".

In view of these realities, some scholars and human rights advocates have argued that the provisions of the law concerning the age of suspects do not adequately protect young persons and should be amended. It has been suggested for instance that there should be a more scientific and empirical way of ascertaining the age of a suspect and where a mistake as to the age of the suspect is made and discovered later, the judgment should be reversed and where damage has been suffered, compensation ought to be made.[33] Prompt identification of persons less than 18 years of age is necessary to ensure that no irreparable damage is caused to them, and that they are not punished for acts done at an age when legislation intends them to be treated differently from adults.

Contrary to what is obtainable in Nigeria, the burden of proof by the State in the determination of criminal responsibility in South Africa is not a task which is exclusively for a probation officer. The court is permitted to request additional information. In this regard, the provision of

[30] Okonkwo, C. O., Nwankwo, Clement, and Ibhawoh, Bonny, *Administration of Juvenile Justice in Nigeria* (1st ed.; Lagos: Constitutional Rights Project (CRP), 1997), 6.

[31] Ibid., 7. See, CLO, Annual Report on Human Rights in Nigeria, 1990.

[32] Ibid.

[33] Ibid., at 6–7.

Section 11(3) of the Child Justice Act, 2008 provides to the effect that "the inquiry magistrate may order a report by a qualified person, which must include an assessment of the cognitive, moral, emotional, psychological and social development of the child". Therefore, in accordance with the South African Children's Act, "three stages are involved in the determination of the age of criminal liability of a child" thus:

> In the first instance, where the police is uncertain as to the age of a child suspect, the law stipulated that the suspect be treated like a child pending the determination of his actual age by a probation officer or medical expert.[34] The second procedure demands that a probation officer makes an estimation of the child age at the time of the commission of the offence. This estimation is usually carried out at the stage of assessment of a child. Probation uses information such as previous determination by a magistrate, statement made by the parent or the child, school registration form or medical expert estimation.[35] The third stage occurs at determination by inquiry Magistrate or child justice court where document submitted by probation officer pursuance to section 13(3) of the Act is considered, request for document information or statement from any person, subpoena a person to produce the documentation.[36]

In the same vein, the decision of the South African reviewing court in the case of *S v. M*[37] is apposite where considering Section 337 of the South African Criminal Procedure Act 51 of 1977, that "it is essential for the district surgeon (medical practitioner) to be called as a witness and for him to be questioned as to the basis of his own estimate of the complainant's age and the possible margin of error".[38] Plasket, J. in *S v. Dial*[39] opined that "in the absence of unequivocal documentary

[34] See Section 12(a-b), Children's Act, 2005 as amended.

[35] See Section 13(1)(a-e), ibid., see also Section 5 of the Child Justice Act 2008 as amended.

[36] See Section 14(1), Child Justice Act.

[37] 1967 (1) SA 70 (N) at 71. See details of the provision of Section 337 of the South Africa Criminal Procedure Act, 51 of 1977 at Chapter 6 of this book.

[38] Case of *R v. Machambere & Another* 1950 (1) SA 315 (SR) is apposite to the above decision where it was held that "the opinion of a medical practitioner must be given under oath and must be subjected to cross-examination". See also, *S v. Reynders* 1972 (1) SA 570 (C).

[39] 2006 (1) SACR 395 (E).

evidence, magistrates should obtain a report from a district surgeon regarding the probable age of a young person or if there is none, by referring the accused to a nearest surgeon or State hospital". Also, the case of *S v. Ngoma*[40] further explicates the above position when it was held by the court that any evidence that can assist the court such as "expert evidence, a birth certificate, and testimony by the parents of the child or of family or other persons knowing the accused" can be considered. By Section 9(1) of the South Africa Birth and Death Registration Act 51 of 1992, "a child born alive must within 30 days after the birth registered". And Sections 3 and 15 of the Identification Act 68 of 1977 further authenticate the above position by allowing a child of 16 years of age to approach any appropriate authority for an identity card. These provisions also provide "*prima facie*" evidence to be used by the presiding judge for the purpose of determination of age.[41] To buttress this position is another case of *S v. Tsankobeb*[42] where the court held that "where there was medical evidence that the accused was 'plus minus' 20 years old, this was *prima facie* evidence by a competent person and the trial court had no power to estimate age as there was no suggestion that there was 'no or sufficient' evidence of age".

From the foregoing, it is clear that the discrepancy in the age with regard to child criminal responsibility at countries level is not uniform. This is irrespective of the fact that at international level the age of criminal liability has been fixed at 12 years.[43] Similarly, South Africa appears to have more elaborated procedure for determining child culpability which could influence the Nigeria response to child justice. Though, more elaborate procedures were established through case laws in Nigeria, it will be more appropriate if incorporated into the Nigerian legislations like that of South Africa. Alternatively, the Nigeria Government can rely on Article 40(3)(a) of the United Nations Convention on the Rights of

[40] 1984 (3) SA 666 (A).

[41] In *S v. Mavhungu* 1988 (3) SA 67 (V), reference was made to "a medical report in terms of section 212(4)(a) of the Criminal Procedure Act 51 of 1977 to establish prima facie proof of the age of the accused".

[42] 1981 (4) SA 614 (A). See also, *S v. Swartz* 1970 (2) SA 240 (NC).

[43] However, South Africa in 2016 has reviewed minimum age for criminal liability to 12 years, whereas a child of 13 and 14 will enjoy special protection measures. See South African Press Report dated 22 February 2016.

the Child[44] and incorporate the procedures via legislation to aid expeditiously mechanism for identification of persons who are below age of criminal responsibility. Furthermore, a definite age of criminal responsibility for children in conflict with the law and children beyond parental control should be determined since ascertainment of age plays a very important role as it ensures that the child offender enjoys the protection he or she is entitled to under the law. Government should as a necessity compel the entry of every child born in the country in the Births and Death Register as the birth certificate is the best proof of age. In the alternative, for proof of age of criminal responsibility, the School Leaving Certificate should be adopted.[45] These options should be considered as documentary evidence for the purpose of determining age in the court of law.

3 Theory of Child Delinquency

Crime is a very complicated phenomenon. It lacks a single theoretical explanation that neatly ties together all the nuances. It appears improbably that a single theory cannot cover the scope and all the facets of illegal behaviour.

[44]Article 40(3)(a) of the United Nations Convention on the Rights of the Child provides that: "States parties shall seek to promote the establishment of laws, procedures, authorities and institutions specifically applicable to children alleged as, accused of, or recognized as having infringed the penal law, and, in particular: The establishment of a minimum age below which children shall be presumed not to have the capacity to infringe the penal law".

[45]A Birth Certificate or School Leaving Certificate produced by the accused person to denote his age may be verified in the event of the court doubting same and this can be done by the police. In the absence of documentary evidence, the opinion of a medical practitioner may be called for. In Modi's Medical Jurisprudence & Toxicology, Butterworths India, New Delhi, 22nd Edition, p. 49 quoted from Adenwalla, Ms. Maharukh, 'Child Protection and Juvenile Justice System: For Juvenile in Conflict with the Law'. The principle means, which enable one to form a fairly accurate opinion about the age of an individual, especially in early years, are teeth, height and weight, ossification of bones and minor signs. However, it has been pointed out in the case of *Jaya Mala v. Home Secretary, Govt. of J & K* (1982) 2 SCC 538; 1982 SCC (Cri) 333; AIR 1982 SC 1297; 1982 Cri LJ 1777 (SC) that the age as ascertained by the medical examination is not conclusive proof of age, and judicial notice has been taken that it is a mere opinion of a doctor and the margin of error could be of 2 years on either side. And in *Bhoop Ram v. State of U.P.* (1989) 3 SCC1; 1989 SCC (Cri) 486; AIR 1989 SC 1329; (1989) 2 Crimes 294, the court held that in case of conflict between documentary evidence and the medical examination report, the age shown in an authentic document will be treated as the correct age of the accused. See also, *SMT. Kamiesh & Anor. v. State of U.P.* (2002) Cri LJ 3680 (Allahabad).

Crime and delinquency have been clarified from different perspectives by several disciplines. The theory of delinquency from the criminological perspective encompasses perspectives from biology, medicine, neurology, psychology, sociology and other social sciences. As a result, delinquency and crime have variously been explained in terms of biological, psychological and socio-economic motivations and inadequacies.[46] Generally, theories of delinquent behaviour fall into many categories. A few criminological notions of crime and delinquency which include naturalism, demonology, classical school, biological, psychological and sociological theories among others were briefly examined in this chapter in order to enhance an appreciation of delinquency, its incidences, prevention and control.

3.1 Naturalism Theory

Naturalism is an old practice of connecting human affairs to the natural world and inferring that human behaviour is derived from the forces of nature which are beyond individual control.[47] In this regard, naturalism can also be referred to as a deterministic theory of crime causation because it removes individual responsibility for one's lack of responsible self-control.[48] Therefore, a conclusion from the ancient civilisations around the Mediterranean region was that "human behaviour is driven by nature". It was observed that "Natural signs" "divine the course of human events, and offerings were given to appeal for favours, or to appease perceived signs of punishment".[49] This is a theory linked with

[46] See Alemika, E. E. O., and Chukwuma, I. C., *Juvenile Justice Administration in Nigeria: Philosophy and Practice* (Lagos: Centre for Law Enforcement Education, 2001).

[47] See Freda, Adler, Gerhard, O. W. Mueller, and Williams, S. Laufer, *Criminology and the Criminal Justice System* (6th ed.; New York: McGraw-Hill, 2007). See also Johnson, H. A., and Travis Wolfe, N., *History of Criminal Justice* (2nd ed.; Cincinnati, OH: Anderson, 1996). Quoted in Juvenile Delinquency: World Youth Report, 2003. Available at http://www.tdh-childprotection.org/documents/world/youth-report-chapter-7-juvenile-delinquency. Accessed on 21 March 2011.

[48] Ibid.

[49] Ibid. For example, the Romans had a propensity for studying flights of birds and reading the entrails of sacrificial beasts to divine their fortunes. Romans also believed that the moon, or *Luna*, influenced human behaviour. Our word *lunatic* comes from the ancient belief that criminal or otherwise bizarre behaviour is caused by phases of the moon. The Greeks consulted oracles, such as the famous one at Delphi, who sometimes divined fortunes by inhaling sacred vapours, hallucinating and babbling fortunes that required interpretation by holy guides.

the beliefs and practice rooted in the customs of people and is thus different from one community to another. Incidentally, criminologists who are naturalist in concept have attempted to explain deviance by applying natural and supernatural forces as factors that can affect human fortunes and behaviour.[50] Thus, some of the early deterministic theories of child criminality held that the natural world is reflected in human appearance and behaviour.

3.2 Demonology Theory

Demonology, like naturalism, is also a deterministic theory of criminal causation where criminal behaviour and delinquency are not considered to be a consequence of free will. Instead, regards were made to these offences to be "a manifestation of conflict between creatures of evil and chaos against deities of goodness and order".[51] Thus, it is believed by humans for many centuries that "evil creatures such as demons or devils wielded great influence over humans, sometimes possessing them and making them commit offences against the greater good or society or against the deified order with remedies and punishments meted out".[52] Thus, painful ordeals (i.e. torture) were devised to elicit confessions or drive out the demonic spirits accordingly.[53]

3.3 Classical/Free-Will Theory

Towards the end of eighteenth and early nineteenth centuries, the classical school propounded the free-will theory of investigating criminal and delinquent causation through scientific methods to explain deviant behaviour in an attempt to apply rationality and the rule of

[50] See Freda, Adler, Gerhard, O. W. Mueller, and Williams, S. Laufer, *Criminology and the Criminal Justice System*, 237. See also Johnson, H. A., and Travis Wolfe, N., *History of Criminal Justice*.

[51] See Juvenile Delinquency: World Youth Report, 2003.

[52] Ibid.

[53] For example, a number of ancient cultures engaged in the practice of drilling holes in the skull (known as *trephining*), which supposedly allowed evil spirits to depart from their human "host".

law to brutal and arbitrary criminal justice processes.[54] This theory[55] concentrated on the personal responsibility of individuals for their behaviour. It rejected the naturalist and demonological explanations of criminality and delinquency, an approach that was typical of the rationalism of the European enlightenment which is grounded in the human desire for pleasure and aversion to pain.[56] It was argued by the classical theorists on this human-centred rationality that "perpetrators should be held personally accountable for criminal and delinquent acts and punished accordingly since the criminal's calculus for making this choice is the acquisition of a benefit from criminal behaviour (pleasure)". They maintained that policies must be developed by the society in order to increase the costs for this benefit (pain).[57] Thus, harsher punishment must be imposed if one's deviance has become more "egregious"; that is, the costs of crime must always outweigh the benefits.

[54] See Freda, Adler, Gerhard, O. W. Mueller, and Williams, S. Laufer, *Criminology and the Criminal Justice System*, 60. See also Juvenile Delinquency: World Youth Report, 2003.

[55] This Classical School Theory of "free will" originated with the writings of Cesare Beccaria in Italy, who published *An Essay on Crimes and Punishment* in 1764. His discussion of why crime occurs and how society should respond to it was groundbreaking, and it resulted in widespread debate. Beccaria advocated the then-radical proposition that punishment should be swift, certain and proportional. He also argued that both corporal and capital punishments should be abolished and that most (if not all) criminal laws should be revised accordingly. The philosopher Jeremy Bentham in England promoted Beccaria's thesis in the late eighteenth and early nineteenth centuries, primarily in his book *An Introduction to the Principles of Morals and Legislation*. Bentham believed that humans rationally seek pleasure and avoid pain, so that rational people can be deterred from criminal deviance. Nevertheless, criminals conclude that the pleasure derived from crime counterbalances the pain of punishment. Bentham further argued that deterrence would be accomplished by the certainty of punishment, and by making the severity of each punishment surpass any benefit derived from the crime. See Becarria, C., *An Essay on Crimes and Punishment* (Wellesley, MA and London: Branden Publishing, 1992) in Juvenile Delinquency: World Youth Report. See also, Burns, J. H., and Hart, H. L. A., *The Collected Works of Jeremy Bentham: An Introduction to the Principles of Morals and Legislation* (Oxford University Press, 1996). See Dambazau, A. B., *Criminology and Criminal Justice*, 6–9.

[56] Ibid.

[57] Ibid.

3.4 *Biological Theory*

Biological theory is one of the scientific explanations of criminal behaviour that focuses on the actors rather than the act.[58] However, many early biological theories such as "somatotype",[59] "physiognomy",[60] "phrenology"[61] and "atavism"[62] are "scientific and quasi-scientific by current standards".[63] They signify a serious effort to bring scientific rigour to the study of criminal causation.[64] Biological inquiry continues unabated, with new fields of inquiry such as "deoxyribonucleic

[58] See Juvenile Delinquency: World Youth Report, 2003.

[59] Somatotype school of criminology, which related body build to behaviour. This originated from the work of Ernest Kretschmer which was later formulated by William Sheldon as the endomorph, the mesomorph and the ectomorph respectively and concluded that a high degree of mesomorphy and a low degree of ectomorphy were found in juvenile delinquents and other aggressive, violent individuals. See Freda, Adler, Gerhard, O. W. Mueller, and Williams, S. Laufer, *Criminology and the Criminal Justice System*, 72. See also Juvenile Delinquency: World Youth Report, 2003.

[60] This is a study of facial features and their relation to human behaviour. The Medieval-era Europeans ascribed the concept of physiognomy to moral and behavioural traits of human physical appearance. In particular, they argued that facial characteristics were deemed to be indicators of moral character, so that facially pleasing people were more likely to be given the benefit of the doubt than facially "displeasing" people. Physiognomists dutifully reported the soundness of a variety of physiognomic traits and measured their prominence among criminals and other undesirables in comparison with the general population. See Freda, Adler, Gerhard, O. W. Mueller, and Williams, S. Laufer, *Criminology and the Criminal Justice System*, 67. See also Juvenile Delinquency: World Youths Report, 2003.

[61] Phrenology is human behaviour that is determined by bodily functions emanating from the organs. During the late eighteenth and early nineteenth centuries, Franz Joseph Gall systematically promoted the science of phrenology by positing that bumps on the head were indications of psychological propensities, and brain is the source of all personality, including deviant personality. See Freda, Adler, Gerhard, O. W. Mueller, and Williams, S. Laufer, *Criminology and the Criminal Justice System*.

[62] Atavism is a reversion to a lower type of evolutionary development. It has been observed by Cesare Lombroso in his evolutionary interpretations of human behaviour that criminals are atavistic creatures with uncivilised criminal dispositions, and the characteristic of these people was called atavism. See Freda, Adler, Gerhard, O. W. Mueller, and Williams, S. Laufer, *Criminology and the Criminal Justice System*. See also Juvenile Delinquency: World Youth Report, 2003.

[63] See Becarria, C., *An Essay on Crimes and Punishment* (Wellesley, MA and London: Branden Publishing, 1992) in Juvenile Delinquency: World Youth Report.

[64] Ibid.

acid" (DNA)[65] research providing new bases for exploring the causes of delinquency and criminality.[66] It is a predictive factor that refers to the effect of congenital (inherited physical)[67] traits on human behaviour. It presents strongly deterministic explanations of delinquency and criminality and holds that some people are "naturally born criminals"[68] with physical qualities[69] that govern their deviant tendencies.[70] It has been observed by Richard Dugdale[71] that "delinquency and crime often run in families". Hereditary explanation of causation is to the effect that criminality is hereditary in some families, and that those born into the family group are encoded with genetic deviance. Thus, it is argued that

[65] Chromosome theory represents an example of the modern approach to heredity theory. Chromosomes, which are composed of DNA, contain the genetic code for human gender differences. Gender is determined from chromosomal arrangements, so that women typically have an "XX" pattern and men have an "XY" pattern. Some people have anomalous patterns, which include "XXX" for some women and "XYY" for some men. During the 1960s, scientists investigated the theoretical implications of the "XYY" pattern. Research was reported in 1965 suggesting that "XYY" males are more prevalent in prison populations than in society. These "super males" were reported to be more aggressive than typical "XY" males, and therefore, more prone to criminal deviance than "XY" males. See Jacobs, P., Brunton, M., Meville, M. M., et al., 'Aggressive Behaviour, Mental Subnormality, and the XYY Male' (1965, December), *Nature*, 208, 1351–1352. Cited in Juvenile Delinquency: World Youth Report, 2003.

[66] Ibid.

[67] To demonstrate that certain traits are inherited, geneticists for example have argued that the predisposition to act violently or aggressively in certain situations may be inherited. In other word, while criminals are not born criminal, the predisposition to be violent or commit crime may be present at birth. For more details, see Freda, Adler, Gerhard, O. W. Mueller, and Williams, S. Laufer, *Criminology and the Criminal Justice System*, 101.

[68] The belief that criminals are born, not made, and that they can be identified by various physical irregularities is reflected not only in scientific writing but also in literature as well. This was evidenced in the postulation of Shakespeare Julius Caesar thus: "Let me have men about me that are fat; sleek headed men and such as sleep o' nights. Yond Cassius has a lean and hungry look; He thinks too much: such men are dangerous".

[69] These qualities include genetic, biological and biochemical profiles that theoretically cause or have a strong effect upon, one's propensity for deviant behaviour.

[70] See James, A. I., *Criminal Justice* (8th ed.; New York: McGraw-Hill, 2007), 49–50.

[71] Richard Dugdale's research on the Juke family, published in 1877, was among the first scientific studies that systematically argued in favour of a genetic basis for immorality, crime and delinquency. See Dugdale, R. L., *The Jukes: A Study in Crime, Pauperism, Disease and Heredity* (3rd ed.; New York: G. P. Putnam's Sons, 1985) cited in Juvenile Delinquency: World Youth Report, 2003.

"a bad seed is theoretically inherited and passed from generation to generation".[72] The central implication of biological determinants is that "free will is at best a secondary cause of delinquency". Rather, there is a shift of fault for deviant behaviour to internal physical qualities, which explain one's predisposition for criminal conduct.[73]

3.5 *Psychological Theory*

Psychological theory ascribes deviant behaviours to "cognitive and personality disorders brought on by one's environment, brain chemistry, or some other condition".[74] Thus, variety of options were considered by the theorists in explaining individual differences such as "defective conscience, emotional immaturity, inadequate childhood socialisation, maternal deprivation and poor moral development" by showing how "aggression is learned", which situations promote violent or delinquent reactions, how crime is related to personality factors and how various mental disorders are associated with criminality.[75]

Again, psychological explanations appear to be rounded in several research traditions, such as "psychoanalysis",[76] "conditioning"[77] and

[72] Ibid.

[73] See Curran, D. J., and Renzetti, C. M., *Theories of Crime* (Boston: Allyn & Bacon). Quoted in Juvenile Delinquency: World Youth Report, 2003.

[74] Ibid.

[75] See Freda, Adler, Gerhard, O. W. Mueller, and Williams, S. Laufer, *Criminology and the Criminal Justice System*, 85.

[76] The psychoanalytic principle of criminality attributed delinquent and criminal behaviour to either a conscience so overbearing that it arouses feelings of guilt or a conscience so week that it cannot control the individual's impulses or the need for immediate gratification. Sigmund Freud suggested that an individual's psychological well-being is dependent on a healthy interaction among the id, ego and superego. Healthy development of the id, ego and superego occurs early in life, so that early experiences are critical for future adult behaviour. Troubling or traumatising events during childhood can become catalysts for delinquency and criminality. Juvenile delinquents and adult criminals are, according to psychoanalytic theory, persons without sufficiently developed egos and superegos. See Freda, Adler, Gerhard, O. W. Mueller, and Williams, S. Laufer, *Criminology and the Criminal Justice System*.

[77] Conditioning, which is also regarded as learning concept, maintains that delinquent behaviour is learned through the same psychological processes as any other behaviour. Ivan Pavlov observed that it is a truism that every person's future behaviour is conditioned by past experiences, and these experiences or environmental stimuli underlie socially acceptable

"psychopathology".[78] These explanations seem not to be deterministic as that of biological theories because they appear to leave open, the possibility of deviant free will. Thus, the psychological explanations of crime and delinquency have several elements that are commonly present in them. For instance, such criminals and delinquents do not (or cannot) "differentiate right from wrong", have "detrimental behavioural conditioning", "suffer from diseased minds", learn from "toxic environments", have "disordered or abnormal personalities", "lack ability to control his or her person or emotion" which affects behaviour during adulthood.[79]

3.6 Sociological Theory

In the examination of individual's behaviour, the approach of sociological theorists is on the effects of structures and processes on the behaviour of individuals and groups of people. They observed to the extent that "societal conditions theoretically affect people's collective perceptions of the availability of opportunities and the intensity of deprivations". They believed that delinquency and crime are reactions to certain types of environments.[80]

The major focus of the sociological theorists is on the "personal idiosyncrasies of individuals" to explain delinquency and crime. Among these personal attributes are individual's physical or psychological makeup which has been used by scholars to "formulate theories of deviance and to design policies to deal with lawbreakers".[81] Sociologists study interrelationships between individuals, "socio-economic groups, social processes, and societal structures".

behaviour, as well as delinquency and criminality. See Freda, Adler, Gerhard, O. W. Mueller, and Williams, S. Laufer, *Criminology and the Criminal Justice System*, 90.

[78]The concept of the psychopathic personality was developed to describe criminals who behaved cruelly and seemingly with no empathy for their victims. Psychopaths (sociopaths) are considered to be people who have no conscience. They are severely dysfunctional in their relationships with other people and are fundamentally selfish, unpredictable, untruthful and unstable. The term is sometimes used to describe very aggressive delinquents and criminals who act spontaneously without an observable motive.

[79]For a good introduction to the work of Jung, see Campbell, J., *The Portable Jung* (New York: Penguin Books, 1976).

[80]See Juvenile Delinquency: World Youth Report, 2003.

[81]Ibid.

In order to improve the understanding of the perception on the nexus between society and human deviance, several elements are commonly present in sociological explanations of delinquency and crime.[82] These are the "socio-economic conditions and pressures" that shape individual and collective behaviour, "inequality and deprivation" that are associated with delinquency and criminality, "sub-cultural norms that are often at odds with accepted norms of the society" creating tensions that can result in "sub-cultural conflict" with the greater society and delinquency and crime that are associated with underclass conditions such as "poverty, neighbourhood degeneration, low educational achievement, inadequate housing, and family dysfunction".[83]

Significantly, therefore, sociologists have historically argued that the broader society has certain inherent features and structures that cause some members to engage in delinquent and criminal behaviour.[84] This theory sometimes reflects the political ideology of the times in which they were designed. Instructively, the sociological theory tends to explain predispositions towards criminal deviance and therefore allows for some degree of free will.[85]

[82] Ibid.

[83] This is evident in the postulation of Gabriel Tarde who served as a provincial judge for 15 years and who was later placed in charge of France's national statistics. After an extensive analysis of these statistics, he concluded that "the majority of murderers and notorious thieves began as children who had been abandoned and the true seminary of crime must be sought for upon each public square or each crossroad of our towns, whether they be small or large, in those flocks of pillaging street urchins who, like bands of sparrows, associate together at first for marauding and then for theft because of a lack of education and food in their homes". See Tarde, Gabriel, *Penal Philosophy* (R. Howell, Trans.; Boston: Little Brown, 1912), 252.

[84] Ibid.

[85] The Belgian mathematician Adolphe Quetelet who reigned between 1796 and 1874 and the French lawyer Andre Michel Guerry who also reigned between 1802 and 1866 were among the first scholars to repudiate the classicist free-will doctrine from their working independently on the relation of crime statistics to such factors as poverty, sex, race, age and climate to mention just but few. They concluded that society and not the decisions of individual offenders were responsible for criminal behaviour. Adolphe Quetelet discovered that behaviour is indeed predictable, regular and understandable. He believed that just as the physical world is governed by the laws of nature, human behaviour is governed by forces external to the individual. The more we learn about those forces the easier it becomes to predict behaviour. He further postulated that the major goal of criminological research should be to identify factors related to crime and to assign to them their proper degree of influence. See Quetelet, *A Treatise on Man*, 103, and Cheatwood, Derral,

In sum, the foregoing brief discussion of the perspectives to delinquency provides us with an understanding of delinquency and crime particularly, their multiple and complex origins and manifestations. The examination of crime and delinquency from different theoretical dispositions or schools of thought, attempted to demonstrate and establish the impact of these theories as predictive causes of child delinquency in Africa.

To this end, in view of all that have been discussed, a question that begs for answer is whether crime and delinquency are related to multiple and complex origins and manifestations or whether scientific and practical literatures need to be used to determine children's crimes and violence. It is however safe to conclude here that the empirical verification by the author broadens the understanding of the theory that fully account for all cases of crime and child delinquency in Nigeria and South Africa.

4 Causes of Child Delinquency and the Sociological Theory

Child delinquency has been explained as an anti-social behaviour that is beyond parental control, and therefore, it is subject to legal adjudication.[86] Society takes this behaviour as an indication that the person is out of control and must therefore be controlled through its legal system. Hence, the causes and conditions for children's crime are usually found at each level of social structure including society as a whole, social institutions, social groups and organisations, and interpersonal relations.[87] In this regard, the sociological theory is singled out as the common explanation for the causes of child delinquency especially in Africa. This is a reason why this part of the chapter focuses on identifying some sociological factors which are commonly said to be causes of child delinquency. They include parental neglect, parental imitation, peer pressure, poor education, school and community influence, child abuse and trauma,

'Is There a Season for Homicide?' (1988), *Criminology*, 26, 287–306. Quoted in Freda, Adler, Gerhard, O. W. Mueller, and Williams, S. Laufer, *Criminology and the Criminal Justice System*.

[86] Ayua, I. A., and Okagbue, I. E., *The Rights of the Child in Nigeria* (Lagos: Nigerian Institute of Advanced Legal Studies, 1996), 240.

[87] Ibid.

lack of opportunities, media influence, poverty and divorce. Each of the causes of child delinquency is explained below.

4.1 Parental Neglect

Children and their families lack a specific description. Family, social and environmental risk factors tend to cluster, and any number of them can occur together within the same family.[88] Currently, there are substantial changes in the family social institutions. The form of family institution is diversifying with, for example, the increase in "one-parent families and non-marital unions".[89] This is supported by findings from a recent field survey by the author where 798 (64%) out of 1258 respondents confirmed that "children from single parenthood are prone to delinquency".[90] It is therefore argued that single parent or absence of fathers can lead boys to seek patterns of masculinity in delinquent groups of peers especially, in many low-income families. In many respects, the delinquent groups of peers may be substituted for the family, define male roles and contribute to the acquisition of such attributes as cruelty, strength, excitability and anxiety.

Studies have also shown that "children who receive adequate parental supervision are less likely to engage in criminal activities".[91] Lack of adequate parenting practices is among the most powerful predictive factors of early anti-social behaviour among children.[92] This conforms with the respondents views in an interview conducted by the author in Nigeria (Lagos, Port Harcourt, Enugu and Ilorin, Kwara States)[93] and South

[88] Patterson, G. R., and Stouthamer-Loeber, M., 'The Correlation of Family Management Practices and Delinquency' (1984), *Child Development*, 55, 1299–1307.

[89] Ibid.

[90] Author's field survey at Lagos, Kaduna, Port Harcourt, Enugu, Bauchi and Ilorin in 2014.

[91] Cicchetti, D., and Rogosch, F. A., 'Finality and Multifinality in Developmental Psychopathology' (1996), *Journal of Development and Psychopathology*, 8. Available at http://www.ncjrs.gov/html/ojjdp/.../contents.ht. Accessed on 20 October 2011.

[92] Hawkins, J. D., Herrenkohl, T., Farrington, D. P., Brewer, D., Catalano, R.F., and Harachi, T. W., 'A Review of Predictors of Youth Violence', in R. Loeber and D. P. Farrington (eds.), *Serious and Violent Juvenile Offenders: Risk Factors and Successful Interventions* (Thousand Oaks, CA: Sage, 1998), 106–146. See also Patterson, G. R., and Stouthamer-Loeber, M., 'The Correlation of Family Management Practices and Delinquency' (1984), *Child Development*, 55, 1299–1307, 25.

[93] Interviews conducted by the author in 2014.

Africa (Grahamstown and Western Cape)[94] where they expressed that "laxity of parents/guardians in child upbringing may lead to development of delinquent acts by youths". From the questionnaire administered by the author in Nigeria, majority of the respondents representing 1136 (90.3%) out of 1258 hold the views that "low socio-economic background may lead children to commit delinquent acts".[95] Dysfunctional family settings—characterised by weak internal linkages and integration, conflict, inadequate parental control and premature autonomy—are closely associated with child delinquency.[96] Children in disadvantaged families that have few opportunities for legitimate employment face a higher risk of social exclusion.[97] It was revealed in the course of the author's interview at South Africa (Pretoria and Western Cape)[98] and in the questionnaires administered to 1258 respondents in Nigeria (Lagos, Ilorin in Kwara, Kaduna and Port Harcourt) that "lack of equal opportunities for social and emotional adjustment for juveniles lead to delinquency".[99] Majority of the respondents representing 1005 (80%) are in support. The findings from the author's fieldwork correspond with the position of Gardner in his study which revealed that:

> families in which the children do not have conduct problems compared with families of children with conduct problems have been found to be eight times more likely to engage in conflicts involving discipline, to engage in half as many positive interactions, and, often unintentionally, to reinforce negative child behaviour.[100]

However, three specific parental practices were identified by many scholars including the author that may be associated with early conduct problems, and they were listed thus: (i) "a high level of parent-child

[94] Interviews conducted by the author in 2015.

[95] Author's field survey at Lagos, Kaduna, Port Harcourt, Enugu, Bauchi and Ilorin in 2014.

[96] Ibid.

[97] Ibid.

[98] Interviews conducted by the author in 2014 and 2015.

[99] Author's field survey at Lagos, Kaduna, Port Harcourt and Ilorin in 2014.

[100] Gardner, F. E. M., 'Positive Interaction Between Mothers and Conduct-Problem Children: Is There Training for Harmony as Well as Fighting?' (1987), *Journal of Abnormal Child Psychology*, 15, 37.

conflict", (ii) "poor monitoring" and (iii) "a low level of positive involvement".[101] The study conducted by Pittsburgh Youth also revealed that "co-occurrence of low levels of monitoring and high levels of punishment increased the risk of delinquency in 7-to 13-year-old boys".[102] Conversely, attachments to conventional parents and to society's institutions are hypothesised to protect against developing anti-social behaviour.

Increasing behavioural problems have also been linked to those children that are witnessing domestic violence at home especially for boys and younger children. In most families, when the woman is battered,[103] children are also battered and as such co-occurrence of child abuse and witnessing domestic violence affect children's adjustment. To support this position is an interview at South Africa (Cape Town) where a respondent agreed with the position of the author that "domestic violence most of time leads to delinquency".[104] This pattern of findings is similar to the respondents views in the questionnaire administered by the author in Nigeria (Ilorin in Kwara, Kaduna Lagos, Enugu, Port Harcourt-Rivers and Bauchi States), where 955 (76%) of 1258 respondents strongly agreed.[105] At the same time, children whose parents divorced[106] and subsequently remarried have been found to be

[101] Wasserman, G. A., Miller, L., Pinner, E., and Jaramillo, B. S., 'Parenting Predictors of Early Conduct, Problems in Urban, High-Risk Boys' (1996), *Journal of the American Academy of Child and Adolescent Psychiatry*, 35, 22. See also, Appendix B of this book.

[102] Hirschi, T., *Causes of Delinquency* (Berkeley: University of California Press, 1996), 22.

[103] Jaffe, P., Wolfe, D., and Wilson, S. K., *Children of Battered Women* (Sage, 1990). See also McKibben, L., De Vos, E., and Newberger, E., 'Victimization of Mothers of Abused Children: A Controlled Study' (1989), *Pediatrics*, 84, 531–535. See also, Reid, W. J., and Crisafulli, A., 'Marital Discord and Child Behavior Problems: A Meta-Analysis' (1990), *Journal of Abnormal Child Psychology* 18, 105–117. See also Hughes, H. M., Parkinson, D., and Vargo, M., 'Witnessing Spouse Abuse and Experiencing Physical Abuse: A Double Whammy?' (1989), *Journal of Family Violence*, 4, 197–209.

[104] Interview conducted at Cape Town, South Africa in 2016.

[105] Author's field survey at Lagos, Kaduna, Port Harcourt, Enugu, Bauchi and Ilorin in 2014.

[106] See Hetherington, E. M., 'Coping with Family Transitions: Winners, Losers and Survivors' (1989), *Journal of Child Development*, 60, 1–17. According to some scholars in their articles notably Pearson, J. L., Ialongo, H. S., Hunter, A. G., and Kellum, S. G., 'Family Structure and Aggressive Behaviour in a Population of Urban Elementary School

more likely to have continuous problems with anti-social, coercive and non-compliant behaviours through age 10 as well as children who lose their parent(s). Parents' anti-social personality disorder,[107] substance abuse, psychopathology and depression[108] show many parenting deficiencies associated with increased anti-social behaviours in children such

Children' (1994), *Journal of the American Academy of Child and Adolescent Psychiatry*, 33, 540–548; Vaden-Kiernan, N., Ialongo, N. S., Pearson, J. L., and Kellam, S. G., 'Household Family Structure and Children's Aggressive Behavior: A Longitudinal Study of Urban Elementary School Children' (1995), *Journal of Abnormal Child Psychology*, 23, 553–568; McLanahan, S., and Booth, K., 'Mother-Only Families: Problems, Prospects, and Politics' (1989), *Journal of Marriage and the Family*, 51, 557–580; and Sampson, R. J., 'Urban Black Violence: The Effect of Male Joblessness and Family Disruption' (1987), *American Journal of Sociology*, 93, 348–382, they postulated that, on average, children from single-mother households are at increased risk for poor behavioural outcome as a result of their fewer economic resources, mental health problems, higher levels of residential mobility, fewer resources to monitor their children's activities and whereabouts. Cumulatively, each of these factors contributes to increased levels of early childhood behaviour problems.

[107]Lahey, B. B., Piacentini, J. C., McBurnett, K., Stone, P., Hartdagen, S., and Hynd, G., 'Psychopathology in the Parents of Children with Conduct Disorder and Hyperactivity' (1988), *Journal of the American Academy of Child and Adolescent Psychiatry*, 27, 163–170. See also Robins, L. N., *Deviant Children Grown Up* (Baltimore, MD: Williams and Wilkins, 1966). See also Cummings, E. M., and Davies, P. T., 'Maternal Depression and Child Development' (1994), *Journal of Child Psychology and Psychiatry*, 35, 73–112. See also Costello, E. J., Farmer, E. M., Angold, A., Burns, B., and Erkanli, A., 'Psychiatric Disorders Among American Indian and White Youth in Appalachia: The Great Smoky Mountains Study' (1997), *American Journal of Public Health*, 87, 827–832. Overall, anti-social parents show increased levels of family conflict, exercise poorer supervision, experience more family breakdown and direct more hostility towards their children.

[108]The Pittsburgh Youth Study has shown that the association between delinquency and parental anxiety or depression was stronger in younger than in older children. See Loeber, R., Farrington, D. P., Stouthamer-Loeber, M., and Van Kammen, W. B., *Antisocial Behavior and Mental Health Problems: Explanatory Factors in Childhood and Adolescence* (Mahwah, NJ: Lawrence Erlbaum, 1998). Available at http://www.ncjrs.gov/html/ojjdp/.../contents.ht. Accessed on 20 October 2011. According to Keller et al., 'Parent Figure Transitions and Delinquency and Drug Use Among Early Adolescent Children of Substance Abusers' (2002), *Journal of Drug and Alcohol Abuse*, 28(3), 399–423, "parental disruption is one of the key predictors for delinquent behavior. These disruptions can be varied in nature from divorce, to parental depression (other serious illnesses), inconsistent parenting, constantly moving from one place to another, and at least one-parent committing a crime" (ibid.). The conclusion here is that lack of stability and consistency in the lives of children leaves them at great risk for delinquent behaviour.

as inconsistency, irritability, lack of supervision and increased rates of psychiatric disorder among school-aged children.[109]

Therefore, children have the opportunity to develop or adopt delinquent behaviour when they are exposed to the influence of adult offenders, and their engagement in adult crimes becomes more real. Thus, the "criminalisation" of the family also has an impact on the choice of delinquent trajectories.[110]

4.2 Child Abuse and Trauma

Child abuse and trauma are significant predictive factors of delinquency in Nigeria and South Africa. Unfortunately, the reality of life in both countries and Africa in general is that, far too many children are abused and traumatised every day.[111] Some of these abuses occur on regular basis while some are infrequent. The nature of the abuse may vary, ranging from "physical, sexual, or psychological, or as a combination".[112] Without a doubt whatever the nature of the abuse, it can have long lasting and profound effects on the children's lives. Another sad fact of childhood trauma in most African countries is that of abuse involving someone the child has come to know and trust such as a parent, sibling, babysitter, relative, caregiver or teacher.[113] This violation of trust only multiplies the effect of the trauma or abuse.

In African countries generally, there is a correlation between abuse of young person and the development of serious problems in life which may in turn be one of the most significant factors in the development of delinquent behaviour.[114] This assertion corresponds with the author's field survey in Nigeria (Bauchi, Enugu, Kaduna, Ilorin-Kwara, Lagos and Port Harcourt-Rivers States)[115] and interviews conducted at South

[109] Ibid.

[110] See Juvenile Delinquency: World Youth Report, 2003.

[111] Ibid.

[112] Siegfried, C. B., Ko, S. J., and Kelley, A., 'Victimization and Juvenile Offending' (2004), *National Child Traumatic Stress Network*. Available at http://www.nctsnet.org/nctsn_assets/pdfs/edu. Accessed on 28 April 2011.

[113] Ibid.

[114] Okonkwo, C. O., Nwankwo, Clement, and Ibhawoh, Bonny, *Administration of Juvenile Justice in Nigeria*, 10.

[115] Author's field survey at Lagos, Kaduna, Port Harcourt, Enugu, Bauchi and Ilorin in 2014.

Africa (Cape Town, Grahamstown and Pretoria).[116] The findings from the field survey that revealed the views of majority of the respondents representing 1051 (84%) that "child abuse by parent may make children vulnerable to child delinquency" are similar to the responses of those respondents interviewed in South Africa especially, the Children's courts and social welfare. For example, a Magistrate at Grahamstown expressed that "most of the children in need of care and protection before the Children's Court are abused from their parents, relatives and caregivers". Interestingly, if a person lives in a violent neighbourhood, it is possible to be affected by the violence.[117] Unlike adolescents that are capable of understanding concepts such as fairness, justice and appropriate behaviour and inappropriate behaviour, children are not capable of understanding these concepts and so adolescents are affected differently by traumatic and abusive incidents.[118]

4.3 Peer Pressure

While child abuse and traumatic factors are connected with the exposure of children to delinquent behaviours, peer pressure involves enticing a child/juvenile to commit crime in the society or other types of delinquent conduct.[119] In many cases in Nigeria and South Africa pressure from peer group may be a principal cause of child delinquency and may inevitably account for young persons' participation in criminal or other anti-social activities in order to feel that they belong.[120] Many studies have revealed that "juvenile gang members consider their group a family".[121] For example, adolescents that are constantly facing violence may consider belonging to a gang will provide them with protection from threats of assault,

[116] Interviews conducted by the author in Pretoria in 2013, Grahamstown in 2015 and Cape Town in 2016.

[117] Kilpatrick et al., 2003(b). Juvenile Delinquency: World Youth Report (2004). Available at http://www.un.org/esa/socdev/unyin/documents/ch07.pdf. Accessed on 2 February 2011.

[118] Ibid.

[119] See Mason, A., 'Self-Esteem and Delinquency Revisited (Again): A Test of Kaplan's Self-Derogation Theory of Delinquency Using Latent Growth Curve Modeling' (2001), *Journal of Youth and Adolescence*, 30, 1.

[120] Okonkwo, C. O., Nwankwo, Clement, and Ibhawoh, Bonny, *Administration of Juvenile Justice in Nigeria*, 15.

[121] World Youth Report, 2003.

oppression, harassment or extortion on the street or at school.[122] This position was alluded by the majority of respondents representing 1103 (88%) out of the total population of 1258 respondents that responded to the questionnaires administered by the author in Nigeria.[123] Those respondents strongly agreed that "peer group influence contributes to involvement of children in delinquency". Nigerian position also conforms with the interviews conducted by the author in South Africa[124] where some of the respondents hold the views that "the need to be recognised makes some children to engage in child delinquency". This also corresponds with the views of 643 (51%) of the respondents in Nigeria when questionnaires were administered on 1258 in another interval.

It is important to point out that children at risk of peer pressure are mostly those who spend their leisure time in unstructured and unsupervised activities on the streets. The punishment for lack of co-operation includes: isolation by friends and physical threats which sometimes lead to violence on the victim of peer pressure.[125] Children who find acceptance from their delinquents peers tend to feel as if they belong and committing acts of delinquency is easier to do within the framework of the group. According to some findings, "statistical data" in many African countries, Nigeria and South Africa inclusive show that "delinquency is largely a group phenomenon; between two-thirds and three-quarters of all child offences are committed by members of various groups".[126] Even those children who commit offences alone are likely to be associated with groups.

[122]As one juvenile from the Russian Federation said, "I become involved in gang when I was in the eighth form (at 13 years old), but I joined it only when I was in the tenth (at 15 years of age). I had a girlfriend and I feared for her, and the gang was able to provide for her safety". See Machel, G., Impact of Armed Conflict on Children: Report of the Expert of the Secretary-General. Ms. Graca Machel submitted pursuant to United Nations General Assembly resolution 48/157 (1996) (A/51/306). See also Klein, M., *The American Street Gang: Its Nature, Prevalence and Control* (New York: Oxford University Press, 1995), 25.

[123]Author's field survey at Lagos, Kaduna, Port Harcourt, Enugu, Bauchi and Ilorin in 2014.

[124]Interviews conducted by the author in Grahamstown, 2015 and Cape Town, 2015 and 2016.

[125]World Youth Report (2003).

[126]Ibid.

Furthermore, there is a sense of elevation by children that are accepted by other young persons of their age even if they are engaging in delinquent behaviours whenever they feel rejected by peers. The implication is that young persons are not necessarily seeking to engage in delinquent behaviour but rather acceptance by their peers.[127]

4.4 *School and Community Influence*

School and community play a significant role in the developmental stage of children. The generality of the environment of these institutions do have positive and negative impact on the children. Thus, school and community organisations can be a predictor of delinquency especially where a child adopts negative behaviour from the environment.

It is opined that a school with fewer teachers and higher students' enrolment may somewhat be susceptible to having higher levels of teacher victimisation and poor rule enforcement. Thus, study has shown that:

> school environment with fewer teachers and higher students' enrolment is capable of generating low levels of teacher satisfaction, little cooperation, poor student-teacher relations, the prevalence of norms and values that support anti-social behaviour, poorly defined rules and expectations for conduct and inadequate rule enforcement, the result of which will be the breeding of child delinquents in the school.[128]

Therefore, low commitment of students which is associated with the failure to bond to school during childhood, low educational aspirations and poor motivation place children at risk for general offending and for child delinquency.[129] Akin to the above scenario is the fact that children

[127] Cole, J. D., Terry, R. A., Lenox, K., Lochman, J. E., and Hyman, C., 'Childhood Peer Rejection and Aggression as Predictors of Stable Patterns of Adolescent Disorder' (2003), *Journal of Development and Psychopathology*.

[128] Herrenkohl, T. I., Hawkins, J. D., Chung, I. J., Hill, K. G., and Battin-Pearson, S., 'School and Community Risk Factors and Interventions', in R. Loeber and D. P. Farrington (eds.), *Child Delinquents: Development, Intervention, and Service Needs* (Thousand Oaks, CA: Sage, 2001), 211–246.

[129] Hawkins, J. D., Herrenkohl, T., Farrington, D. P., Brewer, D., Catalano, R. F., and Harachi, T. W., 'A Review of Predictors of Youth Violence', pp. 106–146. See also Hawkins, J. D., Lishner, D. M., Jenson, J. M., and Catalano, R. F., 'Delinquents and

whose academic performance is poor may fail to develop strong bonds to school and have lower expectations of success, the effect of which may be an inclination for the adoption of anti-social behaviour. This proposition gained credence in the findings of Maguin and Loeber et al.,[130] through their research that "poor academic performance is related to the prevalence, onset, frequency, and seriousness of delinquency". Loeber et al.,[131] further observed that "in young children, ages eight to eleven, academic performance has been related to serious later delinquency even when individual intelligence and attention problems are taken into account". These postulations give strong support that community and schools which are the first contact of children in developmental stage, play significant roles in child delinquency, and this position was confirmed by the author's field survey in Nigeria where 1016 (81%) of the respondents in an administered questionnaire hold the views that "coordinated efforts by the school and community where the child resides would minimise child delinquency".

4.5 Urbanisation Influence

Another significant point of reference on the predictive factor of child delinquency is the problem associated with urbanisation. Study has shown that "geographical analysis suggests that countries with more urbanised populations have higher registered crime rates than those with string rural lifestyles and communities".[132] It is argued that the increase in the population may be attributed to the differences in

Drugs: What the Evidence Suggests About Prevention and Treatment Programming', in B. S. Brown and A. R. Mills (eds.), *Youth at High Risk for Substance Abuse* (DHHS Publication No. ADM 87–1537) (Washington, DC: U.S. Government Printing Office, 1987), pp. 81–131. See also, Le Blanc, M., Coté, G., and Loeber, R., 'Temporal Paths in Delinquency: Stability, Regression and Progression Analyzed with Panel Data from an Adolescent and Delinquent Sample' (1991), *Canadian Journal of Criminology*, 33, 23–47.

[130] Maguin, E., and Loeber, R., 'Academic Performance and Delinquency', in M. Tonry (ed.), *Crime and Justice: A Review of Research* (Chicago: University of Chicago Press, 1996), 145–267.

[131] Loeber, R., Farrington, D. P., Stouthamer-Loeber, M., and Van Kammen, W. B., *Antisocial Behaviour and Mental Health Problems: Explanatory Factors in Childhood and Adolescence.*

[132] Okonkwo, C. O., Nwankwo, Clement, and Ibhawoh, Bonny, *Administration of Juvenile Justice in Nigeria*, 18.

social control and social cohesion. It is observed that rural groupings rely mainly on family and community control as a means of dealing with anti-social behaviour and exhibit markedly lower crime rates. Urban industrialised societies tend to resort to formal legal and judicial measures, an impersonal approach that appears to be linked to higher crime rates.

The process of urbanisation in developing countries like Nigeria is contributing to children's involvement in criminal behaviour, because it is argued that, the basic features of the urban environment foster the development of new forms of social behaviour deriving mainly from the weakening of primary social relations and control, increasing reliance on the media at the expense of informal communication and the tendency towards anonymity. Comparatively, similar situation is obtainable in South Africa due to her long experience with colonial rule. These patterns are generated by the higher population density, degree of heterogeneity and numbers of people found in urban contexts.

It is argued that child delinquency robs society of some of its brightest and brilliant young people, who choose to pursue a lifestyle of criminal behaviour. Some will become institutionalised and engage in further violent behaviour, costing victims their lives and casting further financial burdens on the society. In turn, the general population may view certain areas of a city, usually urban, as undesirable.

4.6 Media Influence

Media influence, particularly electronic media, constitutes a predictive factor of child delinquency.[133] Eron and Huesmann[134] posit that violence can be learned by young persons who watch violence media programmes. They tend to behave more aggressively or violently, replicating violence in the media.[135] These findings are also buttressed with responses garnered from respondents interviewed particularly

[133] Ibid.

[134] Eron, L. D., and Huesmann, L. R., 'Television as a Source of Maltreatment of Children' (1987), *School Psychology Review*, 16, 195–202.

[135] For example, children exposed to high levels of television violence at age 8 were found to be more likely to behave aggressively at that age and subsequently, up to age 30. Ibid., 220.

Grahamstown in Eastern Province, South Africa[136] and Lagos, Kaduna and Port Harcourt, Nigeria[137] that "exposure of children to different types of foreign films aggravates criminal tendency among children". This is similar to the responses of the respondents in the administering of questionnaire phase of the book where majority of the respondents representing 1103 (88%) in Nigeria[138] strongly agreed with the interview phase. In addition, children of parents who frequently watched violence films on television and showed aggression were found to be more likely to exhibit aggression and to prefer violent programmes than other children whose parents are not watching violence films.[139] Study has shown that media brings an individual to violence in three ways[140] thus:

> First, movies that demonstrate violent acts excite spectators, and the aggressive energy can then be transferred to everyday life, pushing an individual to engage in physical activity on the streets. This type of influence is temporary, lasting from several hours to several days. Second, television can portray ordinary daily violence committed by parents or peers (the imposition of penalties for failing to study or for violations of certain rules or norms of conduct). It is impossible to find television shows that do not portray such patterns of violence, because viewer approval of this type of programming has ensured its perpetuation.
>
> As a result, children are continually exposed to the use of violence in different situations and the number of violent acts on television appears to be increasing. Third, violence depicted in the media is unreal and has a surrealistic quality; wounds bleed less, and the real pain and agony resulting from violent actions are very rarely shown, so the consequences of violent behaviour often seem negligible.[141]

[136] Interview conducted by the author at Grahamstown, 2015.

[137] Interviews conducted by the author at Lagos, Kaduna and port Harcourt, 2014.

[138] Author's field survey at Bauchi, Enugu, Ilorin-Kwara, Lagos, Kaduna and Port Harcourt, 2014.

[139] See Loeber, R., Farrington, D. P., Stouthamer-Loeber, M., and Van Kammen, W. B., *Antisocial Behavior and Mental Health Problems: Explanatory Factors in Childhood and Adolescence.*

[140] American Psychological Association, 'Violence and Youth: Psychology's Response', Summary Report of the APA Commission on Violence and Youth (Washington, DC, 1993). Available at http://www.aacap.org/publications/ractsiam/behavior:htm. Accessed on 20 February 2010.

[141] Ibid.

It is therefore argued that, over time, television causes a shift in the system of human values and indirectly leads children to view violence as a desirable and even courageous ways of reestablishing justice. The findings from the study conducted by the American Psychological Association evident the conclusion that "television violence accounts for about 10 percent of aggressive behaviour among children".[142]

4.7 *Availability of Drugs and Alcohol*

Taking of drug and hard substances have become common phenomenon globally notwithstanding the adverse effect on the individual and society at large. There is a very strong linkage globally, between drug abuse and child delinquency[143] in the sense that drug abuse is capable of instigating young persons' to undertake unlawful acts in order to obtain illicit drugs. Thus, in an attempt to get money to buy drugs or to obtain drugs, youths commit a variety of crimes like theft and armed robbery.

Most children who are exposed to drugs at early ages are prone to be delinquents. Studies have indicated that almost 80% of offenders have used illicit psychotropic substances at one point or another; most had shown traces of drugs in their blood or urine after arrest, and many of the offenders too were under the influence of drugs when they committed the crime.[144] There seems to be no variation with the findings and the views expressed by majority of the respondents in the course of administering of questionnaires in Nigeria by the author where 1171 (93%) out of 1258 respondents hold that "drug addiction has the tendency for children involvement in child delinquency".[145] When the author asked some of the respondents to comment on their responses in an interview at Borstal institutions, Nigeria (Ilorin and Kaduna), one of them says: "in fact, 80% of students brought to Borstal institution here are drug addict while the remaining 20% are beyond parental

[142] Summary Report of the APA Commission on Violence and Youth.

[143] Okonkwo, C. O., Nwankwo, Clement, and Ibhawoh, Bonny, *Administration of Juvenile Justice in Nigeria*, 25.

[144] See McBride, D. C., and McCoy, C. B., 'The Drugs-Crime Relationship: An Analytical Framework' (1993), *The Prison Journal*, 73(3–4), 257–278 cited in Dambazau, A. B, *Criminology and Criminal Justice*, 348.

[145] Author's field survey at Bauchi, Enugu, Ilorin-Kwara, Lagos, Kaduna and Port Harcourt, 2014.

control".[146] Some of the respondents interviewed especially the Social Workers at Grahamstown and Cape Town, South Africa[147] expressed their views that: "one of the major problems of child delinquency in South Africa today is drug addiction which aggravated most of the children brought before us to be judged delinquents". One of them went further to say: "we mostly regarded these children to be in need of care, protection and reformation and we do take them to Children's Court for adjudication other than Child Justice Court". The author contends that drug abuse contributes to acting-out behaviours which include certain mental illnesses, which have been directly correlated with criminal activity.

4.8 Accessibility to Firearms

Accessibility to firearms constitutes another important predictive factor of child delinquency in Nigeria and South Africa, although unlike the USA and other industrialised countries. It was revealed that as far back as 1965 and 1992, homicide and other violent crimes committed by children involving firearms increased nearly threefold in the USA and while the number of children arrested for weapons violation increased by 117%.[148] Not until very recent in the history of Nigeria as well as South Africa, children's access to firearms is limited to the locally made or hand-made guns and pistols or other sharp objects to cause harm to victims.[149]

The laws have made it in such a way that it is only a particular set of people with specified age brackets that have access to firearms.[150] Nevertheless, in a study conducted by the National Institute of Justice, findings suggested that one in five children studied carried a gun all or most of the time.[151] The discussion on selected predictive factors and perspectives provides us with an understanding of crime and delinquency especially their multiple and complex origins and manifestations. It

[146] Interview conducted by the author at Kaduna and Ilorin Borstal Institutions, 2014.

[147] Interview conducted by the author at Grahamstown and Cape Town, 2015.

[148] *Combating Violence and Delinquency: Juvenile Offenders & Victims* (Washington, DC: Department of Justice, 1997), 188.

[149] See Dambazau, A. B., *Criminology and Criminal Justice*, 350.

[150] Ibid.

[151] Ibid.

should be noted that the list is not exhaustive of factors that can directly or indirectly affect children in any society. The fact is that children may be criminally disposed internally or externally.

5 Preventive Mechanisms for Child Delinquency

There is a growing realisation that the Nigerian and South African society like many other countries around the world have expended vast resources on crime control and too little for the prevention of crime.[152] Incidentally, the United Nations instruments reflect a preference for "social, rather than judicial, approaches to controlling child delinquency". Also the United Nations Guidelines for the Prevention of Juvenile Delinquency (Riyadh Guidelines 1990) assert that "the prevention of child delinquency is an essential part of overall crime prevention in the society".[153]

The United Nations Standard Minimum Rules for the Administration of Juvenile Justice (the Beijing Rules) recommends "instituting positive measures to strengthen a child's overall well-being and reduce the need for State intervention".[154] Thus, it is the author's contention that early preventive measures are more appropriate in preventing child delinquency in Nigeria and South Africa. Some of the most promising preventive mechanisms and approaches for child delinquency, such as, initiatives and programmes are examined in some details below.

5.1 Assistance to Parents in Dealing with Early Behaviour Problems

The home is the first contact for every child. Thus, home plays a significant role in child's life and may influence his or her attitude either positively or negatively. The family, as the primary institution of socialisation, appears to play the most important role in the prevention of

[152] This is evident from series of criminal activities going on in several parts of the country like the *Boko Haram* insurgence, Niger Delta and Oil Pipeline vandalism, political killing, ethnic violence, kidnapping and mostly corruption in every facet of the Nigeria polity.

[153] United Nations Guidelines for the Prevention of Juvenile Delinquency (The Riyadh Guidelines) 1990.

[154] The United Nations Standard Minimum Rules for the Administration of Juvenile Justice (The Beijing Rules) 1985.

children delinquencies. It is argued that the child's needs for affection, security and opportunities for growth or development in shaping his or her personality are met or thwarted from home.[155] Children feel secured when the emotional maturity of parents, upon justice, truthfulness, regularity, order and serenity in the home are secure. It is argued that opportunities for development can be given to the child only by parents who want to see him or her grows and give him or her every chance to utilise and enlarge his or her own powers.[156] However, several factors may affect the home in the upbringing of children and in preventing child delinquency. For instance, "divorce/separation of couples" is one phenomenon adversely effecting the growth and development of children and strong instigative factor of child delinquency.[157] At least incidence of divorce occurs in one out of every six marriages (about one-third of the divorce cases involving children).[158] Other important factors that can deprive children of their fundamental rights to normal home life are parental separation and desertion.

It is the position of this book that assistance to parents in dealing with the problems of children often involves assistance to parents themselves in solving their marital disputes or problems. Promotion of stability and happiness of family life will aid in the prevention of child delinquency.[159] A complete outline of a preventive programme for early behaviour

[155] In an address on Child Welfare Standards a Test of Democracy at the National Conference of Social Work in 1919, Julia C. Lathrop, the first Chief of the Children's Bureau reiterated that children are not safe and happy if their parents are miserable, and parents must be miserable if they cannot protect a home against poverty. Let us not deceive ourselves. The power to maintain a decent family living standard is the primary essential of child welfare. This means a living wage and wholesome working life for the man, a good and skilful mother at home to keep the house and comfort all within it. Society can afford no less and can afford no exceptions. This is a universal need.

[156] See Blatz, William E., and Helen, B., *Parents and the Preschool Child* (New York: William Morrow & Co., 1929), 340.

[157] Dambazau, A. B, *Criminology and Criminal Justice*. Ibid., 352. See also the findings of the author in a field survey analysed in this book under the "causes of child delinquency"; particularly, the "parental neglect".

[158] Ibid.

[159] See Blatz, William E., and Helen, B., *Parents and the Preschool Child* (New York: William Morrow & Co., 1929), 350.

problems would include reference to the improvement of conditions affecting the family and child's life. For example, a cursory investigation into the countries of South Africa[160] and Nigeria[161] society reveals that the basic incomes of many families are very low.

It is suggested that every community should ensure that there are educational opportunities for parents on the principles of homemaking, family relationships and the education and care of their children. In doing this, suggested model of educational programmes by some scholars[162] must be designed to assist families and children by providing them with information that would assist parents on how to raise healthy children and teach children about the effects of drugs, gang involvement, sex and weapons. These programmes will instill in young persons' awareness that will allow them to exercise discretion in decision-making. Majority of the respondents views in an administered questionnaires by the author summarises this issue when 1042 (83%) out of 1258 of them strongly agreed that "national orientation on the ethical standard of behaviour will reduce incidents of child delinquency".[163] This position also conforms to the respondents' views at South Africa (Pretoria and Cape Town) that "enlightenment programmes for children on the benefits of good behaviour would reduce child delinquency".[164]

[160]Report has shown that "the number of persons living in extreme poverty (i.e. persons living below the 2015 Food Poverty Line of R441 per person per month) in South Africa increased by 2.8 million from 11 million in 2011 to 13.8 million in 2015". In the report, it shows that "the most vulnerable to poverty are the children (aged 17 or young)". See the report released by Statistics South Africa (StatsSA). Available at http://www.statssa.gov.za. Accessed on 28 November 2018.

[161]Report has shown that about 71% of Nigerians live on less than $1 a day and about 92% live on less than $2 a day. See World Resources Institute's environmental resource portal Earth Trends. Available at http://earthtrends.wri.org/povlinks/country/nigeria.php. Cited by Chimobi, Ucha, 'Poverty in Nigeria: Some Dimensions and Contributory Factors' (2010, June), *Global Majority E-Journal*, 1(1). Available at http://pdfs.semanticsholar.org. Accessed on 28 November 2018.

[162]See Blatz, William E., and Helen, B., *Parents and the Preschool Child* (New York: William Morrow & Co., 1929), 350.

[163]Author's field survey at Bauchi, Enugu, Ilorin-Kwara, Lagos, Kaduna and Port Harcourt, 2014.

[164]Interview conducted by the author at Pretoria, 2014 and Cape Town, 2015.

Similarly, special attention must be given to street children, and adolescents who have lost their families and thus have had no appropriate family surveillance.[165]

5.2 *Education and Public Opinion on the Rights of Children*

The plight of children globally, particularly in Africa continent, remains pitiable despite the existence of laws for the promotion and protection of their rights. A crucial approach to prevention of child delinquency starts with educating the public about the rights of children and the need to give them adequate opportunity for development. The author agreed with the study of Dambazau that "enlightened public opinion is one of the most important requisites for a successful programme for the prevention of child delinquency in Nigeria".[166] Therefore, the attitude of the public towards children should be characterised not by irritation or fear but by "understanding that the child needs protection, education, and guidance, in the community if possible and in a well-managed institution if necessary".[167]

It is important that the existence of behavioural problems in homes, schools and communities must be recognised by the public and appreciate that homes and neighbourhood conditions, such as the patience and resourcefulness of parents, relatives and friends, the economic condition of the family, the type of neighbourhood, more often than the degree of badness, determine whether or not a child should be referred to a juvenile/family court.[168]

[165]The United Nations Convention on the Rights of the Child provides a framework for improving the living conditions of children most especially Articles 2, 6, 12, 13, 14, 17, 19, 27.1, 26, 28, 32.1, 33, 34, 36 and 37. These provisions range from children survival's rights, development rights, protective rights and participation rights among others.

[166]Dambazau, A. B., *Criminology and Criminal Justice*, 355.

[167]Murphy, H. A., Hutchinson, J. M., and Bailey, J. S., 'Behavioral School Psychology Goes Outdoors: The Effect of Organized Games on Playground Aggression' (1983), *Journal of Applied Behavioral Analysis*, 16, 29–35.

[168]Facts About Juvenile Delinquency: Its Prevention and Treatment, Publication No. 215 United States Department of Labor Children's Bureau 193. Provided by the Maternal and Child Health Library, Georgetown University.

When the public is brought to an understanding and acceptance of its own responsibilities in the prevention and treatment of delinquency, it will be more willing to give the needed support to that well-rounded and coordinated community programme for the development of constructive, wholesome interests and the early study and guidance of children presenting problems of behaviour and personality.[169] This book contends that distribution of literature, newspapers, magazine, radio talks, lectures and study-club work will provide the very useful opportunity in re-orienting public opinion.

5.3 Social Work in the Schools

Social work in the school is another mechanism for preventing child delinquency in Nigeria and South Africa. When children enrol in school, he or she enters a new world and faces new conditions. Thus, individual differences and needs in children must be given adequate attention. In the modern style of education emphasis is placed on the person taught rather than the things taught.[170] The fact remains that the school undertakes not only to give the child an academic education but also to train him or her to fit into the society's complexities. Whatever the causes of child delinquency may be, it is usually during the school days that the child's most serious delinquencies develop, and the school is, therefore, most intimately involved in the whole problem of delinquency.[171]

[169] See Thom, Douglas A., *Everyday Problems of Everyday Child* (New York: Appleton & Co., 1932), 368.

[170] Kellam, S. G., Rebok, G. W., Ialongo, N., and Mayer, L. S., 'The Course and Malleability of Aggressive Behaviour from Early First Grade into Middle School: Results of a Developmental Epidemiologically Based Preventive Trial' (1994), *Journal of Child Psychology and Psychiatry and Allied Disciplines*, 35, 162–195.

[171] See Truitt, Ralph P., Lowrey, Lawson G., Hoffman, Charles W., Connor, William L., Ethel, T., and Fanny, R. K., 'The Child Guidance Clinic and the Community', a Group of Papers Written from the Viewpoints of the Clinic, the Juvenile Court, the School, the Child-Welfare Agency, and the Parent (New York: Commonwealth Fund Division of Publications, 1928), 106.

In essence, there must be a real programme for the prevention of delinquency and part of this promise should lie in the fact that the school must realise increasingly that the child it teaches has a life outside of that which is passed in the classroom and that he/she must be taught and treated and guided in the light of this fact and that the school must sincerely and vitally situate itself in the environment of the child it tries to teach.[172]

It is argued that school extracurricular activities/programmes will serve as interventions for reducing aggressive behaviour in the classroom. This was evidenced in the postulations of Murphy, Hutchinson and Bailey,[173] Kellam and Rebok,[174] Kellam et al.,[175] that evaluations of the Good Behaviour Game showed that proactive behaviour management can positively affect the long-term behaviour of the most aggressive elementary school children. By the postulation of Greenberg,[176] schools should design programmes that will enhance the development of social competence curriculums to promote norms against aggressive, violent and other anti-social behaviours. Conflict resolution and violence prevention curriculums, bullying prevention programmes, multi-component classroom programmes to improve academic achievement and reduce anti-social behaviours, after-school recreation programmes and mentoring programmes will also help in a greater way.[177] At the same time,

[172]Kellam, S. G., Rebok, G. W., Ialongo, N., and Mayer, L. S., 'The Course and Malleability of Aggressive Behaviour from Early First Grade into Middle School: Results of a Developmental Epidemiologically Based Preventive Trial', 35, 259–281.

[173]Murphy, H. A., Hutchinson, J. M., and Bailey, J. S., 'Behavioral School Psychology Goes Outdoors: The Effect of Organized Games on Playground Aggression', 16, 29–35.

[174]Kellam, S. G., and Rebok, G. W., 'Building Developmental and Etiological Theory Through Epidemiologically Based Preventive Intervention Trials', in J. Mccord and F. G. Tremblay (eds.), *Preventing Antisocial Behavior: Interventions from Birth Through Adolescence* (New York, NY: Guilford Press, 1992), 162–195.

[175]Kellam, S. G., Rebok, G. W., Ialongo, N., and Mayer, L. S., 'The Course and Malleability of Aggressive Behaviour from Early First Grade into Middle School: Results of a Developmental Epidemiologically Based Preventive Trial', 35, 259–281.

[176]Greenberg, M. T., 'Improving Peer Relations and Reducing Aggressive Behaviour: The Classroom Level Effects of the PATHS Curriculum', Paper Presented at the Society for Research in Child Development (Washington, DC, 1997).

[177]Ibid.

this book suggests that the schools and organisations should provide various services to assist in preventing or solving the various problems of school maladjustment and dissatisfaction which are fertile sources of delinquency.

These services should include health services and child-study departments and clinics, attendance departments like social work officers who will be visiting the schools, having conferences at schools with children, teachers and parents; they can equally visit homes and special schools. Classes should also be organised to cater for children whose needs cannot be met in regular classes. By this, such children will be placed in a special class equipped to deal scientifically with their particular difficulty.[178] Such classes include classes for children who have physical handicaps, mental handicaps, classes for retarded children who are mentally deficient and classes for gifted children for whom the challenge of a different school curriculum may be the solution to behaviour problems caused by lack of interest and satisfaction in their work.[179] Putting all these in school academic planning will go a long way in preventing child delinquency in Nigeria and South Africa.

5.4 Community Influences and Leisure-Time Activities

Community is an extension of the home and another world entirely beyond the precinct of home and school in which the child spends more of his/her time as he/she grows older. Community, therefore, helps to shape his/her personality, influence his/her conduct and attitude towards life.[180] The street on which the child lives and the neighbours with peers surrounding the child are but a few of the influences, tangible and intangible, that affect the child's daily life and that help to create what might be called the spirit of the neighbourhood.

[178] See Culbert, Jane F., *The Visiting Teacher at Work* (New York: Commonwealth Fund Division of Publications, 1929), 235.

[179] Kellam, S. G., Rebok, G. W., Ialongo, N., and Mayer, L. S., 'The Course and Malleability of Aggressive Behaviour from Early First Grade into Middle School: Results of a Developmental Epidemiologically Based Preventive Trial', 35, 259–281.

[180] See Rockwood, Edith, and Street, Augusta J., *Social Protective Work of Public Agencies with Special Emphasis on the Policewoman* (Washington: National League of Women Voters, 1932), 22.

The community may work together with its various agencies and NGOs in order to strengthen the child's moral and fit him/her to meet life squarely.[181] However, if the community lacks programme that may shape the life of a child in a positive way, the child may end up to dissatisfy his/her environment, and end up to rebel against his or her community, and thus, may become a delinquent child. Various studies have been done showing that delinquency is most likely to occur where proper community environment is lacking.[182] Therefore, the community should design programmes of prevention of child delinquency that will provide a constructive, wholesome, happy use of leisure time and a programme of protection against harmful and demoralising influences for children.

It is suggested that community resources for preventive and protective work should include, among others, the recreational facilities under public auspices which will accommodate public playground, athletic fields, municipal beaches, swimming pools, play streets, campsites, parks for picnics, public-library service, concerts and musical activities and museums. Summarily, the community should collaborate with private children's organisations such as child-welfare boards and departments including children's aid societies, child-protective associations, and societies for the prevention of cruelty to children in order to make the protection programmes work.

This book argued that, despite the availability of relevant prevention mechanisms, there is still increase in number of child offenders across the two countries.

6 Conclusion

This chapter examines the concept of child delinquency as a main gateway into the child justice system. It starts by defining the concept of childhood especially from the perspective of determining who is a child. This discussion is critical because of the controversies brought by different laws on the age of the child. The chapter went further to

[181] See Truxal, Andrew G., *Outdoor Recreation Legislation and Its Effectiveness* (New York: Columbia University Press, 1929), 218.

[182] Murphy, H. A., Hutchinson, J. M., and Bailey, J. S., 'Behavioral School Psychology Goes Outdoors: The Effect of Organized Games on Playground Aggression'.

examine the theories on child delinquency. In this part, the key theories explaining why children commit crimes are analysed. It is found that the sociological theory prevails most of the discourses on the causes of child delinquency. It is in this regard that the chapter focuses more specifically on examining the sociological theory and the various explanations under the theory. The chapter establishes that child delinquency is largely a group phenomenon and the discussion on selected predictive factors and perspectives in this chapter provide us with an understanding of crime and delinquency especially their multiple and complex origins and manifestations. The chapter observes that there is a correlation between abuse of young person and the development of serious problems in life which in turn is one of the most significant factors in the development of delinquent behaviour. It is found that the law plays a critical role on curbing and controlling child delinquency, and the unique system of child justice has an important role. However, this chapter contends that irrespective of the vast resources expanded by the two countries for the control of crimes particularly, child delinquency; it has been discovered that too little efforts were directed for the prevention of crimes. Thus, it is the chapter's contention that early preventive measures are more appropriate in preventing child delinquency. Furthermore, the chapter examine various preventive mechanisms for child delinquency that can be adopted in Nigeria and South Africa in this paradigm. Some of the most promising approaches, programmes and initiatives for the prevention of child delinquency are described in this chapter. Therefore, the next chapter will examine the nature and features of child justice administration with a specific focus on Africa.

References

Adenwalla, Ms. Maharukh, 'Child Protection and Juvenile Justice System: For Juvenile in Conflict with the Law'. Available at www.childlineindia.org.in/pdf/cp-JJ-JCL.pdf-similar. Accessed on 22 February 2011.

Alemika, E. E. O., and Chukwuma, I. C., *Juvenile Justice Administration in Nigeria: Philosophy and Practice* (Lagos: Centre for Law Enforcement Education, 2001).

Ayua, A. A., and Okagbue, I. E, *The Rights of the Child in Nigeria* (Lagos: Nigerian Institute of Advanced Legal Studies, 1996).

Becarria, C., *An Essay on Crimes and Punishment* (Wellesley, MA and London: Branden Publishing, 1992).

Blatz, William E., and Helen, B., *Parents and the Preschool Child* (New York: William Morrow & Co., 1929).

Burns, J. H., and Hart, H. L. A., *The Collected Works of Jeremy Bentham: An Introduction to the Principles of Morals and Legislation* (New York: Oxford University Press, 1996).

Campbell, J., *The Portable Jung* (New York: Penguin Books, 1976).

Cheatwood, Derral, 'Is There a Season for Homicide?' (1988), *Criminology*, 26, 287–306, cited in Freda, A., Gerhard, O. W. M., and Williams, S. L., *Criminology and the Criminal Justice System* (6th ed.; New York: McGraw-Hill, 2007).

Chimobi, Ucha, 'Poverty in Nigeria: Some Dimensions and Contributory Factors' (2010, June), *Global Majority E-Journal*, 1(1). Available at http://pdfs.semanticsholar.org. Accessed on 28 November 2018.

Cicchetti, D., and Rogosch, F. A., 'Finality and Multifinality in Developmental Psychopathology' (1996), *Journal of Development and Psychopathology*, 8. Available at http://www.ncjrs.gov/html/ojjdp/.../contents.ht.

Cole, J. D., Terry, R. A., Lenox, K., Lochman, J. E., and Hyman, C., 'Childhood Peer Rejection and Aggression as Predictors of Stable Patterns of Adolescent Disorder' (2003), *Journal of Development and Psychopathology*, 7(4), 697–713.

Costello, E. J., Farmer, E. M., Angold, A., Burns, B., and Erkanli, A., 'Psychiatric Disorders Among American Indian and White Youth in Appalachia: The Great Smoky Mountains Study' (1997), *American Journal of Public Health*, 87, 827–832.

Culbert, Jane F., *The Visiting Teacher at Work* (New York: Commonwealth Fund Division of Publications, 1929), 235.

Cummings, E. M., and Davies, P. T., 'Maternal Depression and Child Development' (1994), *Journal of Child Psychology and Psychiatry*, 35, 73–112.

Curran, D. J, and Renzetti, C. M., *Theories of Crime* (Boston: Allyn & Bacon), cited in Juvenile Delinquency: World Youth Report, 2003.

Dambazau, A. B., *Criminology and Criminal Justice* (Ibadan: Spectrum Books Limited, 2007).

Doherty, O., *Criminal Procedure in Nigeria* (Lagos: Blackstone Press, 1990).

Dugdale, R. L., *The Jukes: A Study in Crime, Pauperism, Disease, and Heredity* (3rd ed.; New York: G. P. Putnam's Sons, 1985).

Eron, L. D., and Huesmann, L. R., 'Television as a Source of Maltreatment of Children' (1987), *School Psychology Review*, 16.

Gardner, F. E. M., 'Positive Interaction Between Mothers and Conduct-Problem Children: Is There Training for Harmony as Well as Fighting?' (1987), *Journal of Abnormal Child Psychology*, 15.

Garlard, D., *The Culture of Control: Crime and Social Order in Contemporary Society* (London: Oxford, 2002).

Goldson, B., *The New Youth Justice* (Lyme Regis: Russell House, 2000).

Goldson, B., and Muncie, J., *Youth, Crime and Justice: Critical Issues* (London: Sage, 2006).

Greenberg, M. T., 'Improving Peer Relations and Reducing Aggressive Behaviour: The Classroom Level Effects of the PATHS Curriculum', Paper Presented at the Society for Research in Child Development (Washington, DC, 1997).

Gupte, A. K., and Dighe, S. D., *Criminal Manual* (5th ed., Chapter VI; Pune, Maharashtra: Hind Law House, 2001).

Hawkins, J. D., Lishner, D. M., Jenson, J. M., and Catalano, R. F., 'Delinquents and Drugs: What the Evidence Suggests About Prevention and Treatment Programming', in B. S. Brown and A. R. Mills (eds.), *Youth at High Risk for Substance Abuse* (DHHS Publication No. ADM 87–1537) (Washington, DC: U.S. Government Printing Office, 1987).

Hawkins, J. D., Herrenkohl, T., Farrington, D. P., Brewer, D., Catalano, R.F., and Harachi, T. W., 'A Review of Predictors of Youth Violence', in R. Loeber and D. P. Farrington (eds.), *Serious and Violent Juvenile Offenders: Risk Factors and Successful Interventions* (Thousand Oaks, CA: Sage, 1998).

Herrenkohl, T. I., Hawkins, J. D., Chung, I. J., Hill, K. G., and Battin-Pearson, S., 'School and Community Risk Factors and Interventions', in R. Loeber and D. P. Farrington (eds.), *Child Delinquents: Development, Intervention, and Service Needs* (Thousand Oaks, CA: Sage, 2001).

Hetherington, E. M., 'Coping with Family Transitions: Winners, Losers and Survivors' (1989), *Journal of Child Development*, 60, 1–17.

Hirschi, T., *Causes of Delinquency* (Berkeley: University of California Press, 1996).

Hughes, H. M., Parkinson, D., and Vargo, M. 'Witnessing Spouse Abuse and Experiencing Physical Abuse: A Double Whammy?' (1989), *Journal of Family Violence*, 4, 197–209.

Imran Ahsan Khan Nyazee, *Islamic Jurisprudence* (Islamabad: The International Institute of Islamic Thought, 2000), 111.

Jacobs, P., Brunton, M., Meville, M. M., et al., 'Aggressive Behaviour, Mental Sub-normality, and the XYY Male' (1965, December), *Nature*, 208, 1351–1352, cited in Juvenile Delinquency: World Youth Report, 2003.

Jaffe, P., Wolfe, D., and Wilson, S. K., *Children of Battered Women* (London: Sage, 1990).

James A. I., *Criminal Justice* (8th ed.; New York: McGraw-Hill, 2007).

Johnson, H. A., and Travis Wolfe, N., *History of Criminal Justice* (2nd ed.; Cincinnati, OH: Anderson, 1996), cited in Juvenile Delinquency: World Youth Report, 2003. Available at http://www.tdh-childprotection.org/documents/world/youth-report-chapter-7-juvenile-delinquency. Accessed on 21 March 2011.

Keller, T. E., et al., 'Parent Figure Transitions and Delinquency and Drug Use Among Early Adolescent Children of Substance Abusers' (2002), *Journal of Drug and Alcohol Abuse*, 28(3), 399–427.

Klein, M., *The American Street Gang: Its Nature, Prevalence and Control* (New York: Oxford University Press, 1995), 25.

Lahey, B. B., Piacentini, J. C., McBurnett, K., Stone, P., Hartdagen, S., and Hynd, G., 'Psychopathology in the Parents of Children with Conduct Disorder and Hyperactivity' (1988), *Journal of the American Academy of Child and Adolescent Psychiatry*, 27.

Le Blanc, M., Coté, G., and Loeber, R., 'Temporal Paths in Delinquency: Stability, Regression and Progression Analyzed with Panel Data from an Adolescent and Delinquent Sample' (1991), *Canadian Journal of Criminology*, 33, 23.

Loeber, R., and Farrington, D. P., *Serious and Violent Juvenile Offenders: Risk Factors and Successful Interventions* (Thousand Oaks, CA: Sage, 1998), 106–146.

Maguin, E., and Loeber, R., 'Academic Performance and Delinquency', in M. Tonry (ed.), *Crime and Justice: A Review of Research* (Chicago: University of Chicago Press, 1996).

Mason, A., 'Self-Esteem and Delinquency Revisited (Again): A Test of Kaplan's Self-Derogation Theory of Delinquency Using Latent Growth Curve Modeling' (2001), *Journal of Youth and Adolescence*, 30, 1.

McBride, D. C., and McCoy, C. B., 'The Drugs-Crime Relationship: An Analytical Framework' (1993), *The Prison Journal*, 73(3–4), 257–278, cited in Dambazau, A. B., *Criminology and Criminal Justice*.

McKibben, L., De Vos, E., and Newberger, E., 'Victimization of Mothers of Abused Children: A Controlled Study' (1989), *Pediatrics*, 84, 531–535.

McLanahan, S., and Booth, K., 'Mother-Only Families: Problems, Prospects, and Politics' (1989), *Journal of Marriage and the Family*, 51, 557–580.

Morenike, Franscis, 'Juvenile Justice in Nigeria: Dilemma of a Criminal Justice System'. Available at http://www.jjn/html. Accessed on 25 November 2008.

Murphy, H. A., Hutchinson, J. M., and Bailey, J. S., 'Behavioral School Psychology Goes Outdoors: The Effect of Organized Games on Playground Aggression' (1983), *Journal of Applied Behavioural Analysis*, 16.

Okonkwo, C. O., Nwankwo, Clement, and Ibhawoh, Bonny, *Administration of Juvenile Justice in Nigeria* (1st ed.; Lagos: Constitutional Rights Project (CRP), 1997), 6.

Patterson, G. R., and Stouthamer-Loeber, M., 'The Correlation of Family Management Practices and Delinquency' (1984), *Child Development*, 55, 1299–1307.

Pearson, J. L., Ialongo, H. S., Hunter, A. G., and Kellum, S. G., 'Family Structure and Aggressive Behaviour in a Population of Urban Elementary School Children' (1994), *Journal of the American Academy of Child and Adolescent Psychiatry*, 33.

Reid, W. J., and Crisafulli, A., 'Marital Discord and Child Behaviour Problems: A Meta-Analysis' (1990), *Journal of Abnormal Child Psychology*, 18, 105–117.

Robins, L. N., *Deviant Children Grown Up* (Baltimore, MD: Williams and Wilkins, 1966).

Rockwood, Edith, and Street, Augusta J., *Social Protective Work of Public Agencies with Special Emphasis on the Policewoman* (Washington: National League of Women Voters, 1932).

Sadr al-Shari'ah, Al-Tawdih, Vol. 2, 755, cited in Imran Ahsan Khan Nyazee (Islamabad: The International Institute of Islamic Thought, 2000), 111.

Sampson, R. J., 'Urban Black Violence: The Effect of Male Joblessness and Family Disruption' (1987), *American Journal of Sociology*, 93, 348–382.

Siegfried, C. B., Ko, S. J., and Kelley, A. 'Victimization and Juvenile Offending' (2004), *National Child Traumatic Stress Network*. Available at http://www.nctsnet.org/nctsn_assets/pdfs/edu.

Smith, J. C., and Hogan, B., *Criminal Law* (London: Butterworth, 1983).

Tarde, Gabriel, *Penal Philosophy* (R. Howell, Trans.; Boston: Little Brown, 1912).

Thom, Douglas A., *Everyday Problems of Everyday Child* (New York: Appleton & Co., 1932).

Truitt, Ralph P., Lowrey, Lawson G., Hoffman, Charles W., Connor, William L., Ethel, T., and Fanny, R. K., 'The Child Guidance Clinic and the Community', a Group of Papers Written from the Viewpoints of the Clinic, the Juvenile Court, the School, the Child-Welfare Agency, and the Parent (New York: Commonwealth Fund Division of Publications, 1928).

Truxal, Andrew G., *Outdoor Recreation Legislation and Its Effectiveness* (New York: Columbia University Press, 1929).

Vaden-Kiernan, N., Ialongo, N. S., Pearson, J. L., and Kellam, S. G., 'Household Family Structure and Children's Aggressive Behavior: A Longitudinal Study of Urban Elementary School Children' (1995), *Journal of Abnormal Child Psychology*, 23, 553–568.

Wasserman, G. A., Miller, L., Pinner, E., and Jaramillo, B. S., 'Parenting Predictors of Early Conduct, Problems in Urban, High-Risk Boys' (1996), *Journal of the American Academy of Child and Adolescent Psychiatry*, 35.

CHAPTER 3

The Nature of Child Justice Administration

1 Introduction

This chapter examines the historical evolution of child justice administration generally and with particular focus on Nigeria and South Africa. The examination takes into account the historical development of the countries' pre-/post-colonial periods and the influence on the later developments on policies and legislations which addresses the rights of children generally. An attempt is made to capture how the pre-colonial child justice system was practised and its influence on customary practice of child justice administration in Nigeria and South Africa before and during the colonial era. The chapter shows that the colonialism ushered in the westernisation, urbanisation and industrialisation drifts that led to social problems and rise in criminal offences among children which are alien to the traditional ways of dealing with crimes. It interrogates the colonial style of administration of child justice and further highlighted the challenges that have continued to besiege the entire criminal justice system from the two countries such as inadequacy or otherwise in the provision of separate custodial facilities for children and young persons. Thus, a large number of child offenders were deprived of the salutary impact of rehabilitative custodial environment due to their remand in squalid prison yards.

© The Author(s) 2020

M. A. Abdulraheem-Mustapha,
Child Justice Administration in Africa,
https://doi.org/10.1007/978-3-030-19015-6_3

In furtherance of the author's investigation, focus is made on post-colonial era. For instance, Nigeria experienced several years of military dictatorship, and the attitude of military rule to child right is examined. More so, the impact of the British colonial rule and legacy bequeathed to Nigeria and South Africa were analysed. The chapter explores how the economic policies of the country (i.e. Structural Adjustment Programme [SAP]) impacted negatively on the rights of children. It is not in dispute that SAP unleashed devastating socio-economic problem particularly on Nigeria, consequent upon which the country experienced serious level of poverty, unemployment and decadence in healthcare services, education, etc. It is thus not in doubt that children are one of those group affected particularly with respect to their right, i.e. to education, healthcare and peaceful environment for purposeful development. In the same paradigm, the chapter explicates the effect of the menace of insurgency (*Boko Haram*), cattle rustlers and other fundamentalists to the rights of children generally.

In like manner, the South African experience of incessant attack on foreigners; xenophobia; and the impact of the rights of children are investigated. Arguably, the phenomenon threatens the rights of children who need protection, as such explicating government efforts in protecting the rights of the children. As noted for the two contexts, the above-stated incidences inadvertently affect child rights; for instance, *Boko Haram* has used children as suicide bombers, and mostly, children are also involved in xenophobic attacks. The exposition of these facts and government synergy to protect child rights is significant to this book. Section 2 discusses the general theoretical expositions of child justice administration according to the principle underpinning international instruments on the subject by tracing the fundamental objectives of child justice system from its early development. This is done in order to lay a proper foundation for the objectives of this book. Section 3 of this chapter examines the procedural processes of child justice administration by following the examination of its uniqueness in contradistinction to the normal criminal justice system in Sect. 4. In this way, the basic characteristics of child justice system are elucidated.

2 Historical Development of Child Justice Administration

In the eighteenth and nineteenth centuries, there was little or no distinction between the adult and the child/juvenile offender either procedurally or in terms of punishment in Africa. The child was punished physically, transported or sent to prison or the hulks, under the same conditions as adults.[1] However, in the modern youth court, the predominant philosophy of criminal justice is based on the individual responsibility of actions leading to punishment as against the social work ideology of the welfare of the child (based on diagnosis of the child).[2]

Until the early nineteenth century, children were expected to enter adult world at a young age. Child labour was regarded as universal practice. For instance, in the early part of the nineteenth century, 80% of workers in English cotton mills were children.[3] Similarly, the criminal justice system did little to formally separate children from adults. In other words, there was no separate legal category of "child/juvenile offending". At common law, the age of criminal responsibility was seven years.[4] For children between the ages of seven and fourteen years, there was a presumption that they are "*doli incapax*", that is, *incapable of committing an offence.* However, this presumption is rebuttable by showing that the child knows the difference between right and wrong. It is not clear whether rules relating to the age of criminal responsibility were effective in practice.[5]

It is pertinent to note that different treatments for young offenders were introduced by the British legal system from 1850s onwards, when reformatory and industrial schools were first introduced.[6] In this

[1] Berlins, M., and Wansell, G., *Caught in the Act* (London: Macmillan, 1974), 1.

[2] Ibid.

[3] Ibid.

[4] Chris, C., and Robb, W., *Juvenile Justice: An Australian Perspective* (New York: Oxford University Press, 1995), 9. See also Dambazau, A. B., *Criminology & Criminal Justice* (Ibadan: Spectrum Books Limited, 2007), 337.

[5] Ibid.

[6] Bradley, Kate, *Juvenile Delinquency and the Evolution of the British Juvenile Courts, c. 1900–1950.*

regards, legal protections for children from various types of cruelty were ushered in by the "Children's Charter" of 1889. The Charter enabled the State to intervene in family life. However, this effort snowballed, as campaigners pressed for greater legal protection and coverage for children and young persons in the 1890s and 1900s.[7] These changes were part of a gradual evolution in the concept of childhood,[8] which led to new ideas about the ways in which the delinquent and vulnerable young person should be handled by the State.[9] Another effort was the establishment of the Child Study Movement in 1893,[10] and this Child Study Movement encouraged the view that "all children were individuals, and should be treated as such by parents, teachers, medical and social professionals".[11]

The ideas about the "scientific" application of welfare introduced by the Child Study Movement had an important influence upon the establishment of the "Cook County Juvenile Court" founded in Chicago, Illinois, in 1899[12] with the aim of providing "individual treatment for troubled children and to neutralise the impact of poor adult

[7] Ibid.

[8] Ibid.

[9] Behlmer, G., *Friends of the Family: The English Home and Its Guardians* (Stanford, 1998), 242–247.

[10] The Child Study Movement was founded in 1893 by James Sully, a British psychologist. The movement attracted other experts—such as the American psychiatrist G. Stanley Hall—and it also provided a forum for amateur readers alike to explore the psychology and psychiatry of the young.

[11] The Charity Organisation Society (COS) was concerned with the rational distribution of charitable alms among the needy, which they hoped to achieve through the careful investigation and consideration of the needs of individual families. See Lewis, J., *The Voluntary Sector, the State and Social Work in Britain: The Charity Organisation Society/ Family Welfare Association Since 1869* (London, 1995). Available at http://www.history.ac.uk/ihr/Focus/welfare/articles/bradleyk.html. Accessed on 30 May 2011.

[12] The Illinois Legislature created this nation's first juvenile court in Chicago after being lobbied by Timothy D. Hurley, a judge and former probation officer, and Julia Lathrop, of the Illinois Board of Charities with the help of the Catholic Visitation and Aid Society and the Chicago Bar Association who advocated abandonment of the system that placed child offenders and wayward children in adult jails and prisons and removed children who had been arbitrarily declared wayward from the custody of their parents and placed them in prisonlike institutions.

influence".[13] The development of new innovation by the Child Study Movement motivated some reformist circles in the UK and inspired the establishment of the first British juvenile court in Birmingham in 1900.[14] Similar to what is obtainable in the Cook County Court, the British courts also believed that "the delinquent young person needed to be saved in order to protect the wider society".[15]

These efforts led to the enactment of the British Children's Act of 1908[16] which provided clear provisions on the juvenile justice system. The power of the State was extended to the determination of family matters, and this extension formally introduced the juvenile court to the British legal system.[17] The British juvenile courts drew upon a diverse range of intellectual influences. It owed much to the development of the "social and socio-medical sciences", notably "criminology, psychology and psychiatry". The developments of these disciplines were partly an attempt to discover the causes of, and solutions to, deviant behaviours and social problems.[18]

However, new problems erupted for those involved in the juvenile courts in 1914 due to the outbreak of the First World War. Although before the war, the courts had made progress in establishing a new

[13]Clapp, E. J., *Mothers of All Children: Women Reformers and the Rise of Juvenile Courts in Progressive Era America* (University Park, PA, 1998), 89, 45 and 120.
Ibid.

[14]See Logan, A., 'A Suitable Person for Suitable Cases: The Gendering of Juvenile Courts in England c. 1910–39' (2005), *Twentieth Century British History*, 16, 129–145 and Bradley, K. M., 'Juvenile Delinquency, the Juvenile Courts and the Settlement Movement 1908–50: Basil Henriques and Toynbee Hall' (2008), *Twentieth Century British History*, 19, 133–135. Available at http://www.history.ac.uk/ihr/Focus/welfare/articles/bradleyk.html. Accessed on 30 May 2011.

[15]Ibid.

[16]The Children's Act 1908 had six parts: infant life protection; the prevention of cruelty; the prohibition of juvenile smoking the refining of the roles of industrial and reformatory schools; the creation of the juvenile courts; and a "miscellaneous" division which included such provision as the banning of under-fourteens from public houses.

[17]Hendrick, H., *Child Welfare: England 1872–1989* (London: 1994), 121–125. Available at http://www.history.ac.uk/ihr/Focus/welfare/articles/bradleyk.html. Accessed on 30 May 2011.

[18]Parry-Jones, W. L., 'The History of Child and Adolescent Psychiatry: Its Present Day Relevance' (1989) *Journal of Child Psychology and Psychiatry*, 30, 3–11 in Bradley, Kate, *Juvenile Delinquency and the Evolution of the British Juvenile Courts, c. 1900–1950*.

model for dealing with delinquent and vulnerable young persons, the courts were stretched to the limit by the rise in juvenile crime that occurred during the war.[19] Notwithstanding this, governmental commitment to the task of reducing and ideally preventing child delinquency continued after the First World War, especially as the Home Office became more comfortable with the changes introduced by the Children's Act of 1908.[20] Surprisingly in 1919, the Children's Branch of the Home Office was established for the purpose of extending their remit beyond the inspection of reformatory and industrial schools to include the management of juvenile courts, probation and places of detention.[21] It was through the Children's Branch that subsequent reforms of the 1908 Act were carried out.

Instructively, the campaigners and civil servants in UK registered their displeasure with the limits imposed by the Act and wished to add more proactive measures to reduce delinquency. A commissioned report establishing a link between the high wages earned by boys in "blind-alley" labour, the paucity of constructive leisure activities in some areas and higher rates of juvenile crime was submitted in 1920 by the Board of Education—again picking up themes expressed by Leeson and other researchers as well as those who had been involved in urban youth work.[22] In January 1925, the then Conservative Home Secretary named William Joynson-Hicks appointed a committee, chaired by Sir Thomas Molony, to investigate the treatment of "young offenders" who reported to the Conservative Home in 1927.[23] The report served as

[19] See Whitehead, P., and Statham, R., *The History of Probation: Politics, Power and Cultural Change 1876–2005* (Crayford, 2006). Available at http://www.history.ac.uk/ihr/Focus/welfare/articles/bradleyk.html. Accessed on 30 May 2011.

[20] Behlmer, G., *Friends of the Family*. Available at http://www.history.ac.uk/ihr/Focus/welfare/articles/bradleyk.html. Accessed on 30 May 2011.

[21] Lerman, P., 'Policing Juveniles in London, Shifts in Guiding Discretion, 1893–1968' (1984), *British Journal of Criminology*, 24, 168–184; 175–176.

[22] Ibid.

[23] "The welfare of the child or young person as the primary object of the juvenile court" formed part of the committee's report in 1927. The report committee also called for magistrates with experience in dealing with young people, and that younger magistrates should be recruited to these posts. The committee's report further reiterated the importance of issues raised by the 1908 Act, notably that "juvenile courts should be held at different times and in different places to adult sittings of courts". In addition, the report also

the foundation for "the Children and Young Persons Bill", which was enacted in 1933 in the UK as "The Children and Young Persons Act of 1933" with extended features of the "1908 Act".[24] The need for a comprehensive law that will adequately address the lapses in the child justice system culminated into the enactment of the English Children's Act of 1948. On this background, the discussion of the Nigerian and South African child justice administration in the next subsection can be divulged from the two countries colonialisms.

2.1 Nigerian Child Justice Administration

Although there is a dearth of literature on this aspect of study in Nigeria, the history and theory of child justice system cannot be separated from the linkage of the Nigeria Legal System to that of the colonialist. In the pre-colonial era, child justice system has been regarded as normative practice and being practised in the traditional set-up.[25] Usually, the extended family and the traditional community structures provide the necessary checks on the attitudes and excesses of depraved children within the society.[26] From the Nigerian customary law

demanded that "court proceedings be made as simple as possible in order that children and young people might better understand what was happening around them". But the report went further, calling for children and young people to remain anonymous and to be in no way identifiable in media reporting of cases. It was felt that public knowledge of a child's acts could in future unfairly jeopardise their chances of finding employment. It further demanded that courts be furnished with as much information as possible about the lives of the children brought before it, about their school attendance, their health and their home environment. Probation was an important part of the work of the court with young offenders, a method by which the young person could be reclaimed to good citizenship through the firm and wise guidance of an appropriate adult. See the report of the Departmental Committee on the Treatment of Young Offenders (Cmd 2831, London, 1925–1927), 121–123. Available at http://www.history.ac.uk/ihr/Focus/welfare/articles/bradleyk.html. Accessed on 30 May 2011.

[24] See the report of the Departmental Committee on the Treatment of young Offenders (Cmd 2831, London, 1925–1927), 121–123. Available at http://www.history.ac.uk/ihr/Focus/welfare/articles/bradleyk.html. Accessed on 30 May 2011.

[25] Nwanna, Chinwe R., and Akpan, Naomi, E. N., *Research Findings of Juvenile Justice Administration in Nigeria* (Lagos: Constitutional Right Project [CRP], 2003), 1–2. See also, Okonkwo, C. O., Nwankwo, C., and Ibhawoh, B., *Administration of Juvenile Justice in Nigeria* (1st ed.; Lagos: Constitutional Rights Project [CRP], 1997), 1–2.

[26] Ibid.

perspective, for instance the Yoruba-African society, the institution of punishment is very important and its central purpose is towards reduction or avoidance of crime in the society.[27] Bolaji Idowu in his work posited that:

> punishment in Yoruba society also assumes that one is a rational human being that has a choice of action(s) and can be held responsible for this choice of action. Man is expected to be morally responsible for an action which he has control over.[28]

In the realm of child justice system, it has been argued that "as for children and infants, the traditional Yoruba believed that they are not beyond the law". Hence, the Yoruba would say "*ati kekere latin peka iroko*" ("it is from infancy that we prune the branches of an *Iroko* tree").[29] Thus, children are expected to be curbed from wrongdoing before they become uncontrollable. The underlying assumption is that "the mind of the infant is still young and can be modeled at this age to conform to the ideas of the society. Once the child grows to maturity, he or she would have formed habits which may be detrimental to the society and the habit will not be easily remodeled".[30]

However, most of the times in Yoruba society, punishment goes beyond the offender and can be extended to the people that surround the child offender because of the communal nature of Yoruba society.[31] The underlying principle of Yoruba culture is that "whatever affects one affects also the others". That is why the Yoruba says: "*Ti ara ileeni ban je kokoro tiko da ti a koba so fun kurukere re koni je ka sun ni oru*" ("if your neighbour is eating poison and you do not warn him the result may be disturbing at night for both of you").[32]

[27] Oduwole, E. O, 'Punishment as a Form of Legal Order in an African Society' (2011) *International Research Journals*, 2(5), 1124–1129.

[28] Idowu, E. B, *Olodumare: God in Yoruba Belief* (Ibadan: Longman, 1962) in Oduwole, E. O, 'Punishment as a Form of Legal Order in an African Society'.

[29] Ibid.

[30] Ibid.

[31] Mbiti, J. S, *African Philosophy and Religions* (Heinemann, 1982), 206. See also Ajisafe Moore, E. A., *The Laws and Customs of the Yoruba People in Abeokuta Nigeria* (Fola Bookshops, 2010) in Oduwole E. O., 'Punishment as a Form of Legal Order in an African Society'.

[32] Ibid.

In the Igbo society, there appears to be no distinction in the treatment of adult and the young offender. The retributive and penal justice practices are the major focus of Igbo society in its understanding of the concept of criminal justice, and these practices were demonstrated in the punishments meted to the respective offenders which include death penalty in very extreme cases, "ostracism, banishment, restitution, fine, compensation, forfeiture, seizure of valuable property, caricature" and so on.[33] Significantly, Igbo criminal and penal justice systems are premised on the "important value of reconciliation and peace-making".[34]

With the westernisation, urbanisation and industrialisation, people including young persons and children started migrating to cities for a standard way of life. These created new social problems such as overpopulation and the increasing neglect of the welfare of many children resulting from the rural–urban drift. This development increased the rate of child delinquency; thus, the resultant effect was the rise in criminal offences among young persons.[35] The Second World War exacerbated the situation in 1945 where a large number of children of soldiers serving with the British forces in the war started moving out of their villages to the main urban centres of Lagos, Enugu and Kano resulting in unprecedented influx of idle youths in these urban centres. Many of the young persons who had no means of livelihood later resorted to crime and other acts of delinquency. These and many other problems such as destitution and unemployment were alien to the traditional ways of dealing with crimes. These problems instigated the need for the formal or British style of administration of child justice in Nigeria as well as the procedure for the prosecution of young offenders.[36] The western way of dealing with such anti-social

[33] Ikenga, K. E. O., 'Crime and Punishment in Igbo Customary Law: The Challenge of Nigerian Criminal Jurisprudence'. Available at www.ajol.info/index.php/og/article/download/57917/46285. Accessed on 18 December 2013. See also, Ikenga, K. E. O., 'The Principles and Practice of Justice in Traditional Igbo Jurisprudence'. Available at www.ajol.info/index.php/og/article/viewFile/52335/40960. Accessed on 18 December 2013.

[34] Ibid.

[35] Drug abuse, teenage pregnancies, prostitution, alcoholism, robbery and violence have proliferated among young persons.

[36] Nwanna, Chinwe R., and Akpan, *Research Findings of Juvenile Justice Administration in Nigeria*, 5.

problems was adopted through the introduction of social welfare services, approved schools and remand homes to rehabilitate and reform the delinquent children.[37]

The Nigerian experience of child justice administration like all aspects of her legal system has its historical linkage with British that colonised the country.[38] Laws on child justice administration in Nigeria were based on the British philosophy of justice with oppressive penal institutions that favoured their interests especially on issues of punishment that makes no distinction between adult and child offenders.[39] For instance, it was revealed that the aim of the criminal justice system of which the child justice system is a component was to promote and protect the economic interest of the British colonial government rather than the interest of Nigerians. Historically, therefore, the Nigerian criminal justice agencies were created, not as instruments of security and justice, but as weapons of oppression.[40]

[37] Ibid.

[38] The logic of colonialism is the political subjugation and domination of a people in order to exploit their labour and resources. Colonial rule, therefore, required repressive legal system, especially vicious and oppressive penal institutions with effective capacity to repress, punish and deter individuals and groups that engage in activities that are deemed detrimental to colonial political and economic interests. Thus, colonial legal and penal institutions were not designed to protect the interests of the generality of citizens but rather to defend the political and economic interests of the rulers in Alemika, E. E. O., and Chukwuma, I. C., *Juvenile Justice Administration in Nigeria: Philosophy and Practice*, 25.

[39] Three conferences were held in Nigeria on Juvenile Justice Administration alone in 2002. The three conferences were the National Conference on Juvenile Justice Administration in Nigeria Abuja, 2–3 July 2002, the Northern Zonal Consultative Conference on Juvenile Justice Administration in Nigeria, Kano, 16–17 September 2002, and the Southern Zonal Consultative Conference on Juvenile Justice Administration in Nigeria, Ibadan, 16–17 October 2002. These three conferences were a collaborative initiative by the National Human Rights Commission (NHRC), Constitutional Rights Project (CRP), Penal Reform International (PRI) and UNICEF. http://www.Cleen.org/Juvenile%20justice%20Report.pdf. Accessed on 17 February 2011.

[40] Alemika, E. E. O., and Chukwuma, I., *Police-Community Violence in Nigeria* in Alemika, E. E. O., and Chukwuma, I. C., *Juvenile Justice Administration in Nigeria: Philosophy and Practice*. See also Odekunle, F., 'The Nigeria Police Force: A Preliminary Assessment of Functional Performance' (1979), *International Journal of Sociology of Law*, 6, 73–78; Alemika, E. E. O., 'The Smoke Screen, Rhetoric and Reality of Penal Incarceration in Nigeria' (1988), *International Journal of Comparative and Applied Criminal Justice*, 7(1) 138–149; Alemika, E. E. O., 'Policing and Perception of Police in Nigeria' (1988), *Police Studies: International Review of Police Development*, 11(4),

The philosophy and practice of child justice administration in Nigeria have been hampered with several fundamental defects which can be understood, largely in terms of the evolution of the country's legal system. For instance, the colonial institution was designed to take control of "deprived and destitute natives, including children, so that they do not constitute a threat or nuisance to the colonial order".[41] The fundamental restructuring of the system of criminal justice to serve as an instrument for the promotion of security and justice as well as the protection of human dignity and rights of the citizens was complicated due to the failure of successive government since independence.[42]

The system of child justice in Nigeria was also modelled after the British system, and the system was established in 1914.[43] Children's court proceedings took place in two courts—"a higher court consisting of a single Judge and a Magistrate court consisting of a magistrate and two lay persons, including a woman". Proceedings were formal and were intended to protect the children's rights. In contrast to many countries however, Nigeria places more emphasis on punishment than on rehabilitation of child offenders.[44] Community treatment efforts are generally not well organised in the country. According to some experts, lack of a countrywide rehabilitation system is partly as a result of the breakdown in the extended family system which has previously influenced the socialisation process and control of children.[45]

161–176; Alemika, E. E. O., 'Socio-Economic and Criminology Attributes of Convicts in Two Nigerian Prisons' (1988), *Journal of Criminal* Justice, 16(3), 197–207; Alemika, E. E. O., 'Colonialism, State and Policing Nigeria' (1993), *Crime Law and Social Change*, 187–219; Ahire, P. T., *Imperial Policing Milton Keynes* (Open University Press 1991) in Alemika, E. E. O., and Chukwuma, I. C., *Juvenile Justice Administration in Nigeria: Philosophy and Practice*; Adewoye, O., *The Judicial System in Southern Nigeria 1854–1954* (London: Longman 1977); and Tamuno, T. N., *The Police in Modern Nigeria* (Ibadan: University Press 1970), 45; Milner, W. B. 'Lower Class Culture as Generating Milieu of Gang Delinquency' (1958), *Journal of Social Issues*, 14, 5–19.

[41] Ibid.

[42] Ibid.

[43] Ibid.

[44] See Alemika, E. E. O., and Chukwuma, I. C., *Juvenile Justice Administration in Nigeria: Philosophy and Practice.*

[45] Juvenile Justice Report: 'Juvenile Justice in Nigeria'. Available at http://www.britannica.com/EBcheckedtopic/kuvenilejustice/nigeria. Accessed on 2 February 2009.

It is apposite to note that Nigeria experienced several years of military dictatorship which has an impact on the child justice system. More so and as earlier stated, the British colonial rule and legacy bequeathed to Nigeria have helped shape the child justice system. Another significant influence is certain economic policies (i.e. SAP). It is not in dispute that SAP unleashed devastating socio-economic problem particularly on Nigeria, consequent upon which the country experienced serious level of poverty, unemployment and decadence in healthcare services, education, etc. It is thus not in doubt that children are one of those groups affected particularly with respect to their right, i.e. to education, healthcare and peaceful environment for purposeful development. In the same paradigm, the book explicates the effect of the menace of insurgency (*Boko Haram*), cattle rustlers and other fundamentalists to the rights of children generally. Study has shown that on 10 December 2016, *Boko Haram* used children aged between seven and eight year old to carry out a suicide at Potiskum.[46] On 14 March 2017, at least six persons were confirmed killed by four teenage girls who detonated explosives worn around their bodies at the outskirts of Maiduguri.[47] Further still, on 17 November 2017, three female teenage bombers died in an attack in Maiduguri[48] and a report by CNN stated that:

> of the 134 suicide bombers whose age could be determined, 60% were teenagers or children. The youngest suicide bomber identified to date was just 7 years old. *Boko Haram* has used four times as many young girls as it has young boys.[49]

Emphatically, child delinquency as a global phenomenon is attracting the attention of stakeholders within the domestic and international spheres.

[46] 'Girls "Aged 7 or 8" Staged Maiduguri Suicide Attack—Witnesses', *Punch*, 11 December 2016.

[47] 'Six Killed as Suicide Bombers Attack Maiduguri', *Premium Times*, 15 March 2017. Available at https://www.premiumtimesng.com/news/top-news/226150-six-killed-suicide-bombers-attack-maiduguri.html. Accessed on 10 December 2017.

[48] 'Three Female Suicide Bombers Die in Failed Attacks on Maiduguri—SEMA', *Punch*, 18 November 2017.

[49] Robyn Kriel, 'Boko Haram Favors Women, Children as Suicide Bombers, Study Reveals', *CNN*, 11 August 2017. Available at: https://edition.cnn.com/2017/08/10/africa/boko-haram-women-children-suicide-bombers/index.html.

Nigeria as a member of the international community and a signatory to Regional and International Conventions reformed its child justice laws with the enactment of its Child Rights Act[50] and domestication of the Children and Young Persons Act[51] with corresponding laws in various States of the Federation. The country has in a very short period developed a legal framework for child justice administration in the face of very difficult circumstances that exist presently in Nigeria. The law reforms movement is extremely open about the adversities presently faced by children in Nigeria. The commitment of these participants was focused on ensuring that "the law reform process focuses on a child's rights approach while establishing procedures that are capable of being properly implemented".[52] But this reformation is not offered as a panacea to address the delinquency problems; rather, it only attempts to reform the basic political, economic and social structures of a certain class of individuals.

It is pertinent to note that the coverage of the Nigerian law on child justice system is quite inadequate as a large number of children technically fall outside the purviews of these laws. It may be argued that "the resources and infrastructure required for the effective implementation of children's laws are hardly proportionate to the population and geographical regions covered under it".[53] Children caught in the system are often helpless with very little redress. Despite the establishment of custodial institutions by the Nigerian government to cater for delinquent children, the increase in the number of children getting involved in crimes continues unabated, to the extent that the corrective institutions set up to reform these child offenders are now over-stretched with only minimal care available and child protection becomes more of charity than a commitment. Protection of such children is not seen as a right but as charity or welfare.[54]

[50] Child Right Act Cap C50 Laws of the Federation of Nigeria, 2004.

[51] Children and Young Persons Act came into being in 1943 to guide the administration of the juvenile justice system which in turn constitutes part of the pillars of the Nigerian criminal justice system.

[52] The Dynamics of Youth Justice and The Convention on the Rights of the Child in Juvenile Justice Report: 'Juvenile Justice in Nigeria'. Available at http://www.britannica.com/EBcheckedtopic/kuvenilejustice/nigeria. Accessed on 15 July 2011.

[53] See Juvenile Justice. Available at www.ksrmccs.ac.in/wp-content/.../JUVENILE-JUSTICE.docx. Accessed on 20 June 2011.

[54] See generally, Ladan, M. T., *Rights of the Child in Nigeria: An Overview in Individual Rights and Communal Responsibility in Nigeria* (Abuja, Nigeria: National Human Rights Commission, 1998), 25.

It is argued that very few studies have been conducted in the area of child offenders, although much has been written about victim children and children in need of care and protection. The State machinery keeps this class of offenders in institutions such as prison, Borstal institutions, government-approved schools and remand homes where no outsider is allowed to tread, and leaves them without adequate attention being paid to their well-being and rehabilitation. Child offenders in these institutions are eventually released to the society ill-equipped to handle challenges of life upon completion of their terms of confinement. It is instructive to note that this treatment meted out to child offenders is most deplorable, especially when children legislations recognise that children in conflict with the law require special care and protection. The system of child justice has been based on a balance between the need to punish or control young offenders and to encourage them to take responsibility for their actions. The system also employs strategies which take account of many problems which may have led to the involvement of children and young persons in crime (otherwise known as welfare-based approach). It also carries out intensive monitoring in an effort to control and limit the opportunities for criminal activity.

Instructively, the philosophy behind the evolution of child justice system was premised on the fact that generally, children alleged to have committed an offence should be treated differently from adults.[55] However, the major challenges that have continued to besiege the entire criminal justice system are lack of separate and adequate custodial facilities for children and young persons in Nigeria unlike South Africa. In addition, the system contends with the serious challenges of poor child justice administration. This was evident from the study conducted by Alemika and Chukwuma that "a large number of child offenders are being remanded in squalid prisons and being deprived of the salutary impact of reformative and rehabilitative custodial environments".[56]

An examination of the existing materials on child justice administration shows that the child justice sector remains a weak area with little or no priority from within the adjudicatory system. Also, lack of separate

[55] Roberts, Cynthia H., *Juvenile Delinquency: Causes and Effect* (Yale-Haven Teachers Institute, 1986). Available at http://www.yale.edu/yhnt/curriculum. Accessed on 2 May 2012.

[56] Alemika, E. E. O., and Chukwuma, I. C., *Juvenile Justice Administration in Nigeria: Philosophy and Practice* (Lagos: Centre for Law Enforcement Education, 2001), 30.

and specific courts dedicated to child justice in Nigeria and poor legal representation during prosecution of child offenders most often results in many of them being kept in custody with adults.

Despite years of the enactment of a specific law aimed at dealing with child delinquency, the situation on ground has not changed much. The author therefore calls for a complete overhauling of the child justice system to tackle the sluggish pace of judicial processes and lack of proper care at custodial institutions. There is clearly a need for greater concern about, and discussion of, the current orientation towards delinquent behaviours, and how it can be ameliorated. There is also the need to empirically examine different options currently in use both in the child and in the adult justice systems for those described as young adults. This brings to the fore the need for progressive-minded individuals to investigate all such areas in order to sensitise the public and effectively mobilise the society towards the restructuring and re-orientation of what it sees as moribund institutions and practices. It is hoped that this book would be recommended for various children's institutions in Africa and will be a beginning of an era of improvement in child justice administration in order to enable Africa catch up with the developments in the rest of the world in the field.

2.2 South African Child Justice Administration

It is important to note from the outset that, before the coming of the colonial masters, South African community has its own established traditional modes for the protection and welfare of the children.[57] However, children's rights were sometimes subjugated to broader interests of the community. For instance, a child may be given out to other relatives to look after cattle.[58] In the same vein, customary law rules regulating children's rights existed. That is, a female child family receives cattle from the prospective husband in consideration for marriage, or payment to someone raising another person's child.[59] In the traditional South African community, adulthood was not determined by age; rather, it commences

[57] Maithufi, Ignatius, 'The Best Interest of the Child and African Customary Law', in C. J. Davel (ed.), *Introduction to Child Law in South Africa* (2000), 140.

[58] ibid.

[59] Ibid.

after certain rituals before the transformation of a child to an adult.[60] The contact with colonialism around 1652 ushered in laws relating to the care and protection of children.[61] In gradual development, South Africa witnessed the following on the protection of children:

i. 1674 Dutch East Indian Company established an Orphan Chamber to administer wills so that the interest of children could be protected.[62]
ii. In 1815, Children Home was built by the British through the effort of Margaretha Heyning, widow of Hendrik Moller and called "the South Africa Orphanage".[63] More Orphanage Homes were later established specifically for girls in 1862, House of Mercy for Wayward Girls in 1868 and Orphanage Home for boys and girls in 1882.[64]
iii. The early law of English Child can be found in the practice of apprenticeship which found its way through the Masters and Servants Act, 1856, for the purpose of placement of dependent children under the guardianship of suitable persons and to be taught a trade.[65]
iv. Reformatory Institution Act of 1879 was established as a response to the views that children are victims of their circumstances deserving special care and treatment.[66] This led to the establishment of the Deserted Wives and Children's Protection Act 7 of 1895 which gave powers to the magistrate to issue summons to force husband who had deserted his wife and children to appear before the court unless he could show reasons why he was not

[60] Bekker, J. C., 'Children and Young Persons in Indigenous Law', in J. A. Robinson (ed.), *The Law of Children and Young Persons in South Africa* (1997), 193.

[61] History of Southern Africa South of the Zambezi (1907), 221.

[62] Bekker, J. C., 'Children and Young Persons in Indigenous Law', in J. A. Robinson (ed.), *The Law of Children and Young Persons in South Africa* (1997), 193.

[63] Theal, G. M., History of South Africa Since 1795: The Cape Colony from 1795 to 1828 (Vol. 5, 1964), 286–288.

[64] Midgley, James, *Children on Trial: A Study of Juvenile Justice* (1975), 53.

[65] Eakelaar, J., 'Child Endangerment and Child Protection in England and Wales', in M. Rosenheim, F. Zimring, D. Tanenhaus, and B. Dohm B (eds.), *A Century of Juvenile Justice* (2002), 384.

[66] Alice Saffy, Jacqueline, 'A Historical Perspective of the Youthful Offender', in C. Bezuidenhout and S. Joubert (eds.), *Child and Youth Misbehaviour in South Africa* (2003), 18.

maintaining his wife and children.[67] Similarly, the Cruelty to Animals Act 13 of 1895 dealing with the care and protection of children was also passed which later led to the first comprehensive piece of legislation on care and protection of children found begging and wandering without support or living in a brothel in South Africa in the same year. This Care of Neglected Children Act 24 of 1895 empowered the court to order a child to be committed to an institution or to a boarding school and order the parents to pay for the child's maintenance.[68] This was followed by the enactment of the Child Protection Act 38 of 1901 (hereafter called the Natal Act). The Act empowered the magistrate to make an order to refer a destitute child to a society or government institution, to be apprenticed to a suitable person, to be boarded out with a suitable person or placed at service with a suitable person.[69]

Instructively, South Africa being a Union in 1910 consolidated the laws from the colonies and the Boer Republics with the enactment of the Children's Care and Protection Act 25 of 1913 (hereafter called "the Children's Charter").[70] The Act ushered an important innovation of establishment of places of safety for children against whom offences were committed to be temporarily detained and to seek refuge.[71] This Act was replaced with the Children's Act 31 of 1937 with the raising of the age which a person was considered to be a child from 16 to 19 years.[72] This Act also consolidated the legislative framework for destitute children and included adoption laws within its ambit. For the first time in history, the "Children's courts" were introduced and the Act declared that every magistrate was a "commissioner of child welfare" with the replacement of the term such as "destitute children" with "children in need of care and protection".[73]

[67] Ibid.

[68] Ibid.

[69] Ibid.

[70] Geffen, Irene, *The Laws of South Africa Affecting Women and Children* (1928), 341.

[71] Ibid.

[72] Van der Spuy, E., Scharf, W., and Lever, J., 'The Politics of Youth Crime and Justice in South Africa', in C. Sumner (ed.), *The Blackwell Companion to Criminology* (2004), 172.

[73] Ibid.

In the Apartheid era, Children's Act 33 of 1960 was also enacted. In pursuance to the Act, the age of criminal responsibility and definition of a child was lowered from 19 to 18 years.[74] It introduced temporary placement observation and treatment. The Act was the first South African statute to use the term "Foster Care".[75] It was followed by Child Care Act 74 of 1983. The Act introduced new measures in relation to adoption, allowing the children's court to dispense with the consent of the parent who has assaulted or mistreated the child.[76] It is, however, noted that the Act foresees neither the phenomenon of street children and unaccompanied foreign children that would arise in the following decades, nor the burden of HIV/AIDS.[77]

The development of children protection as one of the priorities of the South African government cannot be separated from its constitutional development. This can be found in the draft of the children's section in the Bill of Right with particular role given to the court to bear the task of interpreting the nature and extent of children's rights.[78] The effort in protecting children eventually metamorphoses into a comprehensive section that provides strong protection of children. In gradual processes of constitutional drafting and expansion of areas of coverage for the children's rights, such name, nationality, parent care, social services, shelter, protection against maltreatment, abuse and degradation and right to legal practitioner eventually accounted for the insertion of Section 28 in the 1996 of the Constitution of the Republic of South Africa (as amended).[79]

[74]Bosman-Swanepoel, H. M., and Wessels, P. J., *A Practical Approach to the Child Care Act* (1995), 5.

[75]Ibid.

[76]Sinclair, June D., and Bedil, Susan, 'Law of Persons' (1983), *Annual Survey of South Africa Law*, 73.

[77]Ibid.

[78]See du Plessis, Lourens, M., and Corder, H., *Understanding South Africa's Transitional Bill of Rights* (1994), 38, 46, 185–187 (Bill of Rights); du Plessis, Lourens, M., 'A Background to Drafting the Chapter on Fundamental Rights', in B. de Villiers (ed.), *Birth of a Constitution* (1994), 90–91; du Plessis, Lourens, 'The Genesis of the Chapter on Fundamental Rights I South Africa's Transitional Constitution' (1994), *SA Public Law*, 9, 10; Sloth-Nielson, Julia, 'Chicken Soup or Chainsaws: Some Implications of the Constitutionalisation of Children's Rights in South Africa', *Acta Juridica* (1996), 6–12; Skelton Thesis, 392–395; and Dutschke, Mira, *Defining Children's Constitutional Rights to Social Services. A Project 28 Working Paper* (2006), 48–52 (*Defining*).

[79]See Technical Committee on Fundamental Rights, *First Progress Report*, 14 May 1993, 4. See also, Section 30 of the Constitution of the Republic of South Africa Act 200 of 1993.

Again, the synergy of advancing the special protection for children during the constitutional drafting in 1993 and 1996 later influenced the South African government being signatory and ratified the UN Convention on the Rights of the Child[80] (CRC), the Hague Conventions on Abduction[81] and Adoption.[82] In effect, the ratifications signified the South African's readiness to apply CRC and acceptance of international body of human rights on children's protection. The important sections giving legal backing to the right of a child are Sections 28 and 36(2) of the Constitution which direct court to consider international law when interpreting a right in the Bill of Rights.[83]

It is regrettable to note at this point that no such provision exists under the Nigerian Constitution even though the country domesticated CRC which informed the enactment of the Child Rights Act by the National Assembly. Aside from the above weakness, the application of the Child Rights Act in Nigeria is not national in nature, and its adoption is subject to its further domestication by States of the Federation of Nigeria that so desires.

Historically, with the Constitution legitimising the children's protection, several other legislations were enacted to complement the constitutional protection with other policies put in place for the welfare of

[80]The Convention on the Rights of the Child was ratified by South Africa ratified in June 1995.

[81]South Africa acceded to the Hague Convention on the Civil Aspects of International Child Abduction with the promulgation of the Hague Convention on the Civil Aspects of International Child Abduction Act 72 of 1996 which is repealed by the present Children's Act 38 of 2005. See Chapter 17 of the Act in particular.

[82]South Africa acceded to the Hague Convention on Protection of Children and Co-operation in Respect of Inter-Country Adoption on 1 December 2003. This was also repealed by the Children's Act. See Chapter 16 of the Act in particular.

[83]Many Constitutional Court judgements referred to the Convention and other international children's rights instruments. See the cases of *Grootboom v Oostenberg Municipality 2000 (3) BCLR 277(C)*; *Du Toit v Minister of Welfare and Population Development (Lesbian and Gay Equality Project as Amicus Curiae) 2003 (2) SA 198 (CC)*; *South African Human Rights Commission v President of the Republic of South Africa 2005 (1) SA 580 (CC)*; *AD v DW (Centre for Child Law as Amicus Curiae) 2008 (3) SA 183 (CC)*; *Director of Public Prosecutions, Transvaal v Minister of Justice and Constitutional Development and Others 2009 (4) SA 222 (CC)*; *Governing Body of the Juma Musjid Primary School and Others v Essay NO and Others (Centre for Child Law and Another as Amicus Curiae) 2011 (8) BCLR 761 (CC) (hereafter Juma Musjid);* and *C and Others v Department of Health and Social Development, Gauteng, and Others 2012 (2) SA 208 (CC).*

children in South Africa. It is instructive at this point to mention some of these legislations:

i. Children's Act: this Act came into existence following the reform on the Child Care Act which was drafted during the apartheid era. The reform for its re-conceptualisation started in 1997 and eventually was enacted in 2005.
ii. Child Justice Act: this Act focuses more on the procedural aspect or better still a criminal adjudication law on children in South Africa, particularly children that are in conflict with the law. It was enacted in 2008 though the Act serves the interest of the children in special needs and enhances their welfare; thus, it (Act) does not alter the position of the South African Constitution, the Criminal Procedure Act and the Common Law.

It is pertinent to note that in the realm of South Africa, the child justice reform started in 1997 with creation of the South Africa reform commission. The reform which targeted promotion of child justice system eventually led to the enactment of the Child Justice Act in 2008 by the parliament. In summary, the effect of South African government in reaction to the protection of children can be underscored from the above explained. The legislations have accounted for the putting in place institutions such as courts and homes for children's welfare generally.

The South African experience of incessant attack on foreigners and xenophobia also heightened the need for the number of juvenile delinquency in the country. These anti-social conducts saw children being key participants. It therefore recently brought about a situation where a lot of children will need to pass through the justice system.

3 Theories of Child Justice Administration

Children, due to mental immaturity, emotional instability, tender and vulnerable age, weak physique, proneness to vices and violence and inability to look after themselves require special care, protection, treatment and kind handling geared to shape their personalities into socially acceptable persons. The rights of children demand well-oriented and guarded protection exploitation that may occur through moral and material abandonment. Parents, society and the State are bound to ensure observance of the rights of all children. Child justice administration in the modern context organises efforts to prevent and treat child's social maladjustment in keeping with the interests and rights of children. Child justice administration covers not only the children coming in conflict with the law but also those likely to drift into criminogenic culture because of various situational compulsions. Child justice administration as an important component of social and distributive justice has to concern itself with the well-being and welfare of all children in need of care and protection.

The practice of child justice administration unlike in South African child justice regime[84] seemingly places the burden of culpability for committed crimes on child offenders themselves, regardless of their age at the time of commission. Whether or not this practice is supported by law is debatable upon due consideration of relevant laws such as the Nigerian Child Rights Acts, 2003. For example, Section 1 of this Act instructs that once a child is arraigned before the court, the best interest of the child should be the prime consideration. Unfortunately, the Nigerian Child Rights Act does not state clearly what acts may be done to ensure the best interest of the child such as ensuring that all necessary investigations have been conducted by qualified professionals in the fields of psychology, sociology, criminology, Mental Health Review Tribunal, etc., compare to the South African Child Justice Act.[85]

[84]See generally Section 7 of the South African Children's Act, No. 38 of 2005 which explicitly laid down the factors to be considered whenever the 'best interest of the child standard is to be applied'. In the same scenario, Section 63 and 'table of contents P under the Schedule' to this Act empowered the court to have two sittings, one for 'ordinary court' for the adult offender and the other as 'a child justice court' for the trial of the child offender.

[85]For example, Prins, Herschel, *Offenders, Deviants or Patients? Explorations in Clinical Criminology* (4th ed.; London and New York: Routledge and Taylor & Francis Group, 2010), 68–101 in the course of examining juvenile offenders, deviants or patients in clinical criminology made a passage for concern about the circumstances of children and young persons under sixteen years of age who have committed homicides and other grave crimes and are being held in various criminal justice institutions. He contended that before any examination on how to handle a juvenile is conducted there must be enquiries into the mental state of the juvenile and allied matters, and there must be hospital and penal provisions. Unlike Nigeria child justice system, South African child justice system has provided in its Schedule the 'categories or classes of persons that are competent to conduct the evaluation of the criminal capacity of a child' to be 'a medical practitioner- a psychiatrist; and a psychologist who have registered under the Health Professional Act, 1974'.

Another practice in Nigeria is that there are those who are of the view that parents should be held responsible for crimes committed by their children.[86] Those in favour of parental responsibility are of the view that the laws are particularly appropriate in cases in which parents know or should know that their children engage in one form of criminality or the other. To them, they believe that the role of parents in child delinquency cannot be overemphasised especially when viewed from the perspective of their contributions to the development of children's rights from their childhood. Therefore, the decision to have children should always be in agreement with the ability to care for them.[87]

Instructively, it is important to note that in some cases, a child may engage in serious crime, such as robbery, murder, housebreaking, drug trafficking and rape. And due to the special procedure for the treatment of child offenders under the Nigerian child justice system, dealing with them is somewhat problematic[88] to compare with what is obtainable under the South African child justice regime.[89] It is therefore observed that exposure of children to formal criminal processes especially in the case of capital offences may have an adverse effect on subsequent attempts at their rehabilitation and reintegration into the society.

Therefore, a young person under the age of eighteen years who gets himself or herself into trouble with the law may ordinarily have his/her case heard in the juvenile/family court, but this is not always the case. It is important to note that the idea of child justice system is as old as antiquity.[90] Therefore, when looking at the problem of youth crime in the early twentieth century, one is confronted with discourse of "clamping down" on youth crime, of "Zero tolerance" and of "anti-social

[86] Alemika, E. E. O., and Chukwuma, I. C., *Juvenile Justice Administration in Nigeria: Philosophy and Practice* (Lagos: Centre for Law Enforcement Education, 2001), 15.

[87] Ibid.

[88] Ordinarily courts are prohibited from trying child offenders in public or open court with the public in attendance irrespective of the crime allegedly committed. But on the contrary, a child offender who committed a crime with an adult is usually tried in the public.

[89] Child Justice Act has empowered the magistrate to separate the trial of a child who has been alleged to have committed an offence with an adult in South Africa.

[90] Alemika, E. E. O., and Chukwuma, I. C., *Juvenile Justice Administration in Nigeria: Philosophy and Practice* (Lagos: Centre for Law Enforcement Education, 2001), 15.

behaviour". Yet, criminologists and practitioners within youth justice administration have attacked this punitive philosophy.[91] This book posits that it is wrong for the modern youth court system to be castigatory in its tone and methods. Rather, this book will demonstrate that the origin of child justice administration lies in attempts to solve youth crime problems. These attempts aim at diverting children from criminal ways and encouraging them to play a constructive role in the society. Thus, the fundamental objective of the child justice system in Africa (South Africa and Nigeria inclusive) from its early development can be viewed from two distinct perspectives: one is clearly punitive and the other supportive and caring.[92] The next section is an examination of these two fundamental objectives.

3.1 *The Punitive Objective*

The punitive objective of child justice system qualifies as the root or origin of child justice administration which emphasises the imposition of criminal liability on children just as in the case of adult. This classification scheme potentially subjected children between ages seven and fourteen to the rigours of adult criminal liability, proceedings and punishments.[93]

The above practice can be equated with the classical criminological school of thought under the leadership of Cesare Beccaria which set the pace in addressing the issue of crime control from the point of view of punishment (penology).[94] The position of this school is derived from their conceived notion of why people commit crimes. They believed

[91] See Goldson, B., *The New Youth Justice* (Lyme Regis, 2000), 309; Goldson, B., and Muncie J., *Youth, Crime and Justice: Critical Issues* (London, 2006), 202; and Garlard, D., *The Culture of Control: Crime and Social Order in Contemporary Society* (Oxford and London, 2002) in Bradley, Kate, *Juvenile Delinquency and the Evolution of the British Juvenile Courts, c. 1900–1950*. Available at http://www.history.ac.uk/ihr/Focus/welfare/articles/bradleyk.html. Accessed on 30 May 2011.

[92] Freda A., Gerhard, O. W. M., and Williams, S. L., *Criminology and the Criminal Justice System* (6th ed.; New York: McGraw-Hill, 2007), 424.

[93] Ibid.

[94] Beccaria, C., On Crimes and Punishment (reprinted; Indianapolis: Bobbs-Merrill) in Nwanna, Chinwe R., and Akpan, Naomi, E. N., *Research Findings of Juvenile Justice Administration in Nigeria* (Lagos: Constitutional Right Project [CRP], 2003), 14.

that human beings are naturally pleasure-loving animals that use their free will to choose acts from which they derive pleasure as against those that will cause them pain and suffering. To this school, therefore, the act of law breaking is a deliberate and conscious decision in pursuit of pleasure. Thus, the school advocates severe punishment to make criminal acts unattractive regardless of the identity and personality of the offender.[95]

However, while the idea of punishment seems justified because of its practical and social usefulness, Wilson[96] and Van den Haag[97] advocated correctional methods. They argued that if young offenders cannot be improved through rehabilitative programmes, they can at least be confined so that potential lawbreakers, especially young offenders, are deterred. However, this approach has been historically described as a hard-line approach in the child justice system.

The hard-line approach sees punishment as an effective deterrent against delinquent behaviour and it is opposed to the welfare-based approach because it claims that youthful offenders do not take the justice process seriously. Therefore, punishment requires long-term confinement in correctional institutions or to adult prisons.[98] Its proponents further claim that rehabilitation is insufficient and has not been effective; hence, punishment should be the purpose of child justice system. They advocated death penalty for vicious crimes committed by young offenders. Their argument is premised on the logic that if one is old enough to kill, he/she is equally old enough to die.[99] This book has demonstrated this position under the historical evolution of child justice administration under Nigeria and South Africa to show that generally in Africa, this hard-line approach was adopted in dealing with child offenders.[100]

[95] Ibid., 15–16.

[96] Wilson, J. Q., *Thinking About Crime* (New York: Basic Books, 1975) in Nwanna, Chinwe R., and Akpan, Naomi, E. N., *Research Findings of Juvenile Justice Administration in Nigeria*, 18.

[97] Van den Haag, E., *Punishing Criminals: Concerning a Very Old and Painful Question* (New York: Basic Books, 1975) in Nwanna, Chinwe R., and Akpan, Naomi, E. N., *Research Findings of Juvenile Justice Administration in Nigeria*, 16.

[98] Ibid.

[99] Ibid.

[100] See Sects. 3 and 4 of this chapter.

3.2 The Supportive/Caring Objective

The second objective of child justice administration which also originated from Roman law is supportive and caring of child offenders. This theory was championed by a segment of the classical school known as the neoclassical which disagreed with the earlier philosophy developed by Cesare and Wilson. This disagreement is on the grounds that children, the insane, imbeciles and morons cannot be said to possess the ability to exercise free will rationally because of their underdeveloped or defective mental state. The position is obvious in the concept of *parens patriae* where the king or queen could exercise "parental power" in loco parentis. This doctrine is a legal philosophy and it was established in the case of *Ex parte Crouse*,[101] when:

> a father challenged the Philadelphia House of Refuge's right to hold his daughter who had been committed there by the mother. The Pennsylvania Supreme Court stated that such placement was not punishment but benevolence, no due process claim could be made by the father, and that the father had no standing anyway because the state had a legal obligation to step in whenever the parents are irresponsible.

A related concept *In Loco Parentis* was also established in *State v. Pendergrass*[102] where the North Carolina Supreme Court said that "a teacher is the substitute of a parent, and can administer moderate punishment if not inflicted out of malice or bad passion".[103] This notion appears to conform to Fogel's theory which cautioned that correctional institutions wherever desirable should be used as a last resort. He further argued that committal to correctional institutions should be restricted to those who have committed serious offences.[104] For those offenders who are sent to institutions, justice-as-fairness connotes that they are sent there for rehabilitation and not for punishment and therefore must be

[101] 4 Wharton, Pa., 9 (1838).

[102] (1837).

[103] Freda A., Gerhard, O. W. M., and Williams, S. L., *Criminology and the Criminal Justice System* (6th ed.; New York: McGraw-Hill, 2007), 424.

[104] Fogel, D., *We Are the Living Proof: The Justice Model for Corrections* (Cincinnati: Anderson, 1985) in Nwanna, Chinwe R., and Akpan, Naomi, E. N., *Research Findings of Juvenile Justice Administration in Nigeria*, 20.

treated fairly and humanely. Thus, while arguing that it is morally wrong to administer punishment on offenders in this category the same way as other normal adult offenders; this second approach posits that these situational factors should constitute mitigating or extenuating circumstances which should lessen criminal responsibility.[105] It is pertinent to point out here that the viewpoint of the neoclassical school greatly influenced penal reforms in the contemporary time in most jurisdictions including Nigeria and South Africa. This has influenced Nigeria and South Africa when they ratified the UN Convention on the Rights of the Child and African Charter on the Rights and Welfare of the Child with the enactments of the Child Rights Act, Children's Act and Child Justice Act.[106]

4 Procedural Processes on Child Justice Administration

As noted earlier in this book, child justice administration is based on the "philosophy that the special status of children requires that they be protected and corrected, not necessarily punished for criminal conducts". A young person can come into contact with child justice administration in a variety of ways. Firstly, a child may indeed be suspected to have or found to have violated the law consequent upon which he may be arrested. The apprehension marks the entrance and beginning of a child offender navigating the child justice administration. Secondly, a child offender may be charged with having committed a status offence, and in this paradigm, the intake agency must determine whether the child is to be released or prosecuted in court. At this stage, the issue of jurisdiction may be considered having regard to the fact that child justice administration demands special procedure for young offenders. Thirdly, navigation process deals with the process of disposition of hearing of the allegation against the child.

The child justice administration then is based on the notions that every child is treatable and that judicial intervention will result in positive behavioural changes. It is argued that the procedural processes of child justice administration through various steps in the criminal justice system need to place significant attention to the special procedure

[105] Ibid.

[106] See Chapters 5 and 6 of this book for detail analysis.

for child offenders and the need for fair treatment. This book, however, poses some questions on the extent of compliance and effective implementation of laws protecting the interests of young persons in the procedural process of child justice system in Nigeria and South Africa, namely: whether young offenders are afforded the necessary procedures/protection for entering the child justice system; that is, whether child offenders navigating the process of litigation in the Nigerian and South African juvenile/family/children/child justice courts are adequately accorded the protection proffered under international, regional and national instruments? Whether the final point in the procedural process of child justice administration is more focused on achieving the requirements of the law in the treatment and placement of child offenders? These two and other relevant questions bordering on all processes involved in the navigation of the child justice system and the inherent problems or lacuna shall be examined in the following sub-chapters.

This book identifies and examines the procedural process in the juvenile justice administration and argues for increased attention on children's due process[107] and in the fundamental rights and interests of young offenders in Nigeria.

The logical arrangement for procedural process of child justice administration examined in this book is shown below.

4.1 Apprehension or Referral

Almost all criminal cases in Nigeria and South Africa begin with a crime being reported to the police, who may, after investigation, prepare information against the person alleged if they believe that there is sufficient evidence for prosecution by the State. In child justice administration, the next stage after the apprehension of a child offender or on allegation of a crime is for the child to speak to an intake officer who in Nigeria is either the police or social welfare officer as the case may be. In the South

[107] Justice Abe Fortas of the US Supreme Court defined due process *In Re Gaults* "due process embodied the rule of law, which was the "primary and indispensable foundation of individual freedom." And he declared that the fact that the accused are not adults, "does not justify a kangaroo court." 'The Bill of Rights, in sum, protects youth as well as adults". Quoted from The Rights of Juvenile Defendants. Available at www.annenbergclassroom.org/Files/.../Chapter_20_Our_Rights. Accessed on 1 March 2013. See Article 40 of the United Nations Convention on the Rights of the Child, 1990.

African perspective, the child will be interrogated by the police or probation officer depending on the age of the child.[108] At this stage in Nigeria, the intake officer is under the responsibility of making his/her recommendation from an interview conducted with the child, the parents, the complainant and the victim. The concept of navigation of child justice administration literally means a child offender's journey through the criminal justice system. At every stage of the journey, decisions are made on him or her, whether to release the child suspect on bail, whether he or she should be kept in custody pending trial or be referred to social welfare. Similar to Nigerian practice, Chapter 9 of the South African legislation also allows "all persons and authorities handling cases involving children the use of discretionary powers at all levels of the child justice system".

4.2 *Intake by the Police*

There are some similarities in the mode of initiation and entrance to child justice system under the Nigerian and South African laws. In Nigeria, the mode of initiation commences with the apprehension of a child upon commission of a crime and/or reasonable suspicion for the commission of crime. The police are an important point of child's intake to the child justice system because they are the first point of contact with a child who is in conflict with the law. This is the first stage where the child comes in direct contact with the child justice system.[109] Although children may be taken to the police station for questioning but if there is probable cause by the police to believe that children were involved in the offence, the police will take step of booking the children. Sometimes, police may through petition or referral take the suspected offenders to court or detention centre and turn them over to court intake workers (probation agents) to begin the court process.

In addition, when a crime is committed, the police undertake an investigation and all cases are referred to the public prosecutor. It is the prosecutor who undertakes necessary investigations, such as "questioning of the suspects and witnesses and evaluation of collected evidence".

[108] See generally, Chapters 2 and 3 of the South African Child Justice Act 78 of 2008.

[109] By virtue of Section 20 of the Police Act, the police are empowered to arrest a person including a child who is reasonably suspected of having committed an offence.

The prosecutor thereafter makes the decision on whether or not to prosecute. Similar to the South African practice,[110] it is noteworthy to state that the Nigerian Child Rights Act compelled the prosecutor to oblige the parent/guardian of the child suspect and the child copy of the written allegation against the child and immediately inform the child on his constitutional rights, including the right to remain silent. These requirements must be fulfilled before the intake interview/interrogation.[111] The Act also enjoys the child to be informed on his or her right to legal representation who may be present during interview/interrogation and a right to talk to his/her parent or demand the parent to be present during the interrogation. The police is empowered to release a child intake in the child justice system to the parents or guardian on bond unless[112] and except the charge is murder or manslaughter or some other grave crime or if it is in the interest of the child to remove him/her from association with an undesirable person or his/her incarceration would not defeat the ends of justice.[113]

Nigerian Child Rights Act[114] prohibits the use of "any incriminating statement by the probation officer who is considering an informal

[110]See generally Chapter 3 of the South Africa Child Justice Act, Sections 63(3), 65 and 80(1) (a)(b) of the Act.

[111]By Section 211 of Child Rights Act, it is the responsibility of the police to inform the parents or guardian of the arrested juvenile as soon as practicable.

[112]The Constitution recognises three exceptional circumstances when the constitutional right to personal liberty of persons including children in conflict may be inoperative. These are: (i) for the purpose of bringing him before a court in execution of the order of a court or upon reasonable suspicion of his having committed a criminal offence or to such extent as may be reasonably necessary to prevent his committing a criminal offence; (ii) In the case of a person who has not attained the age of eighteen years, for the purpose of his education or welfare; (iii) … or vagrants, for the purpose of their care or treatment or the protection of the community. See Section 35 of the 1999 Constitution. See also Section 215(d) of the Child Rights Act which has to the effect that "the child is not deprived of his personal liberty unless he is found guilty of: (i) A serious offence involving violence against another person or (ii) Persistence in committing other serious offences and there is no other appropriate response that will protect the public safety".

[113]See Sections 22–25 of the South Africa Child Justice Act. See also, Harms, P., *Detention in Delinquency Cases, 1990–1999: 2003 Fact Sheet* (Washington, DC: U.S. Department of Justice, Office of Justice Programs, Office of Juvenile Justice and Delinquency Prevention). See also Sections 211 and 212 of the Child Rights Act which provide procedures to be followed during apprehension of a child and if need be for the child to be detained.

[114]See Sections 211(1)(c)(iii) and 211(2) of the Child Rights Act, 2003.

adjustment against the child in any criminal proceedings". However, it is constitutionally right that a legal practitioner is consulted to attend before this interview is conducted. Hence, the child offenders in most cases are summoned by the police majorly for questioning as witnesses. This is one of the problems of child justice administration in Nigeria as such child is deprived of legal representation. Even the public, particularly parents of child offender, are not usually well informed about their rights to be present at the questioning or to demand for their right to be present during the child offender's interrogation.[115] Importantly, there has not been any evidence of adhering to the stipulations on interrogation of child offenders in consonance with the provisions of the Child Rights Act.[116] This procedure is absolutely in contrast with the practice in South Africa jurisdiction. By the combined effects of Section 18(4), 19(3) and 20(3) of the South Africa Child Justice Act, whether a child suspected to have committed an offence is served with a written notice, summons or to be arrested, parents or guardian of a child is adequately involved in preliminary inquiry of the committed crime.[117]

Instructively as noted earlier, the first step in the Nigerian child justice system can take the form of a direct apprehension upon a reasonable suspicion by the police that the child has committed an offence.[118] Similarly, a child may be apprehended by the police if the offence was or is being committed in his presence. Child intake to child justice system may also take the form of an official complaint made to the police by the parents, guardian, neighbours or victim of the crime. Another important form of intake is that relating to apprehension of a child offender by a task force or police raids on juvenile hideout or for an apprehension for wandering.

The child offender's navigation of the child justice system through his/her intake through police apprehensive and investigation/interrogation does not constitute the termination of the police duty especially

[115] Mwangangi, M. M., 'The Role of Kenya Police in Juvenile Justice'. Available at www.unafei.or.jp/english/pdf/PDF_kenya/session2.pdf. Accessed on 4 March 2013. See Section 211 Child Rights Act.

[116] See Sections 209 and 219 of the Child Rights Act.

[117] See Section 44 of the Child Justice listed the people that should attend preliminary inquiry to include: the child, the parents and probation officer.

[118] Section 20 CYPL Kano State.

where it is established that the offence is a minor or non-serious one (i.e. truancy or beyond parental control). The police have the duty to hand-over or transfer the child to the social workers' office who will decide whether to petition the child to the family court.[119]

When dealing with intake of a child in the juvenile justice system by apprehension, the laws do not specifically deal with the manner by which a child offender should be apprehended. However, the UNCRC provides that the apprehension of a child should be carried out in conformity with the law.[120] Without prejudice as to whether the UNCRC is or is being adequately complied with in Nigeria, the provision of the Child Right Act which is *mutatis mutandis* with UNCRC stipulates that "the child detention pending trial should be used only as a measure of last resort, for the shortest possible period of time" and or "replaced by alternative measures such as close supervision by a family, guardian/parent or placement in an educational setting or home".[121] Significantly, navigation of the child through his/her intake by the police may include referring the child offender's case to the court for prosecution; this must be done within a reasonable time.[122] This provision is in line with the general rule under the 1999 Constitution which limits pre-trial detention of any suspect to 24 hours including children before being taken the suspect to court. Due process of law will follow once a child offender's referral or petition is filed in court. The child passes through the stages of arraignment, bail and perfection of bail condition and so forth. It is important to note as explained earlier that for the police to be effective and in cognisance of the rights of the juvenile particularly from the very first point of intake, the child justice system must comply with provisions

[119] See generally Part XX of the Child Rights Act. The police force being the main law enforcement agency recognised by the Constitution with a higher visibility than other agency, the police bear the onerous burden of crime prevention and law enforcement at every level of the criminal justice system. See generally Part III (B) of Chapter 6 of the Constitution of the Federal Republic of Nigeria, 1999.

[120] See Article 37(b) of the UNCRC.

[121] See Sections 209(3) and 212(1) of the Child Rights Act, 2003.

[122] Section 35(5) of the Constitution defines a "reasonable time" to mean—(a) in the case of an arrest or detention in any place, where there is a court of competent jurisdiction within a radius of forty kilometers, a period of one day and (b) in any other case, a period of two days or such longer period as in the circumstances may be considered by the court to be reasonable.

of the Child Rights Act which stipulate the creation of a special unit to handle the cases of child offenders.[123]

In South African perspective, it is firstly the duty of a probation officer under Section 9(2) of the Child Justice Act after receiving notification from the police to "assess the child in terms of the provisions of Chapter 5 which are applicable to children under the age of 10 years", and thereafter, the police may detain the child prior to appearance at a place of inquiry within 48 h, depending on the age of the child.[124] In a similar vein, a child under the age of 10 years having been suspected of having committed an offence in South Africa will "immediately be handed over" by the police:

(a) to his or her parents or appropriate adult or a guardian; or
(b) if no parent, appropriate adult or a guardian is available or if it is not in the best interests of the child to be handed over to the parent, an appropriate adult or guardian, to a suitable child and youth care centre, and must notify a probation officer.[125]

It should be noted that in South Africa, arrest of a child is the last method of securing attendance of a child which must not be exercised by the police on "any offence referred to in Schedule 1 of the Child Justice Act unless there is a compelling reasons justifying the arrest".[126] The first method is through a written notice as provided in Section 18 of the Act, while the second method is a summon to be issued by the police in accordance with the provision of Section 19 of the Act and the last method is by "arrest as provided for in section 20 of the Act".[127] By Section 47 of the Children's Act No. 38 of 2005, when a question as to whether "a child is in need of care and protection as contemplated in section 150 of the Act", the children's court is empowered "to refer the child to a designated social worker for an investigation contemplated in

[123] See generally Section 207(1)-(3) of the Child Rights Act. It has been revealed in Chapter 5 of this study that instead of compliance with the Child Rights Act to provide for children special unit at the Police Force in Nigeria, child suspect is mingled together with women in the 'Juvenile and Women Centres' (JWC).

[124] See Sections 26–27 of the Child Justice Act 78 of 2008.

[125] See Section 9(1) of the South Africa Child Justice Act 75 of 2008.

[126] See Section 20 of the Child Justice Act. Ibid.

[127] See Sections 17–20 of the South Africa Child Justice Act.

Section 155(2) of the Act". By virtue of Section 9(2) of Child Justice Act stated above, the probation office that received notice of a child commission of crime has a duty within seven (7) days to either refer the child to child justice court or refer the child to a counsellor for counselling or accredited designed programme designed especially for child below 10 years old.

By virtue of Section 9(3) of the Act, the probation officer is enjoyed after the assessment to:

(i) refer the child to the children's court on stay of the grounds set out in Section 50;
(ii) refer the child for counselling or therapy;
(iii) refer the child to an accredited programme designed specifically to suit the needs of children under the age of 10 years;
(iv) arrange support services for the child;
(v) arrange a meeting, which must be attended by the child, his or her parent or an appropriate adult or guardian, and which may be attended by any other person likely to provide information for the purpose of the meeting referred to in Subsection (4).

Without prejudice to the Nigerian practice, the South African prosecutor must decide whether or not to prosecute a child by taking into consideration such as "the educational level and environmental circumstances, seriousness of the crime and the impact of the alleged offence on the victim, community, etc.".[128] Summarily, under the South African child justice system, the procedure though a bit similar to that of Nigeria, however, it appears to be more comprehensive and child interest based.

4.3 Intake by the Social Welfare

Another significant process of navigating the child justice system in Nigeria and South Africa is the intake of child offenders through the social welfare. This process unlike that of the police is not strictly based upon commission or likelihood of committing an offence but concerns a situation where the child has gone beyond parental control or the child is in need of care and protection. This may occur on the following grounds:

[128] See Section 10 of the South Africa Child Justice Act.

i. When, after the police interview or interrogation, it was discovered that the child's problem (i.e. in the case of minor offences) is better handled by the social welfare and
ii. When there is an official report by the family/home of the child.

From Nigerian perspective, the social welfare may contact the family to educate them on the need to cooperate with the police and also educate the family on the rights of the child to the extent that they have the right to legal representation.[129] Social welfare takes the child and family through the possible process by ensuring that the child's rights are not abused. These include protecting the child from torture, from putting him/her among adult suspects and by not allowing the child to be remanded unduly.[130] Instructively, Section 217(6)(a) of the Child Rights Act discourages the prosecutor to proffer charges against a child but instead, a report is presented to the court by a social welfare officer.[131] In taking actions for the determination of the fate of the child, the gravity of the crime would be determined by the trained social workers during the interview of the child. If the offence is a mere minor offence, the child would be cautioned and he or she would be counselled and sent home with a serious warning.

It is the responsibility of social workers to determine the nature of the offence. In this regards, the social workers will refer the case to the magistrate after establishment that the nature of the offence is serious. The magistrate will thereafter determine the next stage.[132] Another role usually performed by the social welfare is the conduct of a social investigation and the submission of a report with recommendation to the magistrate. At the hearing stage, the social welfare sees to it that the court is as child-friendly as possible, that is, the police are not in police uniform, that the parents/guardians are the only people from the public in attendance, that the child is addressed in a language that he/she understands, and that the child is not intimidated in any way.[133]

[129] Oanna, W. M., 'The Role of Social Workers Concerning Juveniles in Court', Paper Presented at a 'Seminar on Problem Areas in Juvenile Justice' (Elmina: Cocoanut Grove Hotel, 2007). Available at www.judicial.gov.gh/JTI/jti_documents/Learning%20Materials/THE%20. Accessed on 4 March 2013.

[130] Ibid. See also Section 417 of the Criminal Procedure Act.

[131] See also Section 418 of the Criminal Procedure Act.

[132] Oanna, W. M., 'The Role of Social Workers Concerning Juveniles in Court'.

[133] Social Welfare follows the laid down procedure as provided in Section 217 of the Child Rights Act.

In addition, the family/juvenile courts partner with the social workers, and in most cases, the court refers children's matters to the social workers for investigation and the outcome of such inquiry often provides a sound basis for the family/juvenile courts' decisions. This partnership between the court and social workers constitutes good practice and this has to some extent enhanced the effectiveness of the administration of child justice in Nigeria in the rehabilitation and reintegration of many of the child offenders into the society.[134]

In a situation where the magistrate eventually commits the child to custody, the social welfare office still intervenes and both institutions, i.e. the custodial institution and the social welfare office, will work hand in hand to try to rehabilitate the child offender. By so doing, social welfare sees to it that the child continues his/her education if he/she was already in the system.[135] Social welfare also encourages the child's family to visit and participate in the reformation of the child. Counselling the child to accept himself/herself is a very vital component of the rehabilitation of the child. Writing of reports on the child and submitting to the head office also are other functions undertaken by social welfare.

Social welfare also performs a vital role when the child offender is given a suspended committal by the court which among others includes the following:

(a) advise and help the child and his family to cope with the situation;
(b) visit the child;
(c) supervise the child; and
(d) submit reports on the progress of the child. The reports may give details that could be used, by the court, to determine the success or otherwise of the disposition.[136]

The department of social welfare will continue to play a central role in ensuring that the philosophy and aim of the Child Rights Act in the rehabilitation and prevention of children who are in conflict with the law or beyond parental control are fulfilled. However, like every strata of the

[134] Akinseye-George, Yemi, *Juvenile Justice in Nigeria* (Abuja, Nigeria: Centre for Socio-Legal Studies, 2009). See also Sections 219 and 224 of the Child Rights Act.

[135] Oanna, W. Mensah, 'The Role of Social Workers Concerning Juveniles in Court'.

[136] Akinseye-George, Yemi, *Juvenile Justice in Nigeria* (Abuja, Nigeria: Centre for Socio-Legal Studies, 2009). See also Sections 219 and 224 of the Child Rights Act.

Nigerian polity, the social welfare office is not exempted from inadequate funding and expert personnel in handling children matters.[137] To buttress this position is one of the facilities visited by the author in Nigeria, where social welfare workers had no formal training in social welfare and had never undergone any training.[138]

Similar to the practice in Nigeria, intake of child in need of care and protection[139] in South Africa could be through referral either from the police, probation officer or court[140] to a designated social worker. A child who has been served with a "written notice or a summons or warrant of arrest" as indicated in Chapter 3 (Sections 17–20) of the Child Justice Act and having been assessed under Sections 34 and 35 of the Child Justice Act by the probation officer to be in need of care and protection shall be called upon by the inquiry magistrate for "preliminary inquiry".[141] The "preliminary inquiry" is followed by an order of the inquiry magistrate to the social worker for "an investigation before the child is brought before the Children's Court" as contemplated under Section 154 of the Children's Act. The social worker must "within 90 days compile a report to be submitted to the relevant provincial department of social development"[142] and indicate in the report "the measure recommended to assist the family which may include counselling, mediation, rehabilitation", etc.[143] The social worker is empowered under Section 155(5) of the Children's Act to "bring the child before the Children's Court for adjudication". Another role played by the social worker is "supervisory services" during the "placement of the child in an

[137] Alemika, E. E. O., and Chukwuma, I. C., *Juvenile Justice Administration in Nigeria: Philosophy and Practice* (Lagos: Centre for Law Enforcement Education, 2001).

[138] Author's field survey at Bauchi and Kaduna States, Nigeria, dated 11 and 13 February 2014.

[139] Section 150 of the South Africa Children's Court No. 38 of 2005 provides a detail explanation of a "child in need of care and protection" to include among others a child who "displays behaviour which cannot be controlled by the parent or care-giver"; "lives or works on the streets or beg for a living"; or "lives in or is exposed to circumstances which may seriously harm that child's physical, mental or social well-being", etc.

[140] See Sections 47, 50(3) and 151(1) of the South Africa Children's Act No. 38 of 2005.

[141] A preliminary inquiry by virtue of Section 43(1) of the South Africa Child Justice Act means "an informal pre-trial procedure which is inquisitorial in nature" for the purpose of "considering the assessment report of the probation officer".

[142] See Section 155(2)(3) of the South Africa Children's Act.

[143] See Section 155(4)(b) of the South Africa Children's Act.

alternative care"[144] such as "foster care" or "child and youth care centre" or "reunification of the child with his or her parents", "care-giver" or "guardian".[145] It should be noted that an "approval for leave of absence of a child under the alternative care must be sought and obtained from the designated social worker" in line with Section 168(2) of the Children's Act and such social worker may "at any time cancel any leave of absence".[146] The social worker is empowered "to apprehend a child who has absconded from the alternative care and can enter any premises without warrant in order to apprehend any child who has absconded from the alternative care".[147] The role of social worker also extend:

> to consultation with the child after taken the age, maturity and stage of the development of the child into consideration and the parent, guardian or care-giver of the child together with the child and youth centre or temporary safe care of where the child has been placed and where the child is to be transferred to before the provincial head of social development can issue an order of transfer of the child to any other alternative care.[148] It is the responsibility of a designated social worker to manage a provisional transfer of a child as directed by the provincial head of a social development to another form of care.[149]

It is also the responsibility of a social worker "to report the assessment and reunification of the child and submit same to the provincial head of social development before such child can be discharged from the alternative care by the provincial head of social development".[150] The designated social worker dealing with the matter of a child must be immediately informed of the "injury sustained by the child or if the child is abused or died while in the alternative care centre".[151]

[144] See Section 167 of the South Africa Children's Act. By this Subsection 1 of this section, an alternative care means "a foster care or a child and youth care centre following an order of a court in terms of this Act, Section 29 or chapter 10 of the Child Justice Act, 2008 or a temporary safe care".

[145] See Sections 156(3)(a)(i)(ii) and 157(1)(b)(i)(ii) (2) of the South Africa Children's Act.

[146] See Section 168(3) of the Children's Act.

[147] See Section 170(1)(2) of the Children's Act.

[148] See Section 171(4) of the Children's Act.

[149] See Section 174 of the Children's Act.

[150] See Section 175(2)(b) of the Children's Act.

[151] See Section 178(2)(d) of the Children's Act.

By Section 187 of the Children's Act, a social worker must provide "conditions to facilitate the reunification of the child with his or her biological parents" before the children's court issue a replacement order which must be in the interest of the child. The social worker must "within two months before the expiration of the court order report to the Children's Court the reason(s) behind non-reunification of the child with his or her biological parents and recommend any steps to be taken for stabilising the child's life".[152] A social worker is also under obligation by virtue of Section 230(2) of the Children's Act

> to make an assessment to determine whether or not the child whom the court intends to issue an order placing him or her in a permanent care of an adopter is actually adoptable and the prospective adoptive parent must also be assessed by the social worker for compliance with the provision of section 231(2)(a)(b) of the Children's Act.

It should be noted that it is also the responsibility of the social worker to counsel the child and the parents of the child before his or her adoption.[153] In summary, the role of social worker in the administration of child justice in South Africa cannot be overemphasised as the developmental social welfare principles enshrined in the Children's Act which the social workers should apply when rendering services to children and their families such as self-reliance, empowerment and accessibility[154] have a positive impact in reintegrating the children into the society as law-abiding citizens.

However, lack of comprehensive legal solution for court's orders in respect of Foster Care and Child and Youth Care Centre hinders the effective performance of social worker in the administration of child justice in South Africa.[155] Inadequate funding to solve infrastructural challenges makes the social workers fail to adequately execute their services

[152] See Section 187(2) of the Children's Act.

[153] See Section 233(4) of the Children's Act.

[154] See Department of Social Development: Framework for provision of developmental social welfare services (Draft) (Pretoria: Government Printer, 2011).

[155] See the cases of Centre for Child Law v. Minister of Social Development and others. 2011a. (North Gauteng High Court) Case No. 21726/11. Order of 10 May 2011, unreported and Centre for Child Law v. Minister of Social Development and others. 2011b. (North Gauteng High Court) Case No. 21726/11. Order of 8 June 2011, unreported.

as advocated by the Children's Act. Further to these challenges are inadequate training of social workers[156] and shortage of human resources which causes delays in responding to emergencies by the social workers in South Africa. Study has shown that as of 2012, 40% of the total number of social workers that registered with South African Council for Social Services Professions (SACSSP) were employed by the South African government[157] which shows clearly that the number of social workers is inadequate to effectively handle children's matters.

4.4 Procedure for Adjudication in Juvenile/Family/Children/Child Justice Court

Adjudication is one of the important processes in the Nigerian and South African child justice system which a child offender may navigate. This is, however, subject to the decision of the intake officer (police or social welfare) to refer/petition the child to court in Nigeria. Compare to South African perspective, the navigation of the adjudication processes is through an intake by the police, probation or social workers which of course must be subject to the age of the child at the time of commission of the alleged offence.

From the Nigerian perspectives, the law provides that a legal practitioner may be present at the adjudication hearing of a child offender who, with the help and advice of a legal practitioner, may confess to the commission of the offence. In this regards, such child has given up his or her important rights, including "a right to a hearing, a right to have the prosecution prove its case beyond reasonable doubt, and a right to cross-examine the prosecution's witness(s)". But the judge should make sure that the child offender is aware of these important rights before accepting any admission from him/her and in so doing, the court shall obtain "all necessary information as to the conduct and social inquiry reports of the background of the child offender as to enable the court deal with the case in the best interest of the child".[158]

[156] See September, R., and Dinbabo, M., 'Gearing Up for Implementation: A New Children's Act for South Africa', *Practice: Social Work in Action*, 20(2), 113–122.

[157] See the South Africa Institute of Race Relations (SAIRR): Social Worker Shortage Undermines Effectiveness of Social Welfare Legislation (2012). Available at www.sairr.org.za. Accessed 20 October 2012.

[158] See Section 217(6) of the Child Rights Act, 2003.

Generally speaking, when a child offender admits the offence, the court will determine if the child is in need of treatment, rehabilitation and supervision. If so, the court will enter a finding of delinquency. At the same time, the court will determine if it is the best interest of the child to commit the child to any treatment such as rehabilitation or supervision after the court adjudged the child as a delinquent child.

In the same vein, a full hearing will commence in situation where the child offender denies the commission of the offence and prosecution will first present its evidence and call its witnesses and then the child offender legal representative will present evidence supporting his/her version of defence.[159] This is similar to the procedure in adult criminal justice system.

From the South African perspectives, the adjudicatory system depends on whether the child is alleged to have committed an offence or in need of care and protection.[160] A child "under the age of 10 years who has been alleged to have committed an offence will not ordinarily be taken to court" unless if he or she is "assessed under chapter 5 of the Child Justice Act by the probation officer, to be in need of care and protection" as contemplated under Section 50 of the Child Justice Act. In this situation, the probation officer will "refer the child to the Children's Court". The children's court may further "order a social worker to investigate and report back to the court for the purpose of determining whether the child is in need of care and protection".[161] It should be noted that a child "older than 10 years but under the age of 14 years can only be brought before a child justice court for trial after a preliminary inquiry" by an inquiry magistrate has been conducted against him or her and the inquiry magistrate "refers the child to the Child Justice Act to be dealt with in terms of Sections 63–67 of the Child Justice Act".[162] Similar to what is obtainable under the Nigerian perspectives, the child justice court must by virtue of Section 63(3) of the Child Justice Act

[159] See Section 217 (3)(4)(5) of the Child Rights Act.

[160] The South Africa Child Justice Act No. 75 of 2008 together with the Criminal Procedure Act is used with respect to child alleged to be in conflict with the law, while the Children's Act No. 38 of 2005 together with the Magistrates' Act No. 32 of 1944 and Rules Board for Courts of Law Act No. 107 of 1985 is used to decide children that are in need of care and protection.

[161] See Sections 47 and 50 of the Children's Act No. 38 of 2005.

[162] See Sections 10, 43–50 of the Child Justice Act No. 75 of 2008.

"inform the child of the nature of the allegations against him or her" and "inform the child of his or her rights and explain to the child the further procedures to be followed". It should be noted that similar to the provisions of the Nigerian Child Rights Act, 2003,[163] the best interest of the child is also a paramount consideration. Also, the child justice court can also "elicit additional information from any person and must ensure that the proceedings against the child are fair and not unduly hostile and are appropriate to the age and understanding of the child".[164]

4.4.1 Legal Representation

In Nigeria and South Africa, a young offender like adult offender is entitled to representation by a legal practitioner of his/her choice at the litigation hearing. The child justice system is a complex system and the outcome of the process could have serious consequences on the child. From the tenets of the Nigerian and South African Constitution particularly Section 36(6)(c) of the 1999 Constitution and Chapter 2 of the South Africa Constitution, 1996,[165] every person, including a child, who is accused of an offence, has the right to counsel (legal representation) at every stage of the proceedings. Therefore, it is important to secure the service of a competent legal representation for a child facing trial before the court. The child must be expressly advised of the right to retain counsel and, if financially unable to do so, to have counsel appointed by the court.[166] Failure to advise the child would render any subsequent incarceration illegal and release of the child would be in order.[167] It is the contention of this book that legal representation for child is important because of the tender age of child whose ability to defend himself/herself may be very weak.

[163] See Section 217 (3)(4)(5) of the Child Rights Act.

[164] See Section 63(4) of the South African Child Justice Act.

[165] Section 155 of the Child Rights Act, 2003, has similar provision to the effect that "a child has the right to be represented by a legal practitioner and to free legal aid in the hearing and determination of any matter concerning the child in the Court". See generally Section 217 of the Child Rights Act. This is similar to Sections 54 and 55 of the South African Children's Act No. 38 of 2005 and Sections 80–83 of the Child Justice Act No. 75 of 2008.

[166] Ibid. See also, *In Re Gault* 387 U.S. 1, 42 (1967).

[167] In Applications of *Johnnie J. Billie and Leroy Jewelryman*, 429 P.2d699 (Ariz. 1967), it was held that where parents and petitioners were not advised of their right to counsel, detention in an industrial school was illegal. The petitioners were ordered released.

The introduction of advocacy to the juvenile/family/children/child justice court system was premised on the philosophy that delinquency proceedings must change in several key ways. The proposition for a more jealously guarded constitutional protection of the adult criminal court and their attendant adversarial nature must be extended to child justice system.[168] In this regards, legal representation in these courts was meant to infuse the informal children's court process with more constitutional protection. Perhaps more importantly, with counsel explicitly assigned to advocate on child offenders' behalf, children accused of delinquent acts were to become participants, rather than spectators in their court proceedings. The court observed in *Re Gault*[169] that "juvenile respondents" needed defenders to enable them "to cope with problems of law, to make skilled inquiry into the facts, to insist upon regularity of the proceedings, and to ascertain whether juvenile has a defence and to prepare and submit it".[170] From the foregoing, this section examines the roles of the public defender, waiver of counsel and the defence counsel in delinquency proceedings.

The requirement of legal representation for the child offender is as important as other rights that guaranteed the child offender to benefit from a fair trial. Such rights that are similar to what are obtainable in South Africa[171] include the right to be informed in the language he or she understands about the substance of the alleged offence,[172] to be presumed innocent; the right against involuntary confession or to give incriminating evidence; and the right to expeditious trial.[173] These requirements logically demand courts handling children cases and proceedings to ensure the observance of the constitutional safeguards to the children. The trial itself cannot be deemed "fair" if any of these rights is

[168] See Section 149 of the Nigerian Child Rights Act, 2003, and Section 89 of the South African Child Justice Act No. 75 of 2008.

[169] (supra).

[170] *In Re Gault* 387 U.S. 1 (1967).

[171] See Chapter 2 of the South African Children's Act (particularly Sections 8, 9, 10, 14 and 15) and Section 11 of the South African Child Justice Act. See also, Zaal, F. N., and Skelton, A. M., 'Providing effective representation for children in a new constitutional era' (1998), *South African Journal on Human Rights*, 14, 593.

[172] See Section 217(1) of the Child Rights Act.

[173] See Article 40 UNCRC. See also Section 210 of the Child Rights Act and Section 89 Child Justice Act 2008.

violated.[174] Therefore, it may be argued that the special treatment to be afforded for the child delinquent during trial is consistent with the need to promote the child's dignity and worth.[175] Surprisingly, the author's fieldwork with 1258 respondents on the administration of child justice in Nigeria indicates that 59% representing 744 of the respondents agreed that "the presumption of innocence is not adequately considered by the juvenile/family courts in Nigeria",[176] especially in a situation where the child is alleged to be "beyond parental control" or "in need of care and protection". This was confirmed in interviews conducted in Nigeria (Borstal institutions in Kaduna State and Ilorin in Kwara State),[177] where some officers noted that "one of the reasons for the congestion at Borstal institutions was that the family court did not observe the right of presumption of innocence of the child since many children were adjudged to be beyond parental control". It is the author's contention that the case of a child "in need of care and protection" is actually a status or minor offence and that the practice of committing the child in those custodial institutions is contrary to international standard and what is obtainable in South Africa, which calls for diversionary measures to be applied and "institutionalisation to be the last resort and within shortest period of time".

It is the duty of a counsel in a child delinquency proceeding or in an order to show cause proceeding against an undisciplined child to be the child's voice to the court and to represent the expressed interests of the child at every stage of the proceedings.[178] Counsel owes the same duties

[174]See Sectins 155, 210, 215(3) and 217 of the Child Rights Act for similar provisions.

[175]Articles 18.2 and 40.1 of the Beijing Rules. See also Sections 11, 158 and 214(2)(b) of the Child Rights Act.

[176]Author's field survey at Lagos, Kaduna, Port Harcourt, Enugu, Bauchi and Ilorin in 2014.

[177]Interviews conducted by the author in 2014.

[178]This statement of the role of defence counsel in juvenile delinquency proceedings was derived from a number of sources. See, e.g., National Council of Juvenile and Family Court Judges, *Juvenile Delinquency Guidelines: Improving Court Practice in Juvenile Delinquency Cases* (2005); American Council of Chief Defenders, National Juvenile Defender Center, 'Ten Core Principles for Providing Quality Delinquency Representation Through Indigent Defence Delivery Systems' (2005); Howell, Amy, and Silverthorn, Brook, Southern Juvenile Defender Center, 'Representing the Whole Child: A Juvenile Defender' (2004), Training Manual IV; California Administrative Office of the Courts, 'Effective Representation of Children in Juvenile Delinquency Court'

to the child under the Rules of Professional Ethics and Conduct,[179] including the duties of loyalty and confidentiality, as a counsel owes to an adult criminal defendant. The court observed in *Haley v. Ohio* that "the child stands in particular need of careful advice concerning their constitutional rights"[180] by someone who expressly and solely identifies with their interests.[181] This makes the service of the counsel imperative for the protection of a child against being a victim of fear and/or of panic in the course of litigation in court.[182] The importance of counsel's role in child

(2004); Juvenile Justice Bulletin, Office of Juvenile Justice and Delinquency Prevention, U.S. Department of Justice, 'Access to Counsel'(2004); Katherine R. Kruse, 'Lawyers Should be Lawyers, But What does that Mean? A Response to Aiken & Wizer & Smith' (2004) *Washington University Journal of Law and Policy*; Frank E. Vandervort, Michigan, 'When Minors Face Major Consequences: What Attorneys in Representing Children in Delinquency, Designation, and Waiver Proceedings Need to Know' (2001) *Bar Journal;* National Association of Counsel for Children, 'Recommendations for Representation of Children in Abuse and Neglect Cases' (2001) Part IV; Barbara Butterworth, Will Rhee & Mary Ann Scali, *Juvenile Defender Delinquency Notebook* (2000) American Bar Association Juvenile Justice Center, Chapter 2, p. 2.2; Massachusetts Committee for Public Counsel Services, *Assigned Counsel Manual: Policies and Procedures* (2000) Parts III. A.4 & J 1.2; Kentucky Department of Public Advocacy, *Juvenile Law Manual* (1999) Chapters 1 and 3; IJA/ABA Juvenile Justice Standards, 'Standards Relating to Private Parties' (1996), Standard 3.1; Stephen Wizner, 'The Child and the State: Adversaries in the Juvenile Justice System' (1972), *Columbia Human Rights Law Review*, 4, 389. Available at www.ncids.org/JuvenileDefender/Role/Role%20Statement.pdf Accessed on 6 March 2013.

[179] See Rules of Professional Conduct for Legal Practitioners and Practitioner Act Cap B57 Laws of the Federation of Nigeria, 2004 and S.I. 6 of 2007 respectively.

[180] The principle of defence counsel in juvenile proceedings is to protect the child's constitutional rights. They do this through their practical, everyday duties ranging from interviewing the child outside of the presence of the child's parents to objecting to inadmissible but informative evidence at adjudicatory hearings, to advocating for the least restrictive alternative at disposition, to pressing, at every stage, for the client's expressed interests. For the purpose of this study, "stage" is broadly defined to include each step at which the state's power intersects the child's life, including, but not limited to, arrest, interrogation at the police station, at school or at home, initial detention hearings, the probable cause hearing and post-disposition hearings. Apart from the provisions in the 1999 Constitution on the above subject matter, the Child Rights Act, specifically in its Section 217(5), provides to the effect that upon establishing a prima facie case against the child offender, the court is under obligation to hear the child's defence by taking the evidence of his/her witnesses.

[181] 332 U.S. 596, 599–600 (1948)

[182] *Haley v. Ohio* (supra).

defence counsel has been emphatically explained in *Re Gault*[183] to the extent that juvenile defence counsel's role in delinquency proceedings is unique and critical. The probation officer cannot act as counsel for the child because his role is that of arresting officer and witness against the child.[184]

Thus, no matter how many court personnel were charged with the responsibility of handling the child offender's interests, their skills cannot be equated with the expert knowledge and skill a legal practitioner will exhibit in defending any child facing "the awesome prospect of incarceration" in the proceedings against him". The same reasons accounted for those adults facing criminal charges securing the service of counsel to handle their case.[185] Therefore, counsel for youth is an essential ingredient in establishing a fair, just and stable child justice system.

Instructively, a diligent defence counsel must possess the legal knowledge and courtroom skills of a criminal defence counsel representing adult defendants.[186] In addition, the counsel must be acquainted with the strengths and needs of their child offenders, their families, communities and other social structures. In addition, the defence counsel must put into consideration that the child is undergoing an adolescent development and he should be able to understand this stage in the life of the child and must be able to communicate effectively with the child, and must be able to evaluate the child's level of maturity and competency and its relevance to the delinquency case. Further, the defence counsel must have knowledge of, and contacts at, community-based programmes to compose an individualised disposition plan and be able to enlist the child's parent or guardian as an ally without compromising the legal practitioner–client relationship with the child.[187]

[183] 387 U.S. 1 (1967). The latter case of *In Re Winship* 397 U.S. 358 (1970) expanded the list of mandated procedural guarantees to include the requirement that prosecutors have to prove delinquency charges beyond reasonable doubt.

[184] *In Re Gault*, 387 U.S. at 36.

[185] Ibid.

[186] Sterling, R. W., 'Role of Juvenile Defence Counsel in Delinquency Court'. Available atwww.americanbar.org/…/crimjust_juvjus. Accessed on 2 March 2013. See generally Part A of the Rules of Professional Conduct and Legal Practitioners Act.

[187] Ibid. See also Part B of the Rules of Professional Conduct and Legal Practitioners Act.

In addition, the counsel has a responsibility to advise the child, recommend actions consistent with the child's interest and advise as to the potential outcomes of various causes of action. The counsel for a child shall meet and communicate with the child regularly putting into consideration the child's maturity, physical, mental and/or emotional health, intellectual abilities, language, educational level, special educational needs, cultural background and gender.[188] The counsel should move the court for appointment of an interpreter if the primary language of the child or the child's parents or guardians' language is other than English and the counsel has difficulty in communicating with them.[189]

Furthermore, after the determination by the defence counsel that the child is unable to understand the proceedings or otherwise cannot assist in representing the child, it is the duty of the defence counsel to move the court for an evaluation of the child's capacity to proceed and otherwise proceed according to Rule 14 of the Rules of Professional Conduct.[190] It is pertinent to note that it is also the duty of the defence counsel to appoint a guardian for the child that has no parent if he thinks necessary and if it is in the best interest of the child to do so for the purpose of assisting the child in making decisions outside the scope of the defence counsel's representation.

Thus, because of the unique nature of a child, defence counsel must strictly adhere to his ethical obligations to pursue with vigour the child's expressed interest and safeguard his/her right to due process in the adjudication.[191] The child defence counsel needs to protect and defend the child by positing that youth are categorically less culpable than the average adult offender.[192] At the same time, the defence

[188] Sterling, R. W., 'Role of Juvenile Defence Counsel in Delinquency Court'.

[189] Ibid.

[190] Rules of Professional Conduct for Legal Practitioners; Ibid.

[191] See The American Bar Association (ABA) Model Rules of Professional Conduct (Model Rules): Preamble; 1.14(a) Client with Diminished Capacity; 1.2(a) Scope of Representation and Allocation of Authority between Client and Lawyer. Available at http://www.njdc.info/pdf/cfjfull/pdf and www.njdc.info/pdf/role_of_juvenile_defense_counsel.pdf. Accessed on 26 February 2013. See also Parts A and B of the Rules of Professional Conduct and Legal Practitioners Act. Ibid.

[192] This was evidenced in the United States Supreme Court's opinion in *Roper v. Simmons* (Supra).

counsel has an affirmative obligation to safeguard the child's information or secrets[193] and the defence counsel has an obligation to protect the child's confidences, unless express permission is sought and obtained from the child to reveal the information for the purpose of getting the particular services, or disclosure is impliedly authorised to carry out the child's case objectives.[194] More importantly, the defence counsel has the duty of competence and diligence[195] which are expansive, encompassing the obligations to investigate, to zealously protect the child's due process rights from arrest through the close of the case, to engage in dispositional advocacy and to access ancillary services.

The Nigerian Child Rights Act by its Section 153(5) and Sections 84–86 of the South Africa Child Justice Act indicate that legal representation for child offenders should not stop at disposition. Post-disposition activities include filing appeals, conducting periodic reviews of how the youth is faring, ensuring that the youth is receiving the services ordered that placement remains appropriate and addressing concerns for conditions of confinement. Therefore, it is the author's contention that many child offenders will be placed in more restrictive settings than appropriate and will not receive critical services if the defence counsel does not exhibit more skilful, consistent and zealous representation.

In general, appeals are rare in Nigerian juvenile/family courts, possibly because sentences are short and the appeal process can be lengthy. Another contributing factor, as suggested by Puritz et al.,[196] may be that public defenders' offices are not organised to deal with appeals in children cases.

[193] See The American Bar Association (ABA) Model Rules of Professional Conduct (Model Rules) 1.6 Confidentiality of Information. Ibid. See also Parts A and B of the Rules of Professional Conduct and Legal Practitioners Act.

[194] Sterling, R. W., 'Role of Juvenile Defense Counsel in Delinquency Court'.

[195] See The American Bar Association (ABA) Model Rules of Professional Conduct (Model Rules) 1.1 Competence, 1.3 Diligence. Ibid. See also Parts A and B of the Rules of Professional Conduct and Legal Practitioners Act. Ibid.

[196] Puritz, P., Burrell, S., Schwartz, R., Soler, M., and Warboys, L., *A Call for Justice: An Assessment of Access to Counsel and Quality of Representation in Delinquency Proceedings* (Washington, DC: American Bar Association Juvenile Justice Center, 1995). Available at www.americanbar.org/.../crimjust_juvjus. Accessed on 2 March 2013.

It should be noted that the importance of due process in child delinquency proceedings cannot be overemphasised in the sense that if counsel does not meet the client until the detention hearing, the counsel cannot effectively investigate placement with a relative or other community-based alternatives. Effective representation at the earliest stages can have important effects on the outcome of a case.

Overall, there is no standardised child justice system procedure in Nigeria and South Africa. The author's fieldwork survey and study by Sipho Sibanda and Antoinette Lombard[197] in Nigeria and South Africa have confirmed this position. From the author's fieldwork survey, the majority of the respondents representing 1103 (88%) out of the total population of 1258 respondents hold the views that "Child Justice Administration in Nigeria is not effective to engender full protection of children's rights".[198] According to Sipho Sibanda and Antoinette Lombard[199] in their study, majority of the respondents interviewed hold the views that "most presiding officers in South African's Children's Courts do not have a standardised way of doing things". Some of the participants that they interviewed commented thus:

> The Act goes with regulations and from jurisdiction to jurisdiction, for instance between Benoni and Johannesburg, the implementation of the Act or the interpretation of the Act is different depending on how the presiding officer understands the Act, so you are asked for certain things in one court that may not be required in the next.
>
> When approaching the courts in terms of the attachments they need on the reports, specifically section 159 reports for the extension of orders, where you find that the Johannesburg Court presiding officers have a set of attachments that they require but if you go to the Alexandra court or if you go to Alberton court, they have different attachments that they need and my understanding is that in the regulations, it is left to the discretion of the presiding Officer, so the fact that there is

[197] Sipho, Sibanda, and Antoinette, Lombard, 'Challenges Faced by Social Workers Working in Child Protection Services in Implementing the Children's Act 38 of 2005'. Available at http://socialwork.journals.ac.za/pub. Accessed 15 October, 2018.

[198] Author's field survey at Lagos, Kaduna, Port Harcourt, Enugu, Bauchi and Ilorin in 2014.

[199] Sipho, Sibanda, and Antoinette, Lombard, 'Challenges Faced by Social Workers Working in Child Protection Services in Implementing the Children's Act 38 of 2005'. Available at http://socialwork.journals.ac.za/pub. Accessed 15 October 2018.

> no uniformity in terms of the attachments that are required by different courts, makes it very difficult and it's a cumbersome process that we are encountering because now we have to either memorise or we have to come up with lists of what is required, at which particular court and that makes it very difficult to organise ourselves administratively in terms of those needs.

Therefore, an experienced magistrate must be designated to handle children cases on arraignment of the child offender. The magistrate must ensure due compliance with laws by ensuring that the child's right to presumption of innocence, legal representation, interpretation and consultation with Legal Aid Council for assistance is made available. At the end of the hearing, the court, having been satisfied beyond any reasonable doubts that the child has committed the offence, moves on to decide on the disposition measure. Section 223 of the Child Rights Act and Chapters 8 and 10 of the Child Justice Act and Chapter 4 of the Children's Act have provided quite a variety of disposition measures for the court to apply depending on the age and needs of the individual child that appears before them.[200]

A counsel's role may be extended to identification of appropriate sanctions which the court can make during the sentencing process for the purpose of protecting the best interest of the child. On behalf of the child offender, the defence counsel can present letters of support from teachers and community groups; educational and medical information; and other documents to aid the judge.[201] At the same time, counsel can explain the process to the child and ensure that the child does not inappropriately waive the right to counsel, admit guilt or make other detrimental statements or decisions. Counsel to a child can also quickly identify people who are in a position to speak well of the child (e.g. teachers, ministers) and ask them to testify on the child offender's behalf. He can also provide the detention hearing judge with enough information (e.g. family strengths, possibility of placement with extended family or other alternatives to detention) to warrant release rather than detention.

[200] This has been discussed somewhere in Chapters 5 and 6 of this book.

[201] Jones, Judith B., *Access to Counsel* (Juvenile Justice Bulletin, 2008). Available at www.americanbar.org/…/crimjust_juvjus_13_1jwr.htm. Accessed on 2 March 2013.

4.4.2 Waiver of Counsel

As earlier noted in the above section, it is a constitutional right for a child offender in Nigeria[202] and South Africa[203] to seek the services of a legal representative or the court may order that a child offender be represented by a legal practitioner if it is in the interest of the child to do so. However, in both countries,[204] a child brought before a juvenile/family or child justice or children's court may waive his or her right to counsel and the validity of such waiver would be evaluated using the same standard applicable to the adult in the criminal court in determining whether the person charged or the child referred voluntarily relinquished or abandoned his or her right to legal representation.[205] However, to assist the child in making a valid waiver, the juvenile/family or the child justice or children's court in Nigeria and South Africa must discuss the implications of the waiver with the child, make sure he or she understands the nature and gravity of the charges, and is made aware of the risks of proceeding without counsel.[206] This discussion or warning must be properly

[202] In particular, see Section 36(6)(c) of the Constitution of the Federal Republic of Nigeria, 1999 (as amended).

[203] In particular, see Sections 28(1)(h) and 35 of the Republic of South Africa Constitution, 1996.

[204] See Section 83 of the South African Child Justice Act.

[205] See *In Re Gault*, 387 U.S. at 42. See also *Johnson v. Zerbst*, 304 U.S. 458 (1938); *Carnley v. Cochran*, 369 U.S. 506 (1962); *United States ex rel. Brown v. Fay*, 242 F. Supp. 273 (D.C.S.D.N.Y.1965). *See also State ex rel. Juvenile Dept. Linn County v. Anzaldua*, 109 Or App 617 (1991), *State v. Twitty*, 85 Or App 98, 102 (1987). The Supreme Court held in *U.S. v. Padilla*, 819 F. 2d 952, 956 (10th Cir. 1987): there must be "a showing on the record that the defendant who elects to conduct his own defence had some sense of the magnitude of the undertaking and the hazards inherent in self-representation when he made the election". It was also held in *Von Moltke v. Gillies*, 332 U.S. 708, 723–724 (1948): the defendant must have an apprehension of the nature of the charges, the statutory offences included within them, the range of allowable punishments there under, possible defences to the charges, and circumstances in mitigation thereof, and all other facts essential to a broad understanding of the whole matter. In a similar case of *State v. Johnson*, 112 Ohio St. 3d 210, 2006-Ohio-6404, 858 N.E.2d 1144, 100: the record must reflect that the defendant who elects to represent himself was made aware of the dangers of self-representation, so that the record will establish that "he knows what he is doing".

[206] See *State ex rel Juv. Dept. v. Afanasiev*, 66 Or App 531 (1984). *In Re Haggard*, 3d Dist. Nos. 2-08-20, 2-08-21, 2-08-22, 2-08-23, 2009-Ohio-3821. The court found that the minor validly waived his right to counsel at a probation violation hearing. But there was no recorded finding that waiver was made at the dispositional hearing immediately following the probation violation hearing. The court reversed the dispositional

recorded by the court.[207] In a similar vein, the court has a duty to determine whether the child understands the nature of the charge, the elements of the offence and the punishments which may be exacted. The court has a duty to move further by informing the child the possible implication of defending himself/herself and the possible advantage of securing the service of a counsel to defend him/her.[208]

The book contends that the significance of the above proposition is established on the fact that the child lacks the ability to make an independent judgement and he or she may not be able to make a decision on waiver. Therefore, the judges should be partly responsible for warning the child of the "dangers inherent in self-representation".[209] The dialogue with the child should be such that would allow the child to examine his/her own environment and critically analyse the consequences of waiving his/her right to counsel or entering a plea on his/her own. The child must be made fully aware of all consequences through an exhaustive consultation, taking into consideration the differences in brain development and thought processing between adults and children.[210]

hearing and remanded for a new hearing with reiteration of the right to counsel. In contrast to that is *In Re I.S.P.*, 4th Dist. No. 09-CA-37, 2010-Ohio-410. The defendant was charged with numerous probation violations. At all of his hearings at which his mother was present, the court advised the defendant and his mother of the right to counsel. The court then made a recorded finding that showed the waiver was voluntary, knowing and intelligent. The defendant was familiar with the juvenile court system and the trial court engaged the child to ensure he understood his rights and the charges. The trial court judgement was affirmed.

[207] Child Justice Act Sections 83–85.

[208] Ibid. See also *State v. Verna*, 9 Or App 620, 626 (1972); see also *State ex rel. Juvenile Dept. Linn County v. Anzaldua*, 109 Or App 617 (1991). In *Miller v. Alabama*, 567 U.S. (2012) at 19, the US Supreme Court again relied on physiological differences in the decision-making processes of children versus adults, and noted that "indeed, it is the odd legal rule that does not have some form of exception for children".

[209] Ibid.

[210] *In Re C.S.*, 115 Ohio St.3d 267, 2007-Ohio-4919, 874 N.E.2d 117. Held that: (1) in a delinquency proceeding, a juvenile may waive his constitutional right to counsel, subject to certain standards, if he is counseled and advised by his parent, custodian or guardian; (2) if the juvenile is not counseled by his parent, guardian or custodian and has not consulted with an attorney, he may not waive his right to counsel; (3) a judge must appoint counsel for a juvenile if there is a conflict between the juvenile and his parent, custodian or guardian on the question of whether counsel should be waived; (4) a totality-of-the-circumstances analysis is the proper test to be used in ascertaining whether there has been a

It is pertinent to note that where the child desires to waive his or her right to counsel at the adjudicatory stage and does not already have court-appointed counsel, a counsel must be appointed[211] to advise the child prior to any execution or acceptance by the court of the waiver, to ensure that such waiver is free and voluntary.[212] The apparent intent of this provision is to avoid a child being committed to the child justice custodial institutions without any legal representation.

Surprisingly, findings from the empirical study carried out by the author revealed that despite the protections available in the Nigerian laws to seek the services of a counsel, too many child offenders are in effect denied the right to counsel because they waive that right when clearly it is not in their best interests to do so. For emphasis, in an administered questionnaire by the author, the majority of the respondents representing 818 (65%) out of the total population of 1258 respondents hold the views that "the right of child offender to fair trial is not respected under the administration of child justice in Nigeria".[213] One of the legal practitioners and a parent interviewed[214] by the author compliment this position thus:

valid waiver of counsel by a juvenile; (5) the judge must consider a number of factors and circumstances, including the age, intelligence and education of the juvenile; the juvenile's background and experience generally and in the court system specifically; the presence or absence of the juvenile's parent, guardian or custodian; the language used by the court in describing the juvenile's rights; the juvenile's conduct; the juvenile's emotional stability; and the complexity of the proceedings; and (6) the waiver of the right to counsel must be made in open court, recorded, and in writing. Also, the court clarified that a parent has no authority to waive the juvenile's right to counsel. The minor signed a 7-page waiver, but the court reversed the adjudication because the waiver did not comply with Juv. R. 29 or R.C. 2151.352—the minor never consulted a parent or guardian prior to waiving right to counsel.

[211] See the preamble and Sections 7 and 9 of the Legal Aid Act, Cap L9 Laws of the Federation of Nigeria, 201. See also, the proviso to Section 83(2) of the South Africa Child Justice Act and Section 55 of the Children's Act; Sections 2 and 3A of the South African Legal Aid Act No. 22 of 1969; Botha NO and Others v. MEC for Education, Western Cape and Others (unreported, Case No. 24611/11, Western Cape High Court).

[212] See generally Ferguson and Douglas, 'A Study of Juvenile Waiver' (1970), *San Diego Law Review*, 39.

[213] Author's field survey at Lagos, Kaduna, Port Harcourt, Enugu, Bauchi and Ilorin in 2014.

[214] Interview conducted by the author in Bauchi State, Nigeria, dated 11 February 2014.

> The right of child offender to fair hearing is not recognised by the present juvenile justice administration especially under status offences, i.e. juveniles who are beyond parental control when taken to court.

In the same manner, a parent said: "The current juvenile justice system in Nigeria does not recognise the child's right to fair trial especially in legal representation unlike what is obtainable in other countries of Africa".

Therefore, mandatory representation will not only protect the child offender, it will also assist the court in handling cases efficiently. The "totality" test by which most courts judged the validity of waivers is difficult to administer and invites uncertainty at all stages of the proceedings. Advisably, the presence of defence counsel will facilitate obtaining effective waivers of other rights by the child offender. Therefore, every effort should be made to convince children that it is in their best interest to have a counsel representing them at all hearings.

Instructively, it is argued that legal system is complex as it is based on constitutionally guaranteed rights, common law precedent, and a web of federal and State statutes, local ordinances and procedural rules. Therefore, maintaining an adequate defence in child or criminal court, avoiding self-incrimination and ensuring that rights are upheld require the assistance of competent legal representation. However, it has been observed by the author that many children who become involved with the child justice system never realise these basic rights because they ill-advisedly waive their right to counsel, inappropriately accept plea bargains[215] or receive substandard services.

4.4.3 Disposition/Dismissal

The outcome of adjudication by the juvenile/family or child justice or children's court in Nigeria and South Africa is disposition or dismissal of the case against the child offender. In both countries, the police, social welfare officer in Nigeria or the probation officer in South Africa may decide not to take action against the child after taken due consideration. It is pertinent to note that in Nigeria, at any time prior to trial, defence counsel and the prosecutor may decide to resolve the case.[216] This may

[215] Plea bargains are not inherently bad or even detrimental to the youth as long as they are not made for expediency's sake and the youth clearly is guilty.

[216] See Child Right Act, 2003, Section 209.

arise in a situation where the prosecutor decides to dismiss a case after determining that there is no sufficient evidence to present to the court. For example, the judge may have excluded evidence after a motion to suppress or a witness may be unavailable or uncooperative or the defence counsel may file a motion to dismiss the case on legal grounds. In addition, the court can *suo moto* discontinue the case at any time if circumstances arise which make discontinuation of the case, the best way to dispose of the case.[217]

Similar to the procedure in Nigeria, a prosecutor under Section 10 of the South Africa Child Justice Act may divert the child's matter in line with the provision of Chapter 6 of the Act instead of prosecuting the matter against the child in court. In this case, the court will dispose of the matter and make the diversion option as an order of the court.[218] In the same vein, an inquiry magistrate before trial of the child can also make an order for diversion of the child which may take the form of either "a compulsory school attendance order" or "a family time order" or "a good behaviour order" or "a peer association order" or "a reporting order" or "a supervision and guidance order".[219]

Further to Nigerian perspectives, the court generally sets a date for a dispositional hearing after adjudging the child to be guilty of the offence charged. It is important to note that a pre-dispositional report will be developed by the appropriate officers. This report will contain the background information of the child, the circumstances in which the child is living and the conditions under which the offence has been committed, and the appropriate recommendation will be made to the court prior to the dispositional hearing.[220] It is very important that the child's counsel and the parents develop a dispositional plan and that they both advocate for the child at this hearing. They should be prepared to provide information on their willingness to work with both the child and child officers so that the child can receive the least restrictive disposition. The court's decision will be based not only on the gravity or severity of the offence but also on the circumstances and needs of the child and the needs of the society.[221]

[217] Ibid., see Section 215(2).

[218] See Section 42 of the South African Child Justice Act.

[219] See Section 53(1) of the Child Justice Act.

[220] Ibid., see Section 219.

[221] Ibid., see Section 215(1)(b).

Further to the South African perspectives, a child found guilty of the offence charged unlike in Nigeria may be brought before a "Family group conference"[222] or a "Victim-offender mediation"[223] or "Pre-hearing conferences"[224] or "Other lay-forums"[225] such as "Lay-forum hearings"[226] in order to settle the matter out of court[227] in an informal procedure provided the child and the victim consented to it.[228] However, in the course of disposition by the court, the child justice court under Chapter 10 of the Child Justice Act can impose a sentence after convicting the child and the children's court can make any of the orders stipulated under Section 46 of the Children's Act.

4.4.4 Placement of Child Offender

The final adjudication processes under the administration of child justice in Nigeria and South Africa have given the child an option of fine or placement of the child in diversion places of custodial institutions. A child offender before a juvenile/family or child justice or children's court in Nigeria and South Africa like the adult offender must make his/her plea. The "plea of involved" to the offence charged will warrant a court giving summary judgement and where it's a plea of "not involved" proper adjudication is warranted. At the close of both the prosecution and defence, the court passes appropriate judgement. In Nigeria,

[222] See Section 61 of the South Africa Child Justice Act and Section 70 of the Children's Act. See generally the cases of *S v. M* (*Centre for Child Law as Amicus Curiae*) (2008) 3 SA 232 (CC); *Dikoko v. Mokhatia* (2006) 6 SA 235 (CC) and *Le Roux and Others v. Dey* (*Freedom of Expression Institute and Restorative Justice Centre as Amici Curiae*) (2011) 3 SA 274 (CC). See also, Sloth-Nielsen, J., and Gallinetti, J., 'Just Say Sorry? Ubuntu, Africanisation and the Child Justice System in the Child Justice Act 75 of 2008' (2011), *Potchefstroom Electronic Law Journal*, 14(4), 63.

[223] See Section 61 of the Child Justice Act.

[224] See Section 69 of the Children's Act.

[225] See Section 71 of the Children's Act. See also, South African Law Commission Project 110, *Review of the Child Care Act*. Discussion Paper 103 (2001), 1157.

[226] See Section 49 of the Children's Act.

[227] See Section 72 of the Children's Act.

[228] These are concepts that embrace the notion of restorative justice which involves a balancing of rights and responsibilities. The purpose of these concepts is to identify responsibilities, meet needs and promote healing. See Skelton, A. M., 'Juvenile Justice Reform: Children's Rights and Responsibilities versus Crime Control', in C. J. Davel (ed.), *Children's Rights in Transitional Society* (1999), 93.

the sentencing of the child offender may be in the manner of giving an order that the child offender be placed under care, guidance or supervision.[229] In addition, the court may order the child to do community service or pay restitution, fine, damages, compensation or costs to the victim. The judge could place the child in a non-residential, community-based residential programme or commit the child to the division of juvenile services.[230] The court may also order the child to undergo treatment if a substance abuse or mental health problem exists.[231] In a similar vein, the court may order the parent or guardian of the child offender to pay a fine, damages, compensation or costs, or order the parent or guardian to give security of the child offender that he/she will be of good behaviour or to enter into recognisance to take proper care of the child offender.[232]

In some cases in Nigeria, a child offender may be discharged conditionally on his/her entering into recognisance with the condition that the child offender be under the supervision of a person as may be named in the order during the period specified in the order.[233] Some examples of supervisory terms are restitution to the victim, drug/alcohol evaluation, counselling, random drug screening, school attendance and community service. However, in a situation where the child offender does not comply with the terms in the condition of recognisance, the court can issue a warrant for the apprehension of the child[234] and commit the child offender to custody in place of detention.[235] It should be noted that the placement of child offender in an institution should be a disposition of last resort and should not be ordered unless there is no other way of dealing with the child.[236]

Once the child offender is placed in an institution, such child offender will be committed to either the Children Attendance Centre, Children Centre, Children Residential Centre, Children

[229] See Section 223(1)(c) of the Child Rights Act.

[230] See Section 223(1)(d) of the Child Rights Act.

[231] See Section 223(1)(g) of the Child Rights Act.

[232] See Sections 220(2) and 223(1)(e) of the Child Rights Act.

[233] See Section 242(2)(a) of the Child Rights Act.

[234] See Section 225(1)(a) of the Child Rights Act.

[235] See Section 223(1)(f) of the Child Rights Act.

[236] See Section 223(2)(a) of the Child Rights Act.

Correctional Centre or Special Children Correctional Centre established by the Minister[237] charged with the responsibility of matters relating to children in the Federation of Nigeria or any part of a State in the Federation. Unfortunately, the only effective institution in the Federation of Nigeria is the Borstal training institution[238] situated in Kaduna, Kaduna State, and Abeokuta in Ogun State and Ilorin in Kwara State. However, the comments of some respondents interviewed in Nigeria[239] were that:

> only the Borstal institution in Ilorin seemed to be effectively operational at the moment and that even if all the three facilities were to be in operation, they would still be grossly inadequate to accommodate the large number of children and young persons who are caught in conflict with the law. It is therefore a very severe situation to have only three Borstal institutions serving the entire country.

This pattern of findings is similar to the questionnaire administered by the author[240] to 1258 respondents where 1103 representing 88% of the respondents expressed that:

> the shortage of Borstal facilities is responsible for the remand of juveniles in prison custody and lamented that Police officers often falsify the ages of juveniles to pass them off in court as adults, in order to avoid adhering to the legal requirements for their treatment especially in States without Borstal institution.

[237] See Section 248(1)(a) of the Child Rights Act.

[238] The findings from the author's fieldwork in Nigeria (Lagos, Kaduna, Port Harcourt, Enugu, Bauchi and Ilorin), 2014, revealed the ranking of the custodial institutions in Nigeria thus: Borstal institution was ranked 1st in the juvenile justice administration with 663 out of 1258 respondents representing (53%). With 554 (44%) out of 1258 respondents, remand home was ranked 2nd in the juvenile justice administration. With 517 (41%) respondents, government-approved school was ranked 3rd in juvenile justice administration. This was followed by prison with 501 (39.8%) and lastly the police cell with 457 (36%).

[239] Interview conducted by the Author at Kaduna, Bauchi and Ilorin in 2014.

[240] Author's field survey at Lagos, Kaduna, Port Harcourt, Enugu, Bauchi and Ilorin in 2014.

These findings conform with the position of Abrifor et al.,[241] Uma, Falobi,[242] Wilson,[243] Soyombo[244] and Ngwuoke[245] that:

> the great majority of children in conflict with the law were held together with adults in the regular prisons and as the children advance in age behind bars, their association with adult criminals invariably expose them to the danger of aggravated criminal tendencies and recidivism.

After successful completion of the treatment placement, the child returns to the community, i.e. home, foster care or further placement. The after-care workers/officers/associations established by the minister continues to supervise the child for their welfare and reformation after they might have been discharged from the institution.[246]

From South African perspectives, the court pronouncing sentence as stipulated under Chapter 10 of the Child Justice Act on the convicted child must "use imprisonment only as a measure of last resort and only for the shortest appropriate period of time".[247] The orders that the children's court can make based on Section 46 of the Children's Act range from "an alternative care order", "an order placing a child in a child-headed household", "an adoption order", "a partial care order", "a shared care order", "a supervision order", "a child protection order", "a contribution order", etc. From the provision of Sections 69(3) and 76 of the Child Justice Act, the child justice court may order "a compulsory residence of a child in a child and youth care centre". The child justice court is also empowered to impose "community-based sentences",[248] "restorative justice sentences",[249] "fine or alternative to

[241] Abrifor et al., 'Differences, Trend And Pattern Recidivism Among Inmates in Selected Nigerian Prisons' (2010), *European Scientific Journal.*

[242] Falobi, F., 'Empowering Prison Inmates', 2009. Available at http://www.independentngonline.com/. Accessed on 21 September 2009.

[243] Wilson, H., 'Curbing Recidivism in Our Society', 2009. Available at http://www.pioneerng.com/article.php?title=Curbing_Recidivism_In_Our_Societyandid=2765. Accessed on 20 December 2009.

[244] Soyombo, O., Sociology and Crime Control: That We May Live in Peace, 2009.

[245] Ugwuoke, C. U., *Criminology: Explaining Crime in the Nigerian Context* (2010), 23.

[246] See Sections 250(8)(f) and 259(1)(a) of the Child Rights Act.

[247] In particular, see Section 69(1)(d) of the South Africa Child Justice Act.

[248] See Section 72 of the Child Justice Act.

[249] See Section 73 of the Child Justice Act.

fine",[250] "sentences involving correctional supervision"[251] and "sentence of imprisonment".[252]

Unlike Nigeria, a laudable provision was provided under Section 87 of the Child Justice Act to the effect that the conviction and sentence of a child convicted by the child justice court:

> fall away and the criminal record of the convicted child expunged from the Criminal Record Centre of the South African Police Service after five years has elapsed after the date of conviction in the case of an offence referred to in Schedule 1; or ten years has elapsed after the date of conviction in the case of an offence referred to in Schedule 2 unless during that period, the child is convicted of a similar or more serious offence.

However, the condition attached to the expunging of the criminal record of the child under Section 87(2)(3) and (5) must be strictly adhere to.

5 The Uniqueness of Child Justice Administration

It is important in any discourse on the child justice administration in Africa, Nigeria and South Africa, in particular, to briefly identify or show the connecting links or differences between the child justice system and the adult justice system. The distinctive feature in the two systems of criminal justice which determines the system applicable to an offender is whether the offender is an adult or a child (young person) who is usually and adequately determined by law. The basic fact is that child justice system (which is for youth) is significantly different from the criminal justice system for adults in many respects.[253]

The child justice system is designated for children and youth and considers offences committed by children under the age of eighteen as delinquent acts rather than crimes as it is legally used for adult criminals. In line with this specialty, child justice demands separate courts,

[250] See Section 74 of the Child Justice Act.

[251] See Section 75 of the Child Justice Act.

[252] See Section 77 of the Child Justice Act.

[253] See Rendleman, D. R., '*Parens Patriae*: From Chancery to Juvenile Court' (1971), *South Carolina Law Review*, 23, 205–259 in Akinseye-George, Yemi, *Juvenile Justice in Nigeria* (Abuja, Nigeria: Centre for Socio-Legal Studies, 2009). See Parts XIII and XX of the Child Rights Act, 2003.

and hearing is not open for the public in attendant.[254] Therefore, the child court adjudicatory hearing in contrast to criminal trials of adult is designed to be informal[255] and directed at achieving the well-being of the child offenders. Consequently, while the criminal justice system for the adult is focused on punishment for adult offenders, the child justice system focuses more on care, treatment, rehabilitation and supervision with emphasis on rehabilitation instead of punishment, prevention rather than retribution.

The language of trial and sentencing is another unique identifiable distinction between the child and adult justice systems. For instance, the word "guilty" or "not guilty" would not be employed while sentencing a child, but "court committal" or "facts sustained" or "facts not sustained" are used.[256] The technical and legal word employed by the children's court for children or young person found to have committed an offence charged is "the child is involved or not involved", rather than finding him "guilty" or "not guilty".

The crux of the traditional child court hearing is to dispose of the crime committed by the youth rather than the determination of his/her guilt or innocence. The children's courts are more concerned with how best to reform the deviant's behaviour rather than the determination of guilt.

The reasons for this can be deduced from the decision in the case of *Roper v. Simmons*[257] which postulated that "youths or young persons are less culpable than the average adult offender because they lack maturity and responsibility, they are more vulnerable and susceptible to outside influences, particularly negative peer influences, are not as well formed in character and personality as adults, and have a much greater potential for

[254]See Section 156 of the Nigerian Child Rights Act, 2003. See also Section 63(2) of the South African Child justice Act and Section 56 of the Children's Act which provides for "Children's Court proceedings to be closed, and to be conducted only in the presence of those persons whose attendance is necessary, in order to protect privacy and confidentiality in family issues that generally are not matters of public interest". For instance, in the case of *Gold v. Commissioner of Child Welfare, Durban* (1978) 2 SA 301, "Persons *in loco parentis* are recognised as necessary persons that can be present at a sitting of the Children's Court".

[255]See Section 209 of the Nigerian Child Rights Act and Section 60(3) of the South African Children's Act.

[256]See Section 213(2) of the Child Rights Act.

[257]543 U.S. 551 (2005)

rehabilitation than adults". More importantly, it was emphasised that the reality that children still struggle to define their identity means it is less supportable to conclude that even a heinous crime committed by a child is evidence of an irretrievably depraved character.

6 Conclusion

This chapter examines the nature of child justice administration in Africa using Nigeria and South Africa as case studies. It investigated the workings of child justice administration from the point of entrance of a child offender to the final destination of his/her treatment under the relevant laws. Further, it gives a comparative analysis of the concept of due process with regard to the child delinquency proceedings in the Nigerian and South African contexts vis-a-vis the roles played by the police, social welfare, defence counsel, probation officer and the court. An attempt is also made to expose the level of compliance with the Constitutions' requirements as concern the system of child proceedings, as well as legislative enactment on children's rights. These are the Nigerian Child Rights Act, South African Child Justice and Children's Acts which provide for the right to legal representation and accord special treatment to the child offenders. This posits that the legislations provide far-reaching innovations which could completely transform the administration of child justice in the two countries. In addition, this chapter further examines the differences between adult and child delinquency proceedings in Nigeria and South Africa. This chapter made a position that the practice that aims to prevent offending will need to reflect, and build on, the fact that child offenders appear to make the transition to adulthood at different rates and degrees of success. Therefore, there must be specific interventions for child offenders who are subject to forms of statutory supervision.

The chapter concludes that when child offenders are placed in a residential facility or secure facility, planning and managing their re-entry into the community are critical. Parents should insist on being involved in the planning process and enlist community-based agencies that can provide services to the youth. Similarly, the analysis in this chapter revealed that lawyers in Nigeria are not properly trained to function in the children's court setting. This may mean that the presence of a lawyer, however, might have desirable or undesirable effects on the conduct of the proceedings but in essence, it will go a long way in assisting the court and the children in the adjudication of their cases.[258] Although the Constitution provides for the right to legal representation and the Child Rights Act has introduced far-reaching innovations which could completely transform the administration of child justice in the country, child offenders are usually without legal representation. Thus, the challenge is to move beyond mere enactment of the legal provisions and take practical measures towards the implementation of the reform measures in the Child Rights Act.

However, the empirical analysis in this book[259] reveals that though Nigerian laws require appointment of counsel at all stages of the proceedings, there is no systemic mechanism to connect counsel and child offender either from the earliest point in the process or when formal petition is filed in court.

References

Abrifor et.al., 'Differences, Trend and Pattern Recidivism Among Inmates in Selected Nigerian Prisons' (2010), *European Scientific Journal*, 8(24), 25–44.

Adewoye, O., *The Judicial System in Southern Nigeria 1854–1954* (London: Longman, 1977).

Ahire, P. T., *Imperial Policing Milton Keynes* (Open University Press, 1991) in Alemika, E. E. O., and Chukwuma, I. C., *Juvenile Justice Administration in Nigeria: Philosophy and Practice.*

Ajisafe Moore, E. A., 'The Laws and Customs of the Yoruba People in Abeokuta Nigeria' (Fola Bookshops, 2010) in Oduwole, E. O., 'Punishment as a Form of Legal Order in an African Society'.

Akinseye-George, Yemi, *Juvenile Justice in Nigeria* (Abuja, Nigeria: Centre for Socio-Legal Studies, 2009).

Alemika, E. E. O., 'The Smoke Screen, Rhetoric and Reality of Penal Incarceration in Nigeria' (1988a), *International Journal of Comparative and Applied Criminal Justice*, 7(1), 137–149.

Alemika, E. E. O., 'Policing and Perception of Police in Nigeria' (1988b) *Police Studies: International Review of Police Development*, 11(4), 161–176.

[258] Ernestine Gray's comment on the proposed legislation in the light of standards and policy adopted by the American Bar Association on the Administration of Criminal Justice, 12 May 2004. Available at www.njdc.info/pdf/18_LAaba.pdf. Accessed on 7 March 2013.

[259] Analysis of the Author's field survey and interviews conducted at Lagos, Kaduna, Port Harcourt, Enugu, Bauchi and Ilorin in 2014.

Alemika E. E. O, 'Socio-Economic and Criminology Attributes of Convicts in Two Nigerian Prisons' (1988c), *Journal of Criminal Justice*, 16(3), 197–207.

Alemika, E. E. O., 'Colonialism, State and Policing in Nigeria' (1993), *Crime Law and Social Change*, 187–219.

Alemika, E. E. O., and Chukwuma, I. C., *Juvenile Justice Administration in Nigeria: Philosophy and Practice* (Lagos: Centre for Law Enforcement Education, 2001).

Alice Saffy, Jacqueline 'A Historical Perspective of the Youthful Offender', in C. Bezuidenhout and S. Joubert (eds.), *Child and Youth Misbehaviour in South Africa* (2003).

Barbara Butterworth, Will Rhee, and Scali, Mary Ann, American Bar Association Juvenile Justice Center, *Juvenile Defender Delinquency Notebook*, Chapter 2, §2.2 (2000), Massachusetts Committee for Public Counsel Services, *Assigned Counsel Manual*.

Beccaria, C., *On Crimes and Punishment* (reprinted; Indianapolis: Bobbs-Merrill).

Behlmer, G., *Friends of the Family: The English Home and Its Guardians* (Stanford: Stanford University Press, 1998). Available at http://www.history.ac.uk/ihr/Focus/welfare/articles/bradleyk.html.

Bekker, J. C., 'Children and Young Persons in Indigenous Law', in J. A. Robinson (ed.), *The Law of Children and Young Persons in South Africa* (1997), 193.

Berlins, M., and Wansell, G., *Caught in the Act* (London: Macmillan, 1974), 1.

Bosman-Swanepoel, H. M., and Wessels, P. J., *A Practical Approach to the Child Care Act* (1995), 5.

Bradley, K. M., 'Juvenile Delinquency, the Juvenile Courts and the Settlement Movement 1908–50: Basil Henriques and Toynbee Hall' (2008), *Twentieth Century British History*, 19, 133–135. Available at http://www.history.ac.uk/ihr/Focus/welfare/articles/bradleyk.html.

Bradley, Kate, *Juvenile Delinquency and the Evolution of the British Juvenile Courts, c. 1900–1950*.

Chris, C., & Robb, W., *Juvenile Justice: An Australian Perspective* (New York: Oxford University Press, 1995), 9.

Clapp, E. J., *Mothers of All Children: Women Reformers and the Rise of Juvenile Courts in Progressive Era America* (University Park, PA: Pennsylvania State University Press, 1998), 89, 45 and 120.

du Plessis, Lourens, M., 'A Background to Drafting the Chapter on Fundamental Rights', in B. de Villiers (ed.), *Birth of a Constitution* (1994a), 90–91.

du Plessis, Lourens, M., 'The Genesis of the Chapter on Fundamental Rights I South Africa's Transitional Constitution' (1994b), *SA Public Law*, 9, 10.

du Plessis, Lourens, M., and Corder, H., *Understanding South Africa's Transitional Bill of Rights* (1994), 38, 46, 185–187 (Bill of Rights).

Eakelaar, J., 'Child Endangerment and Child Protection in England and Wales', in M. Rosenheim, F. Zimring, D. Tanenhaus, and B. Dohm (eds.), *A Century of Juvenile Justice* (2002).

Falobi, F., 'Empowering Prison Inmates', 2009. Available at http://www.independentngonline.com/.

Ferguson and Douglas, 'A Study of Juvenile Waiver' (1970), *San Diego Law Review*, 7, 39.

Fogel, D., *We Are the Living Proof: The Justice Model for Corrections* (Cincinnati: Anderson, 1985).

Freda, A., Gerhard, O. W. M., and Williams, S. L., *Criminology and the Criminal Justice System* (6th ed.; New York: McGraw-Hill, 2007).

Garlard, D., *The Culture of Control: Crime and Social Order in Contemporary Society* (Oxford and London: Oxford University Press, 2002).

Geffen, Irene, *The Laws of South Africa Affecting Women and Children* (1928).

Goldson, B., and Muncie, J., *Youth, Crime and Justice: Critical Issues* (London: Sage, 2006), 202.

Goldson, B., *The New Youth Justice* (Lyme Regis: Russell House, 2000).

Harms, P., *Detention in Delinquency Cases, 1990–1999. 2003. Fact Sheet.* (Washington, DC: U.S. Department of Justice, Office of Justice Programs, Office of Juvenile Justice and Delinquency Prevention).

Hendrick, H., *Child Welfare: England 1872–1989* (London: Routledge, 1994), 121–125. Available at http://www.history.ac.uk/ihr/Focus/welfare/articles/bradleyk.html.

Howell, Amy, and Silverthorn, Brook, Southern Juvenile Defender Centre, 'Representing the Whole Child: A Juvenile Defender' (2004), Training Manual IV.

Idowu, E. B., *Olodumare: God in Yoruba Belief* (Ibadan: Longman, 1962) in Oduwole, E. O., 'Punishment as a Form of Legal Order in an African Society'.

Ikenga, K. E. O., 'Crime and Punishment in Igbo Customary Law: The Challenge of Nigerian Criminal Jurisprudence'. Available at www.ajol.info/index.php/og/article/download/57917/46285.

Ikenga, K. E. O., 'The Principles and Practice of Justice in Traditional Igbo Jurisprudence'. Available at www.ajol.info/index.php/og/article/viewFile/52335/40960.

Jones, Judith B., 'Access to Counsel in Juvenile Justice Bulletin', 2004. Available at www.americanbar.org/.../crimjust_juvjus_13_1jwr.htm.

Kentucky Department of Public Advocacy, *Juvenile Law Manual* (1999), Chapters 1 & 3; IJA/ABA Juvenile Justice Standards, 'Standards Relating to Private Parties' (1996), Standard 3.1.

Kruse, Katherine R., 'Lawyers Should Be Lawyers, But What Does That Mean? A Response to Aiken & Wizer & Smith' (2004), *Washington University Journal of Law and Policy*, 14, 49.

Ladan, M. T., *Rights of the Child in Nigeria: An Overview in Individual Rights and Communal Responsibility in Nigeria* (Abuja, Nigeria: National Human Rights Commission, 1998).

Lerman, P., 'Policing Juveniles in London, Shifts in Guiding Discretion, 1893–1968' (1984), *British Journal of Criminology*, 24, 168–184; 175–176.

Lewis, J., *The Voluntary Sector, the State and Social Work in Britain: The Charity Organisation Society/Family Welfare Association Since 1869* (London: Edward Elgar, 1995). Available at http://www.history.ac.uk/ihr/Focus/welfare/articles/bradleyk.html.

Logan, A., 'A Suitable Person for Suitable Cases: The Gendering of Juvenile Courts in England c. 1910–39' (2005), *Twentieth Century British History*, 16, 129–145.

Maithufi, Ignatius, 'The Best Interest of the Child and African Customary Law', in C. J. Davel (ed.), *Introduction to Child Law in South Africa* (2000).

Mbiti, J. S., *African Philosophy and Religions* (Oxford: Heinemann, 1982).

Midgley, James, *Children on Trial: A Study of Juvenile Justice* (1975), 53.

Mwangangi, M. M., *The Role of Kenya Police in Juvenile Justice*. Available at www.unafei.or.jp/english/pdf/PDF_kenya/session2.pdf.

National Human Rights Commission (NHRC), Constitutional Rights Project (CRP), Penal Reform International (PRI), and UNICEF. Available at http://www.Cleen.org/Juvenile%20justice%20Report.pdf.

Nwanna, Chinwe R., and Akpan, Naomi, E. N., *Research Findings of Juvenile Justice Administration in Nigeria* (Lagos: Constitutional Right Project [CRP], 2003).

Oanna, W. M., 'The Role of Social Workers Concerning Juveniles in Court', Paper Presented at a 'Seminar on Problem Areas in Juvenile Justice' at Cocoanut Grove Hotel, Elmina 2007. Available at www.judicial.gov.gh/JTI/jti_documents/Learning%20Materials/THE%20.

Odekunle, F., 'The Nigeria Police Force: A Preliminary Assessment of Functional Performance' (1979), *International Journal of Sociology of Law*, 6, 73–78.

Oduwole, E. O., 'Punishment as a Form of Legal Order in an African Society' (2011), *International Research Journals*, 2(5), 1124–1129.

Okonkwo, C. O., Nwankwo, C., and Ibhawoh, B., *Administration of Juvenile Justice in Nigeria* (1st ed.; Lagos: Constitutional Rights Project [CRP], 1997).

Parry-Jones, William L., 'The History of Child and Adolescent Psychiatry: Its Present Day Relevance' (1989), *Journal of Child Psychology and Psychiatry*, 30, 3–11 in Bradley, Kate, *Juvenile Delinquency and The Evolution of the British Juvenile Courts, c. 1900–1950*.

Prins, Herschel, *Offenders, Deviants or Patients? Explorations in Clinical Criminology* (4th ed.; London and New York: Routledge and Taylor & Francis Group, 2010), 68–101.

Puritz, P., Burrell, S., Schwartz, R., Soler, M., and Warboys, L., *A Call for Justice: An Assessment of Access to Counsel and Quality of Representation in Delinquency Proceedings* (Washington, DC: American Bar Association Juvenile Justice Center, 1995). Available at www.americanbar.org/…/crimjustjuvjus.

Rendleman, D. R., '*Parens Patriae*: From Chancery to Juvenile Court' (1971), *South Carolina Law Review*, 23, 205–259.

Roberts, Cynthia H., *Juvenile Delinquency: Causes and Effect* (Yale-Haven Teachers Institute, 1986). Available at http://www.yale.edu/yhnt/curriculum.

Robyn, Kriel, 'Boko Haram Favours Women, Children as Suicide Bombers, Study Reveals', *CNN*, 11 August 2017. Available at https://edition.cnn.com/2017/08/10/africa/boko-haram-women-children-suicide-bombers/index.html.

September, R., and Dinbabo, M., Gearing Up for Implementation: A New Children's Act for South Africa. *Practice: Social Work in Action*, 20(2), 113–122.

Sinclair, June D., and Bedil, Susan, 'Law of Persons' (1983), *Annual Survey of South Africa Law*, 73.

Sipho, Sibanda, and Antoinette, Lombard, 'Challenges Faced by Social Workers Working in Child Protection Services in Implementing the Children's Act 38 of 2005'. Available at http://socialwork.journals.ac.za/pub.

Skelton Thesis, 392–395; Dutschke, Mira, *Defining Children's Constitutional Rights to Social Services. A Project 28 Working Paper* (2006), 48–52 (*Defining*).

Skelton, A. M., 'Juvenile Justice Reform: Children's Rights and Responsibilities Versus Crime Control', in C. J. Davel (ed.), *Children's Rights in Transitional Society* (Pretoria: Protea Book House, 1999).

Sloth-Nielsen, J., and Gallinetti, J., 'Just Say Sorry? Ubuntu, Africanisation and the Child Justice System in the Child Justice Act 75 of 2008' (2011), *Potchefstroom Electronic Law Journal*, 14(4), 63.

Sloth-Nielson, J., 'Chicken Soup or Chainsaws: Some Implications of the Constitutionalisation of Children's Rights in South Africa', *Acta Juridica* (1996), 6–12.

Soyombo, O., Sociology and Crime Control: That We May Live in Peace, 2009.

Sterling, R. W., 'Role of Juvenile Defence Counsel in Delinquency Court'. Available at www.americanbar.org/…/crimjust_juvjus. Accessed on 2 March 2013. See generally Part A of the Rules of Professional Conduct and Legal Practitioners Act.

Tamuno, T. N., *The Police in Modern Nigeria* (Ibadan: University Press, 1970), 45; Milner, W. B., 'Lower Class Culture as Generating Milieu of Gang Delinquency' (1958), *Journal of Social Issues*, 14, 5–19.

Theal, G. M., History of South Africa Since 1795: The Cape Colony from 1795 to 1828 (Vol. 5, 1964), 286–288.

Ugwuoke, C. U., *Criminology: Explaining Crime in the Nigerian Context* (Great AP Express Publishers, 2010), 23.

Van den Haag, E., *Punishing Criminals: Concerning a Very Old and Painful Question* (Basic Books: New York, 1975).

Van der Spuy, E., Scharf W., and Lever, J., 'The Politics of Youth Crime and Justice in South Africa', in C. Sumner (ed.), *The Blackwell Companion to Criminology* (2004).

Vandervort, Frank E., 'When Minors Face Major Consequences: What Attorneys in Representing Children in Delinquency, Designation, and Waiver Proceedings Need to Know' (2001), *Bar Journal*, 80(9), 36–41.

Whitehead, P., and Statham, R., *The History of Probation: Politics, Power and Cultural Change 1876–2005* (Crayford). Available at http://www.history.ac.uk/ihr/Focus/welfare/articles/bradleyk.html.

Wilson, H., Curbing Recidivism in Our Society, 2009. Available at http://www.pioneerng.com/article.php?title=Curbing_Recidivism_In_Our_Societyandid=2765.

Wilson, J. Q., *Thinking About Crime* (New York: Basic Books, 1997).

Wizner, Stephen, 'The Child and the State: Adversaries in the Juvenile Justice System' (1972), *Columbia Human Rights Law Review*, 4, 389.

Zaal, F. N., and Skelton, A. M., 'Providing Effective Representation For Children In A New Constitutional Era' (1998), *South African Journal on Human Rights*, 14, 593.

CHAPTER 4

International and Regional Legal Framework on Child Justice Administration

1 Introduction

In reordering priorities and strengthening public management, it may be argued that no group deserves greater attention than Nigeria and South Africa's estimated 44.3% and 34% children as at 2010 and 2015, respectively.[1] The term "rights" as proponents continually contend, should apply to all persons irrespective of age[2] and irrespective of whether the

[1] Nigeria has estimated 44.3% of children population according to http://population-action.org/wp-content/uploads/2012/01/DemoDev.pdf; see also Population Division of the Department of Economic and Social Affairs of the United Nations Secretariat, World Population Prospects: The 2010 Revision http://en.wikipedia.org/wiki/Demographics. Accessed on 24 January 2013. Report by Katharine Hall and Winnie Sambu from the Children's Institute, University of Cape Town revealed a "demography of South Africa's Children as at 2015 to be 34%". Those children are below the age of eighteen years while STATs SA report revealed that the total "population of children younger than fifteen years as at 2018 is 29.5%". See "Demography of South Africa's Children Gauge", 2018. Available at https://www.ci.uct.ac.za. Accessed on 15 October 2018 and STATs SA "Mid-year Population Estimate", 2018. Available at https://www.statssa.gov.za. Accessed on 15 October 2018.

[2] By Articles 1 and 2 of the Universal Declaration on Human Rights—"All human beings are born free and equal in dignity and rights. They are endowed with reason and conscience and should act towards one another in a spirit of brotherhood...Everyone is entitled to all the rights and freedoms set forth in this Declaration, without distinction of any kind...or other status".

© The Author(s) 2020

M. A. Abdulraheem-Mustapha,
Child Justice Administration in Africa,
https://doi.org/10.1007/978-3-030-19015-6_4

person is adult or child.[3] However, most human rights scholars will generally agree that because of the particular vulnerability of children, it is imperative that they enjoy additional rights that recognise their special need for protection. For example, the prevalence of the issues of violence against girls, child labour, children living on the streets, children in conflict with the law,[4] child trafficking, violence in school and violence in conflict situations against children, especially in transitioning contexts such as Nigeria and South Africa, well documented in existing literature.[5]

Thus, the need for specific instrumentality for the protection of children in deserving contexts stems from these pressing situations.[6] For instance, the long years of military rule in Nigeria with its flagrant disregard to human rights, added to her huge population, made it impossible for Nigeria to give the desired attention to child's justice

[3] "Human rights are inherent in all human beings all over the world and are not gifts to be withdrawn, withheld or granted at someone's whim or will. In this sense, they are said to be inalienable or imprescriptibly. If you remove them from any human being, he will become less than human. They are part of the very nature of human beings and attached to all human beings everywhere in all societies, just as much as do his arms and legs". See *The Universal Declaration of Human Rights, A Magna Carta for All Humanity* (United Nations Department of Public Information, 1998) cited in Ogbu, O. N., *Human Rights Law and Practice in Nigeria: An Introduction* (Enugu: CIDJAP Press, 1999), 2. Cited in Nnamani, S. O., 'Institutional Mechanisms for Human Rights Protection in Nigeria: An Appraisal'. Available at www.legislation.act.gov.au/a/2008-19/current/pdf/2008-19. Accessed on 18 January 2013.

[4] A Child in conflict with the law has the right to treatment that promotes that child's sense of dignity and self-worth, and such treatments must take into account the child's age. It must also aim at his or her reintegration into society and at his or her assuming a constructive role in society.

[5] See Second Country Periodic Report on the United Nations Convention on the Rights of the Child by the Federal Ministry of Women Affairs, Abuja, 2004. Available at www.unicef.org/wcaro/WCARO_Nigeria_Factsheets_CRA.pdf. Accessed on 20 January 2013. See also, the supplement to the final report of the study on the violent nature of crime in South Africa produced by the Centre for the Study of Violence and Reconciliation (CSVR) for the Justice, Crime Prevention and Security (JCPS) cluster submitted to the Minister of Safety and Security, 2009.

[6] In 1924, the League of Nations endorsed the first Declaration of the Rights of the Child, which set out a series of normative claims to save and protect the "delinquent" and the "waif". See Second Country Periodic Report on the United Nations Convention on the Rights of the Child by the Federal Ministry of Women Affairs, Abuja, 2004.

and children's developmental issues.[7] While the impact of apartheid long stay in South Africa cannot be overemphasised. However, the return to civilian rule in Nigeria in 1999 and South African dispensation in 1994 raised hopes of a new beginning for both countries, as the current democratic dispensations have created a positive and conducive programming environment for children. There is therefore an enormous improvement in the reception of government to the plight of children.

Until very recently, vaccination coverage rates and the number of children in conflict with the law placed in custodial institutions were somewhat above the average rates for sub-Saharan Africa; Nigeria[8] and South Africa[9] in particular. In spite of these challenges, however, efforts have been made through the development of legal frameworks, as well as institutional arrangements involving a number of programmes and initiatives to renew interest in children's rights, child justice and penal reform in Africa generally—Nigeria and South Africa in particular. This renews interest can be directly linked to both countries' desire to infuse criminal justice reform with children-rights approach in order to adopt and ensure the effective and practical implementation of the provisions contained in the Convention on the Rights of the Child.

[7] Ibid.

[8] As at 2013, there were 1306 juveniles held in custody out of custodial institution capacity of 2115 for offences ranging from property offences rated at 30.72%, offences against person, offences against the State, moral offences and victimless offences among others. See an Operational Research Report on Challenges of Borstal Institutions, Remand Homes, Reformatories and Approved Schools in Nigeria submitted to the Federal Department of Social Welfare, Federal Ministry of Women Affairs and Social Development, Abuja, Nigeria by Alamveabee E. Idyotough, June 2013.

[9] As at 2012 in South Africa, the population of prisoners was estimated at 121,023 with an overcrowding rate of approximately 30%. See South Africa (Republic). Department of Correctional Services. 2012a. 'Annual Performance Plan 2012/2013'. Available at www.dcs.gov.za. Accessed on 3 October 2012. While 597 children were incarcerated with approximately 74% for economical, sexual, narcotics and aggressive crimes. See South Africa (Republic). Department of Correctional Services. 2012b. 'Basic Information: Management Information System'. Available at www.dcs.gov.za/WebStatistics/. Accessed on 5 November 2012. See also, South Africa (Republic). National Prosecuting Authority. 2012. 'Annual Report 2011/2012'. Available at www.npa.gov.za. Accessed on 29 September 2012.

As the social statistics seemingly testify, Nigeria[10] and South Africa[11] have made serious efforts to address the interests of children over the years, but much is still required to be achieved, especially in the area of child justice administration in Nigeria. This position was evident from the fieldwork carried out by the author in 2014, where 710 (56.4%) out of 1258 respondents examined hold the views that "the Government is not committed to juvenile justice administration in Nigeria". The respondents attributed these views to inadequate funding and personnel which confirm the views of majority of the respondents where 67.1% hold that "there are no sufficient budgetary allocations for juvenile justice administration in Nigeria". This position was also in tandem with the views of majority of respondents examined in another interval where 52% of them "rated juvenile justice administration in Nigeria as poor". The child justice policy in Nigeria and South Africa is largely governed by the constitutional mandate given under Chapter IV of the Nigerian Constitution, 1999[12] and Chapter 2 of the South African Constitution, 1996 that guarantee special attention to children through necessary and special laws and policies that safeguard their rights.[13] The implication of these provisions appears to be that the Constitutions of Nigeria and South Africa recognise the vulnerable position of children and their

[10]The development of child justice administration in Nigeria was influenced by various developments in the Nigerian criminal justice administration. These developments include the enactment of the 1999 Constitution, the Children and Young Persons Act (CYPA), 1958; the Child Rights Act (CRA), 2003; the Criminal Code Act (CCA), 1965; the Penal Code Act (PCA), 1960; and The Shariah Penal Code Law, 1999. See next chapter for detail discussion.

[11]Formal process of law reform with variety of institutional improvements was launched after democratic dispensation ended apartheid in 1994. UNICEF report of 1990 has revealed the commitment of South African government in prioritising the issues of children by enshrining children's rights in its Constitution in 1996 and ratifications of the UN Convention on the Rights of the Child and African Charter on the Rights and Welfare of the Child. These have been harmonised with the domestications of the Child Justice Act, 2008 and Children's Act 38 of 2005 which replaced the Child Care Act 74 of 1983. See UNICEF, *First Call for Children* (New York: UNICEF, 1990); September, R., and Dinbabo, M., 'Gearing Up for Implementation: A New Children's Act for South Africa', *Practice: Social Work in Action*, 20(2), 113–122.

[12]See generally Chapter 4 of the Constitution of the Federal Republic of Nigeria 1999, Cap C23 LFN, 2004.

[13]See Chapter 2 of this book.

rights to protection. However, it would seem that the extant national laws that seek to translate this constitutional aspiration into reality vis-à-vis the treatment of child offenders, generally and especially in custodial institutions in Nigeria, is limited to some specific aspects of children's rights, which are grossly inadequate as they concern other areas of human rights.[14] This position corresponds with the views of majority of the respondents examined in Nigeria by the author where 63% hold that "the enactment of the Child Rights Act is not sufficient to address the inherent problems in the juvenile justice administration in Nigeria" and in another interval, while 63.9% of them said that "the existing legal measures to regulate juvenile justice administration is inadequate"; 59% of them said that "constitutional presumption of innocence is not adequately considered by Nigerian courts in the trial of juveniles in status offences". In the same vein, 62% of the respondents hold the views that the existing laws and policies on juvenile justice administration are not adequate.[15] In an interview, some respondents said: "the rights of child offenders to fair hearing is not recognised by the present juvenile justice administration especially under status offences, that is, juveniles who are beyond parental control when taken to court".[16] Also, some respondents said: "the current juvenile justice system in Nigeria does not recognise the child's rights to fair trial especially in legal representation unlike what is obtainable in other countries of Africa".[17]

In order to ensure compatibility with the international legal instruments, accordingly, all domestic legislations must take into account the special provisions that need to be made to address the needs of vulnerable children. This book analyses the strengths and weaknesses of existing juvenile justice legislations in Nigeria by drawing vital insight from South Africa Child justice regime. It also examines the statistics relating to implementation of these laws in Nigeria and South Africa, identifies the areas of fragmentation in the juvenile justice system and makes suggestions for a more cohesive legislation in future in Nigeria.

[14]See Lloyd, A., 'A Theoretical Analysis of the Reality of Children's Rights in Africa: An Introduction to the African Charter on the Rights and Welfare of the Child' (2002), *African Human Rights Law Journal*, 2, 13.

[15]Author's field survey, 2014.

[16]Interview conducted by the Author on 11 February 2014.

[17]Ibid.

2 International Legal Instruments for Juvenile Justice Administration

Child's justice administration in Nigeria and South Africa is accorded recognition and protection under the international, regional and national instruments. These international instruments on child justice administration include some aspects of the "United Nations Convention on the Rights of the Child" (UNCRC)[18]; the "United Nations Standard Minimum Rules for the Administration of Juvenile Justice" (The Beijing Rules)[19]; the "United Nations Rules for the Protection of Juveniles Deprived of their Liberty" (United Nations Rules)[20]; the "United Nations Guidelines for the Prevention of Juvenile Delinquency" (The Riyadh Guidelines)[21] and the "African Charter on the Rights and Welfare of the Child" (ACRWC).[22] Nigeria and South Africa are signatories to all aforementioned instruments and have domesticated them in their "Child rights Act, 2003", "Children's Act 38 of 2005" and "Child Justice Act 75 of 2008" which shall be discussed at later part of this book to show their compliance, adequate or otherwise on child justice system. Instructively, those international provisions dealing with child justice administration are examined below.

2.1 The United Nations Standard Minimum Rules for the Administration of Juvenile Justice (The Beijing Rules) 1985

The "Beijing Rules" was the first international comprehensive declaration that specifically focuses on the administration of child justice with approaches on child's right and development. It is aimed at developing a system of child justice that is fair and humane. It lays emphasis on the well-being and rehabilitation of children. In addition, it ensures the proportionality of the reactions of the authorities with the

[18] United Nations Convention on the Rights of the Child (UNCRC) 1989.

[19] United Nations Standard Minimum Rules for the Administration of Juvenile Justice (The Beijing Rules) 1985.

[20] United Nations Rules for the Protection of Juveniles Deprived of their Liberty (United Nations Rules) 1990.

[21] United Nations Guidelines for the Prevention of Juvenile Delinquency (The Riyadh Guidelines) 1990.

[22] African Charter on the Rights and Welfare of the Child (ACRWC) 1990.

circumstances of that of the offender and the offence committed.[23] And this calls for nothing more than a fair reaction in any given cases of child delinquency and crime. It sets forth minimum standards acceptable to the international community and treatment of juveniles who have run afoul of the law and measures that would prevent the act of delinquency.[24]

Thus, the "Beijing Rules" dictates that not only should child sentencing consider the seriousness of the offence, but the proportionality of the reaction of the law and from the society should be influenced by the personal circumstances of the offender.[25] Interestingly, the provisions of the "Beijing Rules" have been incorporated into the Convention on the Rights of the Child and as such become binding on all the States that are parties to the Convention. Incidentally, the "Beijing Rules" has been identified with the following advantages in the area of child justice system and it includes[26]:

> (i) the use of diversion from formal hearings to appropriate community programmes; (ii) proceedings to be conducted in the best interests of the juvenile by respecting the right to due process and the requested procedural safeguards; (iii) careful consideration before depriving a juvenile of liberty; (iv) specialised training for all personnel dealing with juvenile cases; and (v) the consideration of release both on apprehension and at the earliest possible occasion thereafter.

Therefore, the "Beijing Rules" is meant to serve as a "model" for member states in their development of a comprehensive framework of social

[23] Rules 5 and 17(1) (a) of the Beijing Rules require that at all stages the juvenile justice system shall emphasise the well-being of the juvenile and ensure that any reaction to juvenile offenders shall always be in proportion to the circumstances of both the offenders and the offence on the one hand and the circumstances and needs of the juvenile as well as the needs of the society on the other hand.

[24] See Okagbue, I., 'The Treatment of Juvenile Offenders and the Rights of the Child', in I. A. Ayua and I. E. Okagbue (eds.), *The Rights of the Child in Nigeria* (Nigerian Institute of Advance Legal Studies, 1996), 243. See Commentary to Rule 1 of the Beijing Rules.

[25] See Commentary to Rule 5 of the Beijing Rules. Proportionality of the reaction by law and from the society includes social status, family situation, the gravity of the harm caused by the offence and any other factors affecting personal circumstances.

[26] Ibid.

justice.[27] By this, it entails developing a framework that would ensure, for the child, a meaningful life in the community and fostering a process that is as free from crime as possible. It is also meant to design a procedure to minimise the adverse impact of the criminal justice system in the case of young persons who are in conflict with the law and enhance the process of their integration into the community.[28] In view of the above proposition and for achieving the objectives of the "Beijing Rules", the following mandates are embodied:

a. The child's treatment with humanity and respect for the inherent dignity of the human person;
b. Treatment in a manner, which takes into account the needs of persons of his or her age;
c. Separation from adult offenders unless it is not in the child's best interest to do so[29];
d. Maintenance of contact with his or her family through correspondence and visits save in exceptional circumstances;
e. Rights to prompt access to legal and other appropriate assistance;
f. Right to challenge the legality of the deprivation of his or her liberty before a court or other competent independent and impartial authority; and
g. Right to a prompt judicial process and decision.

[27] See Stephenie, J. Mill, 'The Age of Criminal Responsibility in an Era of Violence: Has Britain Set a Vandabult' (1995), *Journal of Transnational Law*, 28(2), 336, Vandabult University Nashville, cited in Okoro, H. C., 'Juvenile Justice Administration in Nigeria and International Standards on the Rights of the Child' (Issues in Justice Administration in Nigeria, 2003), 334.

[28] See Rule 1 of the Beijing Rules. See also, the Report of the Committee on Crime Prevention and Control. 1983/2, Section IVC cited in Osinbajo, Y., 'Juvenile Justice Administration in Nigeria' (1991), *Justice*, 6, 65 in Okoro, H. C., 'Juvenile Justice Administration in Nigeria and International Standards on the Rights of the Child'. Osinbajo argued that the essential perspective of the rules is to perceive juveniles as requiring both an interventionist and preventive action based on the recognition that the young owing to the early stage of their development require particular care and assistance with regard to their physical, mental and social development and legal protection in conditions of peace, freedom, dignity and security. See also the Report of the Seventh Congress on the Prevention of Crime and Treatment of Offenders, United Nations Publication Sales A/CONF. 121/22/rev. 1, No. E. 86. IV. I01650 cited in Okoro, H. C., 'Juvenile Justice Administration in Nigeria and International Standards on the Rights of the Child'.

[29] See Rule 13(4) of the Beijing Rules.

It is significant at this point to examine some important provisions of the Beijing Rules that are connected with child justice administration. At starting point, is Rule 7 dealing generally with the rights of child offender to fair hearing such as "the presumption of innocence" and the "right to be notified of charges". Some important points on the essential elements of fair and just trial which are recognised under the existing international human rights instruments were emphasised by the "Beijing Rules".[30]

Aside from the above, child offender also enjoys protection against infringement of his/her privacy in connection with criminal proceedings that extends beyond the protection enjoyed by adult offenders. The example of such right is the protection against publication in the mass media of information about juvenile cases.[31]

Concerning the reformative object of child justice administration, the "Beijing Rules" emphasises the importance of "community-based alternatives" and such community programmes include "temporary supervision and guidance, restitution and compensation of victims". These diversionary measures may be used at any point of the decision making by the responsible authorities and may be exercised by the police, prosecutor or other agencies. However, the consent of the child offender or his/her parents or guardian must be sought and obtained before referring him/her to the appropriate community or other services.[32] It should be noted that there should be accountability measures in the authority's exercise of discretion on the diversion process.[33] Emphasis on the provision of specific guidelines on the exercise of discretion was laid down in the "Beijing Rules". Although, due to large coverage of child justice system, the "Beijing Rules" does not specify precise mechanisms of review and accountability; it only makes provision for systems of review and appeal in order to permit scrutiny of decisions and accountability in child justice administration.[34] However, this book posits that efforts should be made to ensure sufficient accountability for the exercise of discretion at all stages and levels.

[30] See also Rule 14(1) of the Beijing Rules.

[31] See Rules 8–11, ibid.

[32] See Rule 11, ibid.

[33] See Rule 6, ibid.

[34] Ibid. See also Rules 1.6 and 2.2, ibid.

By virtue of Rule 12 of the "Beijing Rules", attention was drawn to the need for specialised training for all law enforcement officials who are involved in the administration of juvenile justice. As police are the first point of contact within the child justice system, it is important that the police act of arrest and detention must be in an informed and appropriate manner. The combined effects of Rule 13 of the Beijing Rules focus on detention pending trial generally where the welfare of juveniles is of paramount importance, and their rights guaranteed. It emphasises that detention should be used only as a measure of last resort and wherever possible. Detention pending trial shall be replaced by alternative measures. Rule 19 is aimed at restricting institutionalisation or detention of the child offender, in terms of how often it should be used and of the length of sentences.

This author criticises the provisions of the Beijing Rules especially the subject of diversion measures in Rule 11 where both parties must agree to proceed, and in a constructive manner, the offender must also admit to having committed the offence. This of course negates the constitutional right of presumption of innocence enjoyed by a child offender under Section 36(5) of the Nigerian Constitution, 1999 (as amended) and Sections 10, 12, 28 and 38 of the South African Constitution, 1996.

2.2 The United Nations Guidelines for the Prevention of Juvenile Delinquency (The Riyadh Guidelines) 1990[35]

The United Nations Guidelines for the Prevention of Juvenile Delinquency hereinafter referred to as "Riyadh Guidelines" were adopted as a preventive, rather than a curative policy for the administration of child justice.[36] The guidelines focus on the need for preventive actions in respect of child justice. These guidelines see prevention as not merely a matter of tackling negative situations, but rather as a means

[35] The United Nations Guidelines for the Prevention of Juvenile Delinquency proclaimed by the General Assembly Resolution 45/112 of 14 December 1990.

[36] Owasanoye, B., and Wenham, M., *Street Children and Juvenile Justice System in Lagos State of Nigeria* (Human Development Initiative, 2004), 11 cited in Okoro, H. C., 'Juvenile Justice Administration in Nigeria and International Standards on the Rights of the Child'. This publication comprises the report of proceedings, findingsand conclusions of a workshop organised by the Consortium for Street Children (CSR) of the UK (HDI on the fundamental rights of street children).

of promoting the welfare and well-being of child offenders. Thus, the importance of pursuing a child-centred orientation in any preventive programme for child delinquency was stressed by the guidelines.

However, for successful child delinquency preventions, many efforts are required on the part of the society to ensure the well-being and harmonious development of adolescents, with respect to, and promotion of, their personality from early childhood.[37] Children should have active roles and partnership within society and should not be considered as mere objects of control. The policies that have been designed should consider that youthful behaviour or conduct that does not conform to overall norms and values is often part of the maturation and growth process and tends to disappear spontaneously with transition from childhood.[38]

It is pertinent to note that the labelling of young person as "deviant", "delinquent" or "pro-delinquent" by the society often contributes to the development of a consistent pattern of undesirable behaviour by young persons.[39] It is therefore important that such labelling of young persons' should be sparingly subjected to the criminal process. Thus, the criminal process should only be invoked as a measure of last resort because of its criminalising, stigmatising and recidivistic consequences. Thus, Section 6 of the Riyadh Guidelines gives room for "community-based services and programmes" to be developed for the prevention of child delinquency, particularly where no agencies have yet been established and formal agencies of social control should only be utilised as a means of last resort.

From a human rights perspective, it has been argued that the Riyadh Guidelines represent a comprehensive review by the international community of the problems of children in conflict with the law. This is evident in its Section 52 when it states that: "Governments should enact and enforce specific laws and procedures to promote the rights and well-being of all young persons". The implication of the above section is that, children in conflict with the law are entitled to "fair and humane treatment", the "rights to visits, privacy, communication with the

[37] See Section 2 of the Riyadh Guidelines.

[38] Owasanoye, B., and Wenham, M., *Street Children and Juvenile Justice System in Lagos State of Nigeria* (Human Development Initiative, 2004).

[39] See Section 5(f) of the Riyadh Guidelines.

outside world, daily exercise and to education" (provided outside the detention facility by qualified teachers) suited to the child's needs and designed to prepare them for reintegration into the society. It emphasis generally that children should be separated from adults in detention custody.[40]

The overall aim of these guidelines is that priority should be given to children who are at risk of being abandoned, neglected, exploited and abused when designing the prevention programmes. The guidelines advocated a multidisciplinary and inter-sectoral approach to the prevention of children coming into conflict with the law and recognise children to be full participants in the society.

The guidelines also cover measures to prevent child offending on a number of levels, notably:

(i) primary prevention which covers general measures to promote social justice and equal opportunity, which thus tackle perceived root causes of offending such as poverty and other forms of marginalisation;
(ii) secondary prevention which covers measures to assist children who are identified as being more particularly at risk, such as those whose parents are themselves in special difficulty or are not caring appropriately for them;
(iii) Tertiary prevention which deals with involving schemes to avoid unnecessary contact with the formal justice system and other measures to prevent re-offending.[41]

Indeed, the Riyadh Guidelines echo many of the rights set out in the CRC as basic components of primary and secondary prevention and perhaps to a lesser extent, of prevention at the tertiary level. These guidelines are incorporated in the CRC and as such become binding on all states that are parties to CRC.

[40] See generally Part VI of the Riyadh Guidelines.

[41] See Innocenti Digest 3: Juvenile Justice, UNICEF International Child Development Centre, Florence, Italy in Roy, Nikhil, and Wong, Mabel, 'Juvenile Justice: Modern Concepts of Working with Children in Conflict with the Law' (A training seminar on juvenile justice organised by Save the Children UK, 2003). http://www.crin.org/docs/save/jjmodern_concepts.pdf-similar. Accessed on 14 February 2011.

2.3 *The United Nations Rules for the Protection of Juveniles Deprived of Their Liberty 1990*[42]

It puts in place the applicable standards for a child confined in any facility irrespective of whether or not the child is subjected to penal, correctional, educational or protective facility, or whether the child is subjected to such facility on the grounds of conviction or suspicion of having committed an offence, or simply being deemed "at risk". Thus, protection of the child offender under detention includes principles that universally define the specific circumstances under which children can be deprived of their liberty. Emphases were laid on the fact that "deprivation of liberty must be a means of last resort, for the shortest possible period of time and limited to exceptional cases". This is in line with internationally acceptable framework which is intended to counteract the detrimental effects of deprivation of liberty by ensuring respect for the human rights of child offenders and ensuring the dignity and welfare of the children is upheld while in custody.

Okabgue commenting on the Rules postulated that "the principle that the system of child justice should uphold the human rights and safety of children and promote their physical and mental well-being where they are inevitably deprived of their liberty by order of the Court".[43] The Rules were intended to establish minimum standards for the protection of child offenders deprived of their liberty in all forms.[44] Deprivation of liberty is justified as a means of protection, and this has gained a widespread opinion among judicial personnel that the detention of children is a good preventive measure and therefore a better solution than sending the child back to his or her family.[45]

[42]Adopted by the United Nations General Assembly in 1990 via Resolution 451113 of 14 December 1990 (here-in-after referred to as the United Nations Rules or JDLS). Available at http://www.ohchr.org/English/law/juvenile.htm. Accessed on 20 June 2010. By its Rule 11(b), "the deprivation of liberty means any form of detention or imprisonment or the placement of a person in a public or private custodial setting, from which this person is not permitted to leave at will, by order of any judicial, administrative or other public authority".

[43]Okagbue, I., 'The Treatment of Juvenile Offenders and the Rights of the Child', in *The Rights of the Child in Nigeria*, p. 243. See also Rule 1(1) of The United Nations Rules for the Protection of Juveniles Deprived of their Liberty.

[44]See Rules 1(3) of The United Nations Rules for the Protection of Juveniles Deprived of their Liberty.

[45]Roy, Nikhil, and Wong, Mabel, 'Modern Concepts of Working with Children in Conflict with the Law' (Save the Children UK, 2004). Available at http://www.crin.org/docs/savejjmordern-concepts.pdf-similar. Accessed on 14 February 2011.

Rules 1 and 3 of the United Nations Rules for the Protection of Juvenile Deprived of their Liberty emphasise the duty of the States to provide special treatment to detained imprisoned children and adjust to their needs in an expression of the "best interests" approach canvassed by the UNCRC. This is also fundamentally a logical rule given that the child justice system "should uphold the rights and safety and promote the physical and mental well-being of child offenders" with the aim of "counteracting the detrimental effects of all types of detention and ... fostering integration in society".

Rules 2, 12, 17 and 18 guaranteed specifically the right of the child to fair hearing and the adoption of a child-oriented approach which include prompt determination of matters without delay and the guarantee of the following rights—legal representation, presumption of innocence, silence, non-discriminatory treatment, privacy—be heard in defence and the benefit of meaningful activities and programmes that will foster the child's sense of responsibility by developing their potential as members of the society. By Rule 30 of the United Nations Rules for the Protection of Juvenile Deprived of their Liberty calls for the establishment of open detention facilities "with no or minimal security measures. The population in such detention facilities should be as small as possible and the number of child offenders detained in closed facilities should be small enough to enable individualised treatment".

Instructively, more detailed instructions with regard to the rights of the child detained or imprisoned in custodial institutions were provided under Rules 31–55 and 59–62. These provisions also create room for the child's contact with the wider community such as family and friends. The Rules further provide rights to facilities and services for the child which should meet all the requirements of health and human dignity such as medical care, good physical environment and accommodation, education,[46] vocational training and work, recreation and religion, etc.

In addition to provision of Article 37 of UNCRC with respect to the child's right to "prompt access to legal assistance" and to "legal

[46]It has to be noted that Rule 40 specifically emphasises that certificates awarded to juveniles while in detention should not indicate in any way that the juvenile has been institutionalised.

challenge of detention", the provision of Rule 18(a) extends the rights of the child offenders to "free legal aid" where such aid is available and to communicate regularly with their legal advisers, while "privacy and confidentiality shall be ensured for such communications". However, the rules are binding on all the states that are parties to the Convention on the Rights of the Child because the Rules are incorporated in the Convention and they constitute facets of rights enshrined in the Convention.

In order to be consistent with international standards, the deprivation of liberty of a child must consequently:

> (i) be lawful and not arbitrary; (ii) be imposed as a measure of last resort, that is when no other appropriate alternative measures are at the authorities' disposal to deal with the child concerned; and (iii) last only for the shortest appropriate period of time.[47]

2.4 The United Nations Convention on the Rights of the Child (UNCRC) 1989

It is surprisingly observed that despite the existence of various human rights documents in the world, there is no single document that is child-specific and that is adequate in addressing the peculiar needs of the child. In solving this problem, a "diplomatic manoeuvres by the Polish government in 1979"[48] began with the proposal that the "1959 Declaration of the Rights of the Child" be made a binding agreement.[49] In this regard, the "Civil Society Organisations" (CSOs) began to mount

[47] See Rules 1 and 2 of the UN Rules.

[48] Jones, Gareth A., 'Children and Development: Rights, Globalization and Poverty' (2005), *Progress Development Studies*, 5(4), http://eprints.lse.ac.uk/16971/. Accessed on 30 January 2013.

[49] Prior to the adoption of UNCRC, children had been at the centre of the brief 1959 Declaration of the Rights of the child, which does not however cover the various issues relating to the administration of justice per se. The post-1960s witnessed an ideological shift in perception of child rights from protection to autonomy, from nurturance to self-determination, from welfare to justice.

pressure on the United Nations and this pressure eventually motivated the "United Nations Commission for Human Rights" in 1986 to draft a "Convention on the Rights of the Child" (CRC). This Convention was subsequently adopted by the "United Nations General Assembly on 20th November, 1989".[50]

Globally, the issues relating to children were brought into focus with the adoption of the Convention, and this gained importance among countries that ratified it. The Convention serves as a reference legal document for the development of new laws and public policies by all states that are parties.[51] The Convention made emphasis that children are "holders of rights", and their rights cover all aspects of their lives. It applies to all human beings irrespective of age.[52]

However, the Convention has not taken into consideration whether or not childhood should begin at birth or at some other particular point, such as the moment of conception. Basically, four of the rights set out in the articles in the Convention have been identified as general principles that are to be considered for the purpose of its implementation and in all situations concerning children. These rights are[53]:

(i) Rights against discrimination (Article 2)[54]
(ii) Rights in the best interests of the child (Article 3)

[50]The CRC adopted in 1989 came at a time when the need for improvement in the situation of children all over the globe was clearly apparent. The preparation of the CRC started in 1979, declared by the UN as the International Year of the Child. See Glenn, Mower A., *The Convention on the Rights of the Child* (USA: Greenwood Press, 1997), 17.

[51]It is also possible to assure that the Child Rights Convention has been enormously influential indeed, to many, it is regarded as the touchstone for children's rights throughout the world. It constitutes the most comprehensive list of human rights creates for a specific group. International bodies refer to it with approval on the basis that it can be utilised to promote a change in the way children, as individual with rights, are viewed and also to encourage their active and responsible participation within the family and society.

[52]See Article 1 of UNCRC 1989.

[53]See www.aecf.org/~/media/PublicationFiles/Juvenile_Justice_issuebrief3.pdf. Accessed on 20 January 2013.

[54]Article 2(1) provides: "States Parties shall respect and ensure the rights set forth in the present Convention to each child within their jurisdiction without discrimination of any kind, irrespective of the child's or his or her parent's or legal guardian's race, colour, sex, language, religion, political or other opinion, national, ethnic or social origin, property, disability, birth or other status".

(iii) Rights to life, survival and development (Article 6)[55]
(iv) Right to be heard (Article 12)[56]

Importantly, the above rights have connection with child justice administration with respect to the treatment of child offenders. Suffice to say that the effects of the above provisions consider the differences in the physical and psychological development between adults and children and consider the emotional and educational needs of children which should constitute the basis for the lesser culpability of children in conflict with the law. These and other differences are the reasons for a separate child justice system which presupposes a different treatment for children. The provision for the protection of the best interests of the child in Article 3 of the Convention can be viewed from the perspective that "the traditional objectives of criminal justice, such as repression/retribution, must give way to rehabilitation and restorative justice objectives in dealing with child offenders". The author argues that the provision can be achieved with concert attention to effective public safety. In that sense, the interest of the child must be the subject of active consideration, and it needs to be demonstrated that children's interests have been explored and taken into account as a primary consideration.

Article 2(2) states thus: "States Parties shall take all appropriate measures to ensure that the child is protected against all forms of discrimination or punishment on the basis of the status, activities, expressed opinions, or beliefs of the child's parents, legal guardians, or family members".

[55]These are rights to the resources, skills and contributions necessary for the survival and full development of the child. They include rights to adequate food, shelter, clean water, formal education, primary health care, leisure and recreation, cultural activities and information about their rights. These rights require not only the existence of the means to fulfil the rights but also access to them. Also the inherent right of every child should guide and inspire States parties in the development of effective national policies and programmes for the prevention of juvenile delinquency, because it goes without saying that delinquency has a negative impact on the child's development. Furthermore, this basic right should result in a policy of responding to juvenile delinquency in ways that support the child's development. The death penalty and a life sentence without parole are explicitly prohibited. See Article 37(a) of UNCRC.

[56]Children are entitled to the freedom to express opinions and to have a say in matters affecting their social, economic, religious, cultural and political life. Participation rights include the right to express opinions and be heard, the right to information and freedom of association. Engaging these rights as they mature helps children bring about the realisation of all their rights and prepares them for an active role in society.

Interestingly, most provisions in the Convention such as "right to education",[57] "protection against abuse and exploitation", "right to freedom of movement", "right to adequate information", "right to adequate standard of living and appropriate moral guidance" are very relevant to the system of child justice.[58] These rights will help in keeping children out of criminal activities. It thus means that to prevent children from committing, there is the need to promote and protect rights of children as provided by the Convention. The main thrust of the Convention is to emphasise and support the role of the parents or the family as the primary caregivers to children and to prevent institutionalisation of child offenders whenever possible. The section dealing with the aspect of child justice is those related to the arrest, liberty, trial and treatment of child offenders in order to achieve the object of punishment of child offenders.

The convenient starting point is the provision relating to child offender's entrance to child justice administration and his/her rights. While the law condemns anti-social conducts and empowers the law enforcement agencies to arrest, detain and even prosecute the offender, it recognises/protects the right of the citizen to liberty as a safeguard against arbitrariness. In the spectrum of child justice system, Article 37 deals with the liberty of children, and it posits that "a child cannot be deprived of his/her liberty unjustly".[59] Here, no child shall be the subject of arrest unlawfully or arbitrarily, neither can he/she be detained nor imprisoned unjustly. The measures (arrest, detention or imprisonment) though significant in addressing children issues, can only be employed to deal with the child offender as "a measure of last resort, and for a shortest appropriate period of time".[60] The reason behind these provisions is to accord child offender dignity and respect and to prevent him or her from issues

[57] See Article 29 of UNCRC.

[58] See Article 29 of UNCRC.

[59] The use of deprivation of liberty has very negative consequences for the child's harmonious development and seriously hampers his/her reintegration in society. Instructively, it is noted that the rights of a child deprived of his/her liberty, as recognised in CRC, apply with respect to children in conflict with the law, and to children placed in institutions for the purposes of care, protection or treatment, including mental health, educational, drug treatment, child protection or immigration institutions.

[60] Ibid.

that may affect his or her development in life. Instructively, these rights apply to all situations irrespective of whether or not his or her liberty is at stake and regardless of the reason for the deprivation, that is, whether the child is detained for interrogation, investigation, awaiting trial, convicted or placed for purpose of care and protection.

The provisions of the Convention are *in tandem* with "Chapter IV of the Constitution of the Federal Republic of Nigeria 1999" (as amended), and "Bill of Rights" under "Chapter 2 of the South African Constitution, 1996". The object of these provisions is to protect the rights of Nigerian and South African citizens generally, irrespective of age, sex or religion. Additionally, Article 37 of the Convention "prohibits the torture or other cruel treatment or punishment of any child and the capital punishment or life imprisonment without possibility of release of persons below eighteen years of age".

Another significant aspect of the Convention is the provision dealing with rights of the child offender against allegation of crime or acts that infringe the penal law. Just like an adult offender, Article 40 of the Convention guarantees the child's rights which apply to all phases of the child justice process. The processes start from the stage when a child is a suspect and under interrogation to the processes of prosecution or waiting for trial, and those who are on trial up to the stage when pronouncement is made by court on conviction or discharge and acquittal. These provisions guaranteed the child's rights in matters relating to procedural process (due process rights) such as minimum age for criminal responsibility, diversion and the availability of alternatives to institutional care (superior orders, counselling, probation, foster care, education, for example). The provisions also safeguard the authorities and institutions dealing with children alleged of as having infringed the penal law.

In the generality of the safeguard, the right of a child offender to fair trial or hearing is paramount. Article 40(b)(iii) of the Convention specifically guarantees the right to fair hearing including prompt determination of matters without delay by a competent authority, independent and impartial authority, right to legal representation, presumption of innocence, right to silence, right to be punished for only crime that if committed by an adult, non-discriminatory treatment, respect of privacy at all stages of the proceedings and right to be heard in defence.

Significantly, Article 40(2)(a) of the Convention protects the child from being tried for retrospective offences when it emphasises that the child shall not be accused of "infringing the penal law by reason of acts or omissions" which were not prohibited by law at the time they were committed.[61] Article 40(2)(b)(iv) of the Convention contains two separate rights to wit; the right of the child "not to be compelled to give testimony or to confess guilt" and the right "to examine or have examined adverse witness and to obtain the participation and examination of witnesses on his or her behalf under conditions of equality".

It is pertinent to note that the aim of criminal justice system generally is the prevention of crime and rehabilitation/reformation of the offender to become a useful member of the society; the same applies to the child offender. Article 39 of the Convention recognises the right of child offenders to rehabilitation and social reintegration, and it also extends to children who are "victims of neglect, exploitation and abuse".

All African countries have ratified the Convention and have heightened recognition of the fundamental human dignity of all children and the urgency of ensuring their well-being and development. The Convention makes clear the idea that a basic quality of life should be the right of all children, rather than a privilege enjoyed by a few. Instructively, Nigeria and South Africa ratified the Convention on 16th April 1991 and June 1995. The Convention offers a vision of the child as an individual and as a member of a family and community, with rights and responsibilities appropriate to his or her age and stage of development. By recognising children's rights in this way, the Convention firmly sets the focus on the whole child. The role of parents in the bringing up of children was equally recognised in the Convention. For instance, Article 5 of the Convention encourages "parents to deal with rights issues with their children in a manner consistent with the evolving capacities of the child".

It is the belief of the author that the principles articulated in the Convention can only be achieved when they are respected by everyone within the family, in schools and other institutions that provide services for children, in communities and at all levels of administration. It is therefore understandable while Article 43 establishes the Committee on the Rights of the Child (CRC).[62] This is the body of independent

[61] This is a principle of *nullum crimen sine lege.*

[62] See Article 43 of the UNCRC.

experts that monitors the implementation of the Convention by its State parties.[63]

The notion of the "global child" as the subject of rights has provoked a critique of the Convention's claim to universalism against what many observers suggest[64] is a hardly "obscured Western-centric view" of "normal child-adult and child-society relations that condemns other' styles of upbringing as outside childhood".[65] The Convention, for example, has been argued to have prioritised the family as the "primary care-giver" undermining the cultural role of "community networks and

[63]All State parties are obliged to submit regular reports to the Committee on how the rights are being implemented. States must report initially two years after acceding to the Convention and then every five years. The Committee examines each report and addresses its concerns and recommendations to the State party in the form of "concluding observations". The Committee reviews additional reports which must be submitted by States who have acceded to the two Optional Protocols to the Convention. The CRC Committee is empowered not only to monitor implementation of the Convention, but also to render technical and development assistance to State Parties. This commitment to technical assistance constitutes a change in the very concept of a treaty monitoring body. The role of the Committee is not only to evaluate the efforts made by States to fulfil their obligations under the Convention but also to help them, when appropriate, to obtain assistance needed to overcome to full implementation. The Committee has identified four fundamental principles which underpin the CRC and by extension the rights of the juvenile which are: in all actions concerning children, the best interests of the child must be a primary consideration; children have a fundamental right to life which includes promoting their survival and development to the maximum extent possible; recognising children's right without discrimination of any kind; and children have the right to have their views respected in all matters affecting them. See http://www.ohchr.org/Documents/Publications/FactSheet10Rev.1enpdf. Accessed on 30 January 2013. See Article 43 of UNCRC. See also http://www.bestinterest.org. Accessed on 31 January 2013.

[64]Nieuwenhuys, O., 'Global Childhood and the Politics of Contempt' (1998), *Alternatives*, 23. Available at www.ajol.info/index.php/naujilj/article/download/82393/72548. Accessed on 18 January 2013.

[65]Panter-Brick, C., 'Nobody's Children? A Reconsideration of Child Abandonment', in C. Panter-Brick and M. Smith (eds.), *Abandoned Children* (Cambridge: Cambridge University Press, 2000), 1–26. See also Nieuwenhuys, O., 'Global Childhood and the Politics of Contempt' (1998), *Alternatives*, 23, 267–289. See also Pupavac, V., 'Misanthropy Without Borders the International Children's Rights Regime' (2001), *Disasters*, 25(2), 95–112. See also White, B., 'A World Fit for Children? Children and Youth in Development Studies and Policy', 51st Dies Natalis Address (Institute of Social Studies, The Hague, 2003). See also White, S. C., 'From the Politics of Poverty to the Politics of Identity? Child Rights and Working Children in Bangladesh' (2002), *Journal of International Development*, 14, 725–735.

responsibilities to parents" that partly motivate the acceptance of child work.[66] However, the book observed that the Convention does not create legally binding obligations as such; the Convention is only binding on States that ratify it. Similarly, the notion of deprivation of liberty as applicable to children and child offenders is not defined under the Convention.

This book observed the review of minimum age at which criminal responsibility can be imputed on a child as a welcome provision and urges all States that are parties to amend their respective domestic legislation in this regards. South Africa has been singled out as the State party that has complied with the international standard. However, Nigeria is staggering with this implementation as same is evident in the next chapter of this book.

3 The African Charter on the Rights and Welfare of the Child (ACRWC) (African Child Rights Charter) 1990

The African Child Rights Charter is argued to be the first regional treaty that specifically recognised the peculiar needs and protection of all African children.[67] This Charter considered the need for all African children to be fully prepared to live an individual life in society. It was declared in the Charter that African children should be brought up in the spirit of the ideals particularly, in the "spirit of peace, dignity, tolerance, freedom, equality and solidarity". This Charter was proposed in 1979 by "the Organisation of Africa Unity (O.A.U.) Assembly of Heads of States and Government" (AHOSG)[68] and eventually "adopted on

[66]Burr, R., 'Global and Local Approaches to Children's Rights in Vietnam' (2002), *Childhood* 9(1). Available at https://www.ajol.info/index.php/naujil/article. See also White, S. C., 'Being, Becoming and Relationship: Conceptual Challenges of a Child Rights Approach in Development' (2002), *Journal of International Development*, 14, 1095–1104. See also Nieuwenhuys, O., 'Global Childhood and the Politics of Contempt' (1998), *Alternatives*, 23.

[67]No. 138. Paragraphs 2, 3, 9 and 12 of the Declaration.

[68]Commentary on the UN Convention of the Rights of the Child: Article 3—The best interest of the child, University College London, Nijhoff Publishers 2007 quoted from Adegbola, R. E., 'Children's Rights in Africa: An Appraisal of the African Committee of Experts on the Rights and Welfare of the Child' (Unpublished, Master of Law Dissertation, University of Pretoria, 2007).

11 July 1990 at the 26th Ordinary Session" of the Assembly and same "entered into force on 29 November 1999" (nine years later) after obtaining the "requisite number of ratifications".[69] The rationale for its adoption was premised on the recognition of specific cultural setting in which Africa operates. The Charter calls for consideration of the "cultural heritage, historical background and the values of the African civilisation" which inspired and characterised the concept of the rights and welfare of the child.

In assessing and comparing the core provisions of the Charter, it is not in doubt that the Charter put in place a higher level of protection on the rights and welfare of the African children despite the numerous similarities with the Convention on the Rights of the Child.[70]

This has been evident from the study of Ankut,[71] that "the Charter complements the Convention on the Rights of the Child". According to Murray[72] the Charter attempts "to add an African perspective to be defined or accepted". The Charter has been described as "Africa sensitive",[73] "the most progressive of the treaties on the rights of the child"[74] and "the most forward thinking of all the regional systems on children".[75] On this note, beyond addressing children's rights from an African perspective, this book discovered that it also helps in the understanding of children's rights globally because it complements the Convention.

[69] Article 47(3) provides that the ACRWC will come into force after it has received 15 ratifications from member states. Available at http://www.chr.up.ac.za/statorat_14.html. Accessed on 15 October 2007. As at 2007, the states' ratification stands at 41. The study was carried out by Adegbola, R. E., 'Children's Rights in Africa: An appraisal of the African Committee of Experts on the Rights and Welfare of the Child'. The researcher is grateful to her.

[70] Ankut, P., *The African Charter on the Rights and Welfare of the Child: Linking Principle with Practice* (Open Society Initiative of West Africa [OSIWA], 2007).

[71] Ibid.

[72] Murray, R., *Human Rights in Africa: From the OAU to the African Union* (Cambridge University Press, 2004), 167.

[73] Lloyd, A., 'Evolution of the African Charter on the Rights and Welfare of the Child and the African Committee of Experts: Raising the Gauntlet' (2002), *International Journal on Children's Rights*, 10, 179.

[74] Van Bueren, G., *The International Law on the Rights of the Child* (Martinus Nijhoff Publishers, 1995).

[75] Lloyd, A., 'Evolution of the African Charter on the Rights and Welfare of the Child and the African Committee of Experts: Raising the Gauntlet' (2002), *International Journal on Children's Rights*, 10.

Article 17[76] of the Charter gives detailed provisions applicable to child justice administration. Thus, it affords a child alleged to have committed an offence the opportunity of having the right to "special treatment in a manner consistent with the child's dignity and worth". And this reinforces the respect for the child's rights and fundamental reforms by reintegrating and rehabilitating him/her back to his/her family and the society. It is designed to "suit the social and cultural values of Africa". This regional instrument, which places the child at the centre of the family and community, together with the Convention provide a comprehensive framework of child justice administration in Africa.[77]

However, this book questions the provision of Article 2 of the Charter where a child is defined as more concisely as "every human being below the age of eighteen years". There are no exceptions or caveats included in the definition. Although the Charter is very clear on age limitations, its definition of age does not seem to fit with the African culture and tradition, where childhood is determined, not based on years but on other factors[78] such as the determination of puberty under the Shar'iah law.[79]

[76]See Article 17(1) of the ACRWC and part of the provisions of Article 17 is the enjoyment accorded to a child to be informed promptly in a language he understands and in details the charge against him and be afforded legal and other appropriate assistance in the preparation and presentation of his defence.

[77]The ACRWC consists of 48 Articles where the first chapter contains the 31 substantial articles about the rights and welfare of African children. Of the States Parties that have ratified the ACRWC, only some have domesticated the instrument and Nigeria being convinced that the family, as the fundamental group of society and the natural environment for the growth and well-being of particularly children should be afforded the necessary protection and assistance so that it can fully assume its responsibilities within the community, signed this Instrument on 13 July 1999 and ratified it on 23 July 2001. See http://www.africaunion.org/root/au/Documents/Treaties/List/African%20Charter%20on%20the%20Rights%20and%20Welfare%20of%20the%20Child.pdf. Last accessed on 31 October 2007.

[78]For example in *Joseph Uwa v. The State* (1965) I ANLR, 356, the Supreme Court took into consideration the fact that when an Ibo villager says that he is thirteen years old, it does not necessarily mean that he is thirteen years old as one would expect. The court accepted the fact that 200 villagers reckon their ages by certain festivals and that the result may well be that an Ibo boy who says he is thirteen may only actually be twelve. See Okonkwo, C. O., Nwankwo, Clement, and Ibhawoh, Bonny, *Administration of Juvenile Justice in Nigeria*, p. 6.

[79]See the "concept of childhood" discussed in Chapter 2 of this book.

4 Conclusion

This chapter examines the strengths and weaknesses of the international legal instruments on child justice administration and the custodial institutions from an African perspective. Emphasis is made to the UNCRC; the Standard Minimum Rules for the Administration of Juvenile Justice; Rules for the Protection of Juveniles Deprived of their Liberty; Guidelines for the Prevention of Juvenile Delinquency and the African Charter on the Rights and Welfare of the Child. The chapter further examines the statistics relating to implementation of these laws and identifies the areas of fragmentation in the child justice system. It linked the legal instruments concerned to the promulgation of the Nigerian Child Rights Act, 2003 (which is a legislation that combined the issue of children in conflict with the law and children in need of care and protection) and South Africa Child Justice Act 78 of 2008 (as amended) (regulating children in conflict with law) and South Africa Children's Act 38 of 2005 (as amended) (dealing with children in need of care and protection). It demonstrates their compliance, adequacy or otherwise on child justice system.

References

Adegbola, R. E., 'Children's Rights in Africa: An Appraisal of the African Committee of Experts on the Rights and Welfare of the Child' (Unpublished, Master of Law Dissertation, University of Pretoria, South Africa, 2007).

Ankut, P., *The African Charter on the Rights and Welfare of the Child: Linking Principle with Practice* (Open Society Initiative of West Africa [OSIWA], 2007).

Burr, R., 'Global and Local Approaches to Children's Rights in Vietnam' (2002), *Childhood*, 9(1). Available at https://www.ajol.info/index.php/naujil/article.

Glenn, Mower A., *The Convention on the Rights of the Child* (USA: Greenwood Press, 1997).

Idyotough, Alamveabee E., *Operational Research Report on Challenges of Borstal Institutions, Remand Homes, Reformatories and Approved Schools in Nigeria* (Abuja, Nigeria: Federal Department of Social Welfare, Federal Ministry of Women Affairs and Social Development, 2013).

Jones, Gareth A., 'Children and Development: Rights, Globalization and Poverty' (2005), *Progress in Development Studies*, 5(4), http://eprints.lse.ac.uk/16971/.

Lloyd, A., 'A Theoretical Analysis of the Reality Of Children's Rights in Africa: An Introduction to the African Charter on the Rights and Welfare of the Child' (2002a), *African Human Rights Law Journal*, 2.

Lloyd, A., 'Evolution of the African Charter on the Rights and Welfare of the Child and the African Committee of Experts: Raising the Gauntlet' (2002b), *International Journal on Children's Rights*, 10.

Murray, R., *Human Rights in Africa: From the OAU to the African Union* (Cambridge University Press, 2004).

Nieuwenhuys, O., 'Global Childhood and the Politics of Contempt' (1998), *Alternatives*, 23. Available at www.ajol.info/index.php/naujilj/article/download/82393/72548.

Nnamani, S. O., 'Institutional Mechanisms for Human Rights Protection in Nigeria: An Appraisal'. Available at www.legislation.act.gov.au/a/2008-19/current/pdf/2008-19.

Ogbu, O. N., *Human Rights Law and Practice in Nigeria: An Introduction* (Enugu: CIDJAP Press, 1999).

Okagbue, I., 'The Treatment of Juvenile Offenders and the Rights of the Child', in I. A. Ayua and I. E. Okagbue (eds.), *The Rights of the Child in Nigeria* (Nigerian Institute of Advance Legal Studies, 1996).

Okonkwo, C. O., Nwankwo, Clement, and Ibhawoh, Bonny, *Administration of Juvenile Justice in Nigeria* (1st ed.; Lagos: Constitutional Rights Project [CRP], 1997), 6.

Osinbajo and Kalu, *Law Development and Administration in Nigeria* (Lagos: Federal Ministry of Justice, 1990).

Owasanoye, B., and Wenham, M., *Street Children and Juvenile Justice System in Lagos State of Nigeria* (Human Development Initiative, 2004).

Panter-Brick, C., 'Nobody's Children? A Reconsideration of Child Abandonment', in C. Panter-Brick and M. Smith (eds.), *Abandoned Children* (Cambridge: Cambridge University Press, 2000).

Pupavac, V., 'Misanthropy Without Borders the International Children's Rights Regime' (2001), *Disasters*, 25.

Roy, Nikhil, and Wong, Mabel, 'Juvenile Justice: Modern Concepts of Working with Children in Conflict with the Law' (A training seminar on juvenile justice organized by Save the Children UK, 2003). http://www.crin.org/docs/save/jjmodern_concepts.pdf-similar.

September, R., and Dinbabo, M., Gearing Up for Implementation: A New Children's Act for South Africa', *Practice: Social Work in Action*, 20(2).

Stephenie, J. Mill, 'The Age of Criminal Responsibility in an Era of Violence: Has Britain Set a Vandabult' (1995), *Journal of Transnational Law*, 28(2), Vandabult University Nashville.

Van Bueren, G., *The International Law on the Rights of the Child* (Martinus Nijhoff Publishers, 1995).

White, S. C., 'From the Politics of Poverty to the Politics of Identity? Child Rights and Working Children in Bangladesh' (2002a), *Journal of International Development*, 14.

White, S. C., 'Being, Becoming and Relationship: Conceptual Challenges of a Child Rights Approach in Development' (2002b), *Journal of International Development*, 14.

CHAPTER 5

Legal and Institutional Frameworks on Child Justice Administration in Nigeria

1 Introduction

The development of the administration of child justice in Nigeria was influenced by various developments in the Nigerian criminal justice administration. These developments include the enactment of the 1999 Constitution, the Children and Young Persons Act (CYPA), 1958; the Child Rights Act (CRA), 2003; the Criminal Code Act (CCA), 1965; the Penal Code Act (PCA), 1960; and The Shar'iah Penal Code Law, 1999. These laws addressed issues relating to children in crisis situations such as children in conflict with the law. The chapter also analyses the structures of children's custodial institutions in the achievement of the primary objective of reintegration of child offender into the society. The chapter further interrogates the establishment of police force, court, prison service and approved/Borstal/remand institutions.

2 The Constitution of the Federal Republic of Nigeria, 1999

One of the important instruments that regulate the child justice system and promote and protect the rights of the children is the Constitution. The Constitution is the ***grund norm*** of the laws in the Nigerian legal system.

© The Author(s) 2020

M. A. Abdulraheem-Mustapha,
Child Justice Administration in Africa,
https://doi.org/10.1007/978-3-030-19015-6_5

An examination of any institution in Nigeria must begin with the examination of the Constitution where it derives its status and legitimacy.[1]

There are several provisions of the Constitution pertaining to child justice system and rights of children like any individual. This has been the position even in the successive Nigerian Constitutions from "independence" from British imperialism in 1960.[2] A very good and relevant example is the provisions which accord an accused the right to fair trial and due process; the right to life[3]; the right to personal liberty[4]; the right to fair hearing[5] and the right to freedom of movement.[6] These rights are granted to all persons irrespective of whether you are an adult or young person. These provisions conform to the relevant United Nations Rules and Guidelines on the treatment of offenders inclusive of child offenders.

Other significant constitutional provisions relating to the rights of children like adults are contained in Chapter 2 of the 1999 Constitution, particularly Sections 13, 14(2)(b), 17(3)(c) (d) and (f). The sections enjoin all the tiers of government—the federal, State and local governments, and all persons and authorities exercising legislative, executive and judicial powers, to ensure that the welfare and security of children and adult persons remain the primary purpose of government including protection against any exploitation whatsoever and against moral and material neglect. However, although Chapter 2 is not justiciable,[7] the chapter lays down ideas that should enhance the development of policies or a social order for the protection and promotion of the rights of

[1] This assertion gains credence from the Constitution. For instance, Section 1(1) of the 1999 Constitution provides that "this Constitution is supreme and its provisions shall have binding force on all authorities and persons throughout the Federal Republic of Nigeria". Furthermore, Section 1(3) of the Constitution provides that "if any other law is inconsistent with the provisions of this Constitution, this Constitution shall prevail, and that other law shall to the extent of this inconsistency be void".

[2] 1960, 1979, and 1999 as amended.

[3] See Section 33 of 1999 Constitution.

[4] See Section 35, ibid.

[5] See Section 36, ibid. By Section 36(4)(a) of the 1999 Constitution, right to fair hearing in a competent Court is guaranteed and the Court can exclude the public in the interest of the welfare of persons under eighteen years or the protection of the private lives of persons where the Court is of the opinion that publicity will be contrary to the interest of justice.

[6] See Section 41, ibid.

[7] It should be noted that the non-justiciability of the directive principle as declared by Section 6(6)(c) of the 1999 Constitution is not sacrosanct as the effect is if the Constitution otherwise provides in another section, which will make any section of

children in Nigeria. These policies if well implemented will ensure social justice for the child. This book posits that, in the alternative, protection of children's rights should be specifically included under the enforceable rights enshrined in Chapter 4 of the Constitution.

Thus, the significance of the Constitution in any discussion or examination of child justice administration as it relates to the treatment of child offender like adult cannot be overemphasised. As the *grund norm* which provides basis for the government/institutions, child justice administration, the rights and protection of child offenders must be examined in the light of the Constitution.[8] It is based on this proposition that the Children and Young Persons Act and the Child Rights Act were enacted by the Federal government.

3 The Children and Young Persons Act (CYPA)

Another significant law which addresses the issue of child justice system is the Children and Young Persons Act which was initially enacted as an ordinance in 1943. It is the earliest law on child justice system to have undergone several amendments.[9] Although the Act was intended to be a national law,[10] provisions were made for its adoption as regional laws[11] and subsequently as State laws.[12] Despite the recent adoption of

Chapter 2 to be justiciable. This gains credence in the case of *Federal Republic of Nigeria v. Alhaji Mika Anache & Others* (2004) 14 WRN 61 where the Court held that Section 6(6) (c) of the Constitution provides a leeway by the use of the words "except as otherwise provided by this Constitution".

[8]This is amply demonstrated by the Court of Appeal's decision in the celebrated case of *Karimatu Yakubu v. AlhajiPaiko* Appeal No. CA/K/80s/85—unreported, Court of Appeal, Kaduna where the Court allowed the appeal in favour of a teenage girl on the ground that her right to consent in marriage and to marry her suitor was of paramount consideration even under the Shariah family law notwithstanding her father's right to exercise the power of Ijbar (compulsion), according to the Maliki school of Law widely followed in Northern Nigeria.

[9]i.e. Ordinances 44 of 1945; 27 of 1947; 16 of 1950 as well as the Laws of Nigeria 131 of 1954; 47 of 1955; and Order in Council 22 of 1958.

[10]Cap 32 laws of the Federation of Nigeria and Lagos 1958.

[11]The law was extended to the Eastern and Western Regions of Nigeria in 1946 by Order in Council, No 22 of 1946. The law was enacted for the Northern Region in 1958 and constituted the Children and Young Persons Law, Cap 21 of the Laws of Northern Nigeria 1963.

[12]Lagos State adopted the law in 1970—Children and Young Persons Law Cap. 26 of the Laws of Lagos State.

the Child Rights Act 2003, the CYPA remains an important legislation in Nigeria that deals with the treatment of child offenders especially in those States that are yet to domesticate the Child Rights Act.[13] It was enacted to make provision for the welfare of young persons, the treatment of young offenders and the establishment of juvenile courts.

An important part of the CYPA is Section 3 which deals with rights of juvenile to freedom of movement through bail. For instance, where a juvenile offender is apprehended with or without warrant by a police officer, the child is entitled to be released on bail.[14]

Due to this special treatment, a juvenile arrested may be released on "a recognisance entered into by him or by his parents or guardian, with or without sureties, for such an amount as will, in the opinion of the officer, secure the attendance of such person upon the hearing of the charge". Section 5 of CYPA enjoins "the Inspector General of Police to make arrangements to prevent so far as practicable, a child or young person (until the age of 17) while in custody, from associating with an adult charged with an offence". This provision is in line with Article 37(c) of the United Nations Child Rights Convention. The rationale behind this provision is "to prevent the criminal contamination or indoctrination of young offenders by adult criminals". Apart from the above rationale, the provisions are also desirable for the protection of young offenders from abuse and exploitation by adult criminals. The provision of Section 5 of CYPA also conforms with the empirical survey carried out by the author where 808 (64%) out of 1258 respondents strongly agreed that "prison should not be used as a substitute for custody of child offenders". These respondents in an interview commented that "keeping the child or juvenile offender in prison will only increase his/her criminal inclination because he/she will be mixed up with adult inmates". Whereas, keeping child offender in remand home will be a corrective measure in the control of child delinquency. This is in tandem with the author's field survey where 690 (55%) out of the total population of 1258 respondents strongly agreed to this position.

[13] List of those states that are yet to domesticate the Child Rights Act was later enumerated in this study.

[14] It is important to note that this bail condition, however, does not apply to a person: (a) accused of homicide or other grave crimes or (b) to situation where "it is necessary in the interest of such person to remove him from association with any reputed criminal or prostitute" or (c) to a situation where "the officer has reason to believe that the release of such person would defeat the ends of justice". The last condition (c) appears too vague and may be abused to unnecessarily deny bail to young offenders.

However, in reality, this provision is not always enforced, especially in police cells. A recent survey by the author confirms this position where 849 (71%) out of 1258 respondents hold the views that "there are no children cells in police stations in Nigeria". Some of the police officers interviewed state that "we do not have separate police cells for child offenders; we do put them behind the counter or in an empty adult cell". It is pertinent to also note that a large number of child offenders were incarcerated in the Nigerian prisons,[15] and mingled together with adult inmates. This conforms with the position of Abrifor et al.,[16] Uma, Falobi,[17] Wilson,[18] Soyombo[19] and Ngwuoke[20] that "the great majority of children in conflict with the law were held together with adults in the regular prisons and as the children advance in age behind bars, their association with adult criminals invariably expose them to the danger of aggravated criminal tendencies and recidivism".

In proceedings against a juvenile, the law under Section 6 deals with the issue of juvenile trials. The provision of Section 6, for instance, guarantees the right of the child to be tried in a separate court and to the exclusion of the public. The purpose of this provision is "to protect the privacy of the young offenders and also protect him or her from the effects of stigmatisation that may result from public trial".

Instructively, in the process of committing the child offender in custody, Section 7 of CYPA specifies the conditions of custody or remand. It provides that: "A court on remanding or committing for trial a child or

[15]See the tables on age composition of prisoners in Nigerian prisons published in Annual Abstract of Statistics published by the Federal Office of Statistics. Quoted in Alemika E.E.O. and Chukwuma I.C., Juvenile Justice Administration in Nigeria: Philosophy and Practice. This can also be confirmed from the report gathered from The Vanguard Newspaper of 5 September 2008 at p. 10 that "No fewer than 200 juveniles are currently languishing in Port Harcourt Prison as they have been put behind bars amongst over 2,400 inmates, in (sic) which over 1,800 of the adults and children are awaiting trial".

[16]Abrifor et al., 'Differences, Trend and Pattern Recidivism Among Inmates in Selected Nigerian Prisons' (2010), *European Scientific Journal.*

[17]Falobi, F., (2009). 'Empowering Prison Inmates', http://www.independentngonline.com/ (last visited 21 September 2009).

[18]Wilson, H., (2009). 'Curbing Recidivism in Our Society', http://www.pioneerng.com/article.php?title=Curbing_Recidivism_In_Our_Societyandid=2765 (last visited 20 December 2009).

[19]Soyombo, O., Sociology and Crime Control: That We May Live in Peace, (2009).

[20]Ugwuoke, C. U., Criminology: Explaining Crime in the Nigerian Context 23, (2010).

young person who is not released on bail, shall instead of committing him to prison, commit him to custody in place of detention[21] provided under this Ordinance and named in the commitment, to be there detained for the period for which he is remanded or until he is then delivered in due course of law". It also provides that in case of a young person, it shall not be obligatory on the court to commit him or her if the court certifies that he is of "unruly a character that he or she cannot be safely committed, or that he or she is of depraved character that he or she is not a fit person to be detained". The above provision appears to safeguard the child offender who should not be detained in prisons, except in exceptional circumstances. Unfortunately, inadequate remand centres, approved schools and Borstal institutions led to the detention and imprisonment of young offenders in the prisons.[22] This position was evident in the empirical survey carried out by the author where 663 (53%) out of 1258 respondents ranked Borstal institution as first in the hierarchy of custodial institutions on the basis that "Borstal institution is the only institution that provides for both educational and vocational trainings". Surprisingly, in another interval, 808 (64%) of the respondents said that: "currently Nigeria has three Borstal facilities which situate at Kaduna, Abeokuta and Ilorin". One of the respondents interviewed said:

> Only the Borstal institution in Ilorin seems to be effectively operational at the moment and even if the three Borstal institutions were to be in operation, they would still be grossly inadequate to accommodate the large number of children and young persons who are caught in conflict with the law. It is therefore a very severe situation to have only three Borstal institutions serving the entire country.

Another respondent interviewed expressed that:

> the shortage of Borstal facilities is responsible for the remand of juveniles in prison custody and the more pathetic situation is that; the Police officers

[21] The places of detention referred to in many sections of CYPA are remand homes, approved institutions including Borstal institutions and prisons. A native or local authority or a local government council with prior approval of competent authority "may establish remand homes and may make rules for the management, upkeep and inspection of such homes." See Sections 15 and 18 of CYPA.

[22] See Alemika, E. E. O., and Chukwuma, I. C., Juvenile Justice Administration in Nigeria: Philosophy and Practice, p. 49.

often falsify the ages of juveniles to pass them off in court as adults; in order to avoid adhering to the legal requirements for their treatment especially in States without Borstal institution.

In the realm of punishment or treatment of juveniles, the law takes cognisance of the risk involved in keeping juveniles in prison where adults are kept. Thus, by the spirit and letters of Section 15(3), a child can only be detained in an approved institution, i.e. remand home. However, the court may use its discretion (where there is no available remand home) to order that the juvenile be detained in a prison but he shall not be allowed to associate with adult prisoners.[23] Importantly, the Act has provided that institutions and schools for juveniles be established which shall be responsible for corrective punishment ordered on the juvenile.[24] It is important to note that corrective order is meant for the child offender who is below eighteen years.[25]

Note that Section 8 of the CYPA regulates the trial procedure of juvenile courts, including the right of juvenile offenders to proper proceedings. The provision satisfies the requirements of Article 40 of the CRC and Section 36 of the Constitution of the Federal Republic of Nigeria to a very large extent. In spite of these provisions, there are reported cases of non-compliance and violation against the police and judges in the observance of proper procedure as stipulated by law.[26]

A careful analysis of the provisions of CYPA relating to the detention of juvenile offenders in custody particularly Sections 15(3), 18 and 21 thereof lays too much emphasis on confinement of juvenile offenders in custody. This may be due partly to the fact that the Nigerian CYPA is an old colonial law predating many of the contemporary international standards that encourage non-custodial sentences.[27]

[23] In an earlier discussion under this section of the book, studies by the author, Abrifor et al., Uma, Falobi, Wilson, Soyombo and Ngwuoke, shown that in practice, "great majority of children in conflict with the law were held together with adults in the regular prisons" which negate the provision of Section 15(3) of CYPA.

[24] See Section 18 of CYPA.

[25] See Section 21 of CYPA.

[26] Human Rights Monitor, Administration of Juvenile Justice: The Example of the Borstal Training Institution, Kaduna, 1997.

[27] See Alemika, E. E. O., and Chukwuma, I. C., Juvenile Justice Administration in Nigeria: Philosophy and Practice, p. 49.

It is worthy to note that although the CYPA provides for diversion which is an alternative treatment of juvenile confinement in custody at the pre-trial stage and as a means of disposition after determination of guilt of juvenile offender, most importantly, it does not emphasise the community-based options which are considered very important in international standards (i.e. Rule 11 of the Beijing Rules 1985).

Also, the several diversionary measures contained in the CYPA have not been effectively utilised in the treatment of juvenile in Nigeria.[28] This is evidenced in the population of juveniles in remand homes, approved schools and Borstal institutions.[29] The alternative diversionary measures enshrined in CYPA include "dismissing the charge against the juvenile"; "discharging the offender on his entering into a recognisance"; "discharging the offender and placing him under the supervision of a probation officer"; "committing the offender by means of a corrective order to the care of a relative or other fit person"; "sending the offender by means of a corrective order to an approved institution"; "ordering the offender to be whipped"; "ordering the offender to pay a fine, damages, or costs"; "ordering the parents or guardian of the offender to pay a fine, damages, or costs"; "ordering the parent or guardian of the offender to give security for his good behaviour"; "committing the offender to custody in a place of detention under this ordinances"; where the offender is a young person, "ordering him to be imprisoned"; and dealing with the case in any other manner in which it may be legally dealt with.[30]

The dispositions provided for in the law differ in a variety of ways from the provisions in Rules 18 and 26 of the UN Standard Minimum Rules on Juvenile Justice Administration. Moreover, the provisions of Section 15 of the CYPA are more inclined towards the punishment of young offenders who are in conflict with the law. Consider, for instance, Section 44 of the CYPA which prohibits the death penalty for the child in accordance with the international law standards. Yet, the child

[28] Section 15 CYPA.

[29] See an Operational Research Report on Challenges of Borstal Institutions, Remand Homes, Reformatories and Approved Schools in Nigeria submitted to the Federal Department of Social Welfare, Federal Ministry of Women Affairs and Social Development, Abuja, Nigeria by Alamveabee E. Idyotough, June, 2013.

[30] See generally Section 15 CYPA and Section 14 CYPL of Lagos State.

offender may still be committed to custody at the pleasure of the Head of State. Section 12(2) of the Act allows corporal punishment as a form of retribution. Part V of the CYPA contains provisions that are prohibited under the international and regional legal instruments. For instance, these provisions among other things constitute the "criminalisation and punishment of destitution and deprivation and the conviction and institutionalisation of the disadvantaged children in need of care and protection" as against the international standards.

Section 27 of the Act which gives the court powers to make direction in respect of a child whose parent or guardian proved that he/she is beyond parental control, fall short of the international standard of treating juveniles. The provision may create hardship for juvenile rather than correcting him or her. It may be argued that correcting a juvenile within this category is better brought under social welfare within the jurisdiction of the juvenile court. This is because the section will portray the juvenile who is merely beyond parental control as a criminal or a person who has committed a crime.

The provision created a conflicting situations which render a person who had attained seventeen years of age or older and a person who has not attained the age of seventeen years to be tried by different court.

It is pertinent to note that while CYPA is relevant in juvenile justice administration, it is not without some weakness or shortcomings. One such shortcoming is the fact that it failed to articulate the principle of the best interest of the child. For instance, CYPA emphasises more on the punitive measure rather than the welfare of the child,[31] for example,

[31]This is evident few cases reported showing the attitudes of Nigerian courts in literally throwing juvenile offenders into prisons. For instance, in the case of *C.O.P v. Friday Idehen (Unreported) B/BCA/71*, High Court Benni, where the accused a juvenile offender was sentenced to six months imprisonment with hard labour or one hundred naira fine for assault occasioning harm in the course of a fight. On appeal, a sentence of six strokes of the cane was substituted and the High Court of Benni observed that "if the Magistrate had taken account of his youth he would have been persuaded that the accused is adolescent youth who needed correction rather than punishment..." Also in a similar vein, in the case of *Oyeneye v. C.O.P* (1983) 1 N.C.R. 245 where a young offender was sentenced to four years imprisonment for offence of theft and while reducing the sentence to two years imprisonment on appeal, the High Court observed that not giving these matters due consideration as required by the relevant authorities and a four-year jail sentence for a young offender are more likely to harden than reform; indeed, it will make reform and rehabilitation difficult.

Section 27 dealing with the issue of juvenile beyond parental control. The section directs the court to order that he/she be kept with a probation officer whereas under international instrument[32]; however, such a measure should be a last resort. The rationale behind this is that such a measure is capable of criminalising, stigmatising and having recidivistic consequences on the child.

4 The Child Rights Act 2003

The concern and need to focus, promote and protect children is now a global phenomenon. Part of this book provides an analysis of the relevant provisions of the Child Rights Act relating to child justice administration. In order to be able to give effect to a country's obligations deriving from many international and regional legal instruments governing the administration of child justice, States parties are required to pass specific child rights laws and regulations at the national level.[33] Prior to the Nigerian ratification of the Child Rights Convention in 1991, child right issues were guided by various legislations at both Federal and State/Regional levels. Notable among these were the Constitution of the Federal Republic of Nigeria (1999 as amended) and the Children and Young Persons Act (1958 as amended), which dealt mainly with Juvenile Justice Administration. For instance, similar to the provisions of Chapter 4 of the 1999 Constitution, Section 3 enshrined all the fundamental human rights, and in addition, Section 11 of the Act provides specifically for the "rights to dignity of the child, including sexual abuse, neglect or maltreatment, torture, inhuman or degrading treatment or punishment", among others. This is to combat child delinquency in Nigeria as these factors may lead to child delinquency.

The Act which contains 24 parts and about 278 sections came into existence ten years after a heated debate at the National Assembly in July

[32] See Section 5(f) of the Riyadh Guidelines, 1990.

[33] Article 4 of UN Convention 1989 provides to the effect that the Convention on the Rights of the child enjoins that "Member States shall undertake to disseminate the Conventions principles and take all appropriate legislative, administrative and other measures for the implementation of the rights recognized in the present Convention." See also Article 40(3) of the UNCRC.

2003.[34] The Act was enacted after Nigeria being signatory and ratified the Convention on the Rights of the Child. The Act[35] domesticates the provisions of the Convention and covers the broad themes, namely the "rights of the Nigerian Child to survival and development, protection and participation".

The most important starting point in the analysis of the Act is the area which deals with child justice system, particularly the provision which prohibits the use of imprisonment as means of punishing child below the age of eighteen years.[36] The Act goes further to make the following types of punishment forbidden for child offenders such as corporal punishment.[37]

In determining the individual criminality, the age of a criminal is very important and for the child offenders. The Act stipulates that a child below the age of eighteen years is not criminally liable. The superior court in Nigeria has decided in line with the above decision in the case of *Kachi v. State*[38] when the court postulated thus:

[34]Child Rights Act, Cap C 50 Laws of the Federation of Nigeria 2004. This is a Federal Act which seeks to incorporate the contemporary principles, philosophy and standards of juvenile justice administration into the Nigerian legal system. It is equally seen as an attempt to provide a comprehensive uniform law on the protection of child rights nationwide. However, as a Federal Act on a subject which is not within the exclusive legislative competence of the Federal Government, the Act (with the exception of the Federal Capital Territory, Abuja which has direct application) can only become binding on States if it is approved by a simple majority of all the States or if in the alternative, interested States pass their own version with or without reference to the Federal Statute. See Owasanoye B., Wenham M., Street Children and Juvenile Justice System in Lagos State of Nigeria, p. 11 cited in Okoro, H. C., 'Juvenile Justice Administration in Nigeria and International Standards on the Rights of the Child'.

[35]The Child Rights Act is a law to consolidate and amend the legal framework relating to juveniles in conflict with law and children in need of care and protection. It provides for proper care, protection and treatment by catering to a child's development needs. It attempts to adopt a child-friendly approach in the adjudication and disposition of matters in his/her best interest and secure his/her ultimate rehabilitation through various institutions established under this enactment.

[36]The laudable goals of the provision of the Act have not gained full implementation as shown in a report on human rights violations monitored in Nigeria by the Network of Human Rights Violations Monitors in collaboration with the National Human Rights Commission between 2005 and 2006 at pages 89–91 where children ranging from fifteen years to seventeen years of age were detained at Prisons.

[37]See Section 221(1)(b) CRA 2003.

[38](2015) 9 NWLR (pt. 1464) 213.

> Young offenders should be given opportunity for correction, reformation and rehabilitation to be restored into society as useful law abiding citizens. Thus, prosecutors and adjudicators should not claim ignorance of or deliberately sidetrack the provisions of the Child Rights Act, 2003 in the course of administration of criminal justice in respect of a child or juvenile.

Therefore, a child within this spectrum cannot be subjected to the adult criminal processes, but can only be subjected to the child justice administration process.[39] Even where a child is involved in a crime with an adult, the child cannot be tried with him.[40] Similarly, in making special provision for child justice it provides for the separation of children from adults in detention in all circumstances.[41] The significance of the Act is that it is directly related to the child justice system with the aim of protecting the under-aged.

Part XX is another significant paradigm of the Act that is germane to the system of child justice in Nigeria. Part XX together with Sections 204 to 259 extensively deals with the "policy framework", "institutional provisions" and the "procedures" for the administration of child justice in Nigeria.[42] It establishes the "guidelines, rules and prohibitions regarding the apprehension, treatment, judicial processes and detention" of child offenders. It also makes far-reaching provisions for "institutional reforms in the police, the judicial system and social policies" regarding the enforcement and protection of the rights of the child as provided for by the CRC includes the provisions for "diversionary programmes" that can be implored.

In compliance with international standards, Section 207 of the Act regulates the apprehension and investigation of alleged child offenders by specially trained police officers. In order to deal adequately with children, the Act[43] allows all "persons and authorities handling child

[39] See Section 204 CRA, 2003.

[40] See Section 205 CRA, 2003.

[41] See Section 222 CRA, 2003.

[42] Those provisions aim at enhancing capacity and use of programmes for diversion and appropriate sentence of children by stipulating that every role player exercising discretion under the child justice system must be specially qualified and trained particularly the police, probation/social workers, magistrates, judges, lawyers and any other person who makes a determination on child offenders.

[43] Section 208(1) provides: "In view of the varying special needs of children and the variety of measures available, a person who makes determination on the child offenders shall

cases the use of discretionary powers at all levels" of the child justice system. This is in view of the varying needs of children and varieties of measures available which extend to diverting children from the formal justice system to community-based programmes wherever possible. Section 208(2) of the Act allows the use of discretionary powers. It provides for accountability and the requirement for special training in the use of discretion for the people handling the affairs of child offenders. To safeguard the rights of the child offenders, the police, prosecutors or any other person dealing with a case involving a child offender is empowered "to dispose of cases without resorting to formal trial"[44] by using other means of settlement including "supervision, guidance, restitution and compensation of victims especially in non-serious offences".[45]

However, in cases of a serious nature and where it demands that a child offender be tried in court, the provisions of Sections 210–222 of the Child Rights Act must be strictly adhered to. That is, in compliance, these provisions range from the constitutional rights to fair hearing and proceedings conducted with the best interests of the child offender; avoiding detention of the child unless there is no alternative measure; and where found delinquent, he or she shall not be imprisoned or subjected to corporal punishment or the death penalty.

By Section 223 of the Act, the court is enjoined to exercise discretion on how to deal with the case after determination of the guilt of the child including the omnibus clause[46] to deal with the matter in any other

exercise such discretion, as he deems most appropriate in each case, at all stages of the proceedings and at the different levels of child justice administration, including investigation, prosecution, adjudication and the follow-up of dispositions."

[44] See Section 209 CRA, 2003.

[45] See Owasanoye, B., and Wenham, M., Street Children and Juvenile Justice System in Lagos State of Nigeria, Human Development Initiative. 2004. p. 31. Here, the police have the first opportunity to divert child offenders from the formal Court system followed by the prosecutors and then the magistrates and judges who are empowered to operate a model of justice that is restorative then rehabilitative and in the least retributive.

[46] The judges are empowered under Section 223 above to dispose of cases where they are satisfied that an offence has been committed, with alternatives to custodial or institutional placement. The section also provides for situations where there is sufficient evidence to prosecute, and where decisions have been taken to proceed to trial that diversion must be considered in each and every case in order to meet the needs of the child and encourage the child to be accountable to the harm caused. Also, Section 213 of the Child Rights Act does not permit the use of the terms "conviction" or "sentence" to be used in relation to a child dealt with in the Court.

manner legally permitted. The objective principle is to make the imposition of confinement a last resort and to be ordered only where there is no other way of dealing with the child.[47]

The Act makes provisions for the establishment of "Family Courts".[48] A family court at the High Court and another at the magisterial levels. These courts have been vested with the "jurisdiction to hear all cases in which the existence of a legal right, power, duty, liability, privilege, interest, obligation or claim in respect of a child is in issue, and any criminal proceeding",[49] relating thereto.

The Act has provided for "Child Justice Administration",[50] to replace the old "Juvenile Justice Administration" in Nigeria. In addition, the above provisions

> prohibit the subjection of any child to the criminal justice process, and guarantees that due process be given to any child subjected to the child justice system, at all the stages of investigation, adjudication and disposition of any case against such a child.

The Act further "prohibits the use of capital punishment", "use of imprisonment"[51] and "use of corporal punishment for children less than eighteen years". In the same vein, it provides for the "use of scientific tests

[47] See Section 223(2) CYPA.

[48] See Section 149 of Child Rights Act, 2003.

[49] See Part XX of the Child Rights Act.

[50] Ibid.

[51] The act of imprisonment before the advent of the Child Rights Act can be seen from the few cases reported showing the attitudes of Nigerian courts in literally throwing juvenile offenders into prisons. For instance, in the case of *C.O.P v. Friday Idehen (Unreported) B/BCA/71*, High Court Benin, where the accused a juvenile offender was sentenced to six months imprisonment with hard labour or one hundred naira fine for assault occasioning harm in the course of a fight. On appeal, a sentence of six strokes of the cane was substituted and the High Court of Benin observed that "if the Magistrate had taken account of his youth he would have been persuaded that the accused is adolescent youth who needed correction rather than punishment…" Also in a similar vein, in the case of *Oyeneye v. C.O.P* (1983) 1 N.C.R. 245 where a young offender was sentenced to four years imprisonment for offence of theft and while reducing the sentence to two years imprisonment on appeal, the High Court observed that not giving these matters due consideration as required by the relevant authorities and a four-year jail sentence for a young offender are more likely to harden than reform; indeed, it will make reform and rehabilitation difficult.

in deciding paternity cases".[52] "Children Residential" and "Correctional Centres"[53] are to be established to replace the "Approved Schools" established under the CYPA and where the court decides against institutionalisation of the child offender, the court is enjoyed to utilise such disposition measures as "dismissing the charge, placing the child under care, guidance and supervision". Interestingly, the provisions are novel as they do not exist in the old CYPA. Unfortunately, the author observed from the field survey and interviews[54] conducted that in practice, the provisions for the new institutions in the Act were not implemented. For instance, the replacements of the "approved schools" or "remand homes" or "Borstal institutions" as indicated in the Child Rights Act are still in use till date. The provisions get more complicated especially as they conflict with the Laws of the Federation of Nigeria (LFN), 2011. The old names were still retained in the LFN as "the Borstal Institutions and Remand Centre Act".[55] It is, therefore, the argument in this book that retaining the old names in the LFN results in non-uniformity in the treatment of a child alleged to have committed an offence or a child in need of care and protection committed to those custodial institutions.

In the same vein, some differences were observed in the treatment and other procedure relating to case in some States of the federation.[56] This hampers the uniformity on the national level. The Child Rights Act prescribes for the creation of different institutions for the custody, adjudication, trial and treatment of child offenders. The non-setting up of such institutions in some States is a major setback to the

[52] See generally Part VII of the Child Rights Act, 2003.

[53] See Part XXII of the Child Rights Act, 2003. The wide objective of those provisions is to provide treatment with a view to enable the child play a constructive and productive role in the society.

[54] Analysis of the Author's field survey and interviews conducted at Lagos, Kaduna, Port Harcourt, Enugu, Bauchi and Ilorin in 2014.

[55] Borstal Institutions and Remand Centre Act 32 1960, now Cap B38 Laws of the Federation of Nigeria 2011.

[56] Child Rights Act has been promulgated into Law in only twenty-three States which are Abia, Anambra, Bayelsa, Eboniyi, Ekiti, Imo, Jigawa, Kwara, Lagos, Nassarawa, Ogun, Ondo, Plateau, Rivers, Taraba, Kogi, Oyo, Benue, Osun, Edo, Delta, Cross River, Akwa Ibom Available at www.unicef.org/wcaro/WCARO_Nigeria_Factsheets_CRA.pdf (accessed on 18 January 2013). It leaves thirteen States without Child Rights Law and these States one way or the other are still using the Children and Young Persons Laws of their respective States.

successful implementation of the Child Rights Act. To give credence to this position were the findings of the author in a recent survey where 938 (75%) out of 1258 respondents strongly agreed that "refusal to enact Child Rights Law by some States adversely affect the administration of child justice". Out of the respondents, one of them commented that "in fact, the inability to implement the child Rights Law in some States in the Federation affects child justice administration". In another interval, majority of the respondents 960 (68.3%) views on whether the enactment and implementation of Child Rights Law by some States will improve the administration of child justice were in the affirmative. Some respondents from the fieldwork conducted by the author representing 765 (61%) of the total population of 1258 respondents lamented that "the enactment of Child Rights Act is inadequate for juvenile justice administration in Nigeria".[57] Another set of respondents in an administered questionnaire by the author[58] supported the views of the above respondents when 655 (51%) of them strongly disagreed that "Child Rights Act adequately provide for effective child justice administration in Nigeria". In an interview by the author at Enugu State, Nigeria; a respondent said: "I can say that the Child Rights Act is not sufficient to address the inherent problems in the juvenile justice administration".[59] Majority of the respondents representing 928 (74%) out of 1258 respondents in an administered questionnaire further confirmed the above views when they hold that "laws and policies on the rights of the child are inadequate to address juvenile offences".[60]

Another shortcoming militating against the effectiveness of this Act in dealing with child offenders is related to the unconcerned and apathetic attitudes of the officials associated with this Act. This results from the lack of adequate training of the officials handling the affairs of children.[61] Secondly, there are considerable failures in implementing the laws

[57] Author's field survey at Lagos, Kaduna, Port Harcourt, Enugu, Bauchi and Ilorin in 2014.

[58] Ibid.

[59] Interview conducted by the author at Enugu State, Nigeria dated 13 March 2014.

[60] Author's field survey at Lagos, Kaduna, Port Harcourt, Enugu, Bauchi and Ilorin in 2014.

[61] Ibid.

regulating child offenders stemming from the poor coordination among various institutions involved in the process. In addition, inadequate fund to cater for the institutions involved is also cited as a factor discouraging the progress of implementation of this law. The author's argument above gains support from the views of majority of the respondents representing 845 (67.1%) that "there are insufficient budgetary allocations for the juvenile justice administration in Nigeria".[62] In another interval, almost all the respondents totalling 1158 (92%) out of 1258 respondents strongly agreed that "inadequate funding of the juvenile justice institutions hinders the effective performance and have negative impact on juvenile justice administration in Nigeria".[63] The career growth of the staff involved in the implementation of this Act has also to do with the fate of this Act.[64]

It is evident from the author's field survey[65] where 897 (71.3%) of total population of 1258 respondents strongly agreed with the author that "laws and policies on the rights of the child are inadequate to address the role of police in juvenile justice administration in Nigeria". In another interval, 820 (66%) of respondents also expressed their views in support of the above position that "the role and functions of Nigeria prison service as relate to custody of juveniles are not well spelt out in the laws and policies in juvenile justice administration"[66] and this was further confirmed by 1041 (83%) of the respondents that "the responsibilities of rehabilitation/correctional homes are not fully provided in the laws and policies on the rights of the child".[67] It is the views of 1003 (79.7%) of the respondents that "observance of the rights of the child by the stakeholders in the administration of child justice in Nigeria is likely to reduce incidence of child delinquency".[68]

This book has identified bottlenecks in the child justice system from the operation of the Child Rights Act as including the following:

[62] Ibid.

[63] Ibid.

[64] Ibid.

[65] Ibid.

[66] Ibid.

[67] Ibid.

[68] Ibid.

(i) The Act fails to express the minimum age, below which the Act would not be applicable. The definition of child delinquency provides very little scope for petty acts to be dealt within the community.
(ii) There is no concept of parental responsibility in generating situations ripe for delinquency under this Act. In many cases, the parents place the children in situations where their exploitation and abuse become imminent.
(iii) The education, training and recreation of children, who are in observation homes, have not been provided for. Besides, basic or school education, even higher education and training of these children should be considered in this Act.
(iv) Child justice thrives under the shadow of the adult criminal justice agencies and institutions (like the police). Moreover, the child justice adjudicatory cadres are drawn from the pool of the magistrates who handle adult cases.
(v) The Act does not cast any obligation on the part of the state. A rights-based perspective is a missing dimension in this Act. In its present shape, child protection becomes more of charity than a commitment. Protection of such children is not seen as a right but as charity or welfare.

It is the opinion of the author that addressing the requirement of children needs a regular coordination among parallel government agencies working in similar areas, the absence of which may affect the core objectives for child justice policy. This is borne out of the fact that the Child Rights Act does not have any procedures, which could ensure the continuous supervision, monitoring and evaluation of the functioning of the child justice system as a whole. It is a fact that the resources and infrastructure required for the effective implementation of this law is hardly proportionate to the population and geographical regions covered under it. Thus, because of this inadequacy, children caught in the system are often rendered helpless with very little redress provision. For example, children affected by the problems like HIV/AIDS, drug abuse, militancy and other disasters which may result to them being delinquents do not have any redress under this law.

Furthermore, some states in the federation lacked institutional infrastructure and trained manpower. Non-implementation of the Act with respect to the establishment of "Child Welfare Committees and Child Justice Boards" resulted in the delay of disposal of cases.

Similarly, the provisions of the Child Rights Act have also placed relatively greater emphasis on institutional set-up, and unfortunately, non-uniformity in the services in these institutions and insufficient effort by the government to standardise them have hindered the effectiveness of these institutions. More importantly, the practice has derogated from the international standards which encourage diversionary measures as against institutionalisation. Dearth of services and programmes for the children of special needs lack of index of performance measurement of the institutions in the area of child justice also hinder the quality performance of these institutions. Another disappointing feature has also been observed about the indifference of the police towards the application of the provisions of the Act. Instances of bringing the ages of children into the adult range while writing the False Information Report (FIR) by the police are often heard. Handcuffing and keeping the child offenders in police lock-up are also not unusual.[69]

Overall, it has been argued that the basic idea of the Child Rights Act has not been internalised by the police due to "insufficient training and orientation". The basic idea of child justice was to reintegrate the child into family and society. This book, therefore, calls for proper network of rehabilitation and aftercare services as this arrangement is almost non-existent. The situation gets more difficult because the current child justice policy does not have a preventive approach and the delinquency-prone situations are increasing daily without having substantial mechanism to check the situations.

5 The Criminal Code Act and Criminal Procedure Act

In discussing child justice administration, the relevance of the Criminal Code Act and the Criminal Procedure Act cannot be overemphasised. Thus, in line with the international standard, for instance, the United Nations Convention on the Rights of the Child (UNCRC) and the African Charter on the Rights and Welfare of the Child (ACRWC),[70] the Criminal Code Act and Criminal Procedure Act set down the minimum age below which children shall be presumed not to have capacity to infringe the penal law.

[69] See Ahire, P. T., 'Native Authority Police in Northern Nigeria: End of an era?'

[70] Going by the provisions of Article 40 of UNCRC and Article 17 of the ACRWC, a child in conflict with the law has the right to treatment which promotes the child's sense of dignity and worth, takes the child's age into account and aims at his or her defence. Judicial proceedings and institutional placements shall be avoided wherever possible.

By virtue of the said laws, a person under the age of seven years shall not be criminally responsible for any act or omission and a person under the age of twelve years[71] shall also not be criminally responsible for an act or omission unless it is proved that at the time of doing the act or making the omission he had capacity to know that he ought not to do the act or make the omission.[72]

Here, the court is saddled with the responsibility of determining whether the child has capacity to commit the crime or not, and one of the tests a court can employ is finding out whether a child can distinguish between right and wrong. The test is subjective and this was confirmed in the common law case of *R vs. Corrie*[73] where the jury was directed that they must be satisfied that "when the boy did this he knew what he was doing was wrong-not merely what was wrong, but what was gravely wrong, seriously wrong". By the same provision, "a male person under the age of twelve years is presumed to be incapable of having carnal knowledge".[74]

Significant to determination of the age of a child are Sections 208 and 209 of the Criminal Procedure Act that empower a court to look into the age of any person. Therefore, where there is a dispute as to the age of a person alleged for an offence before a court, the court must make inquiry as to the age of that person or by adducing evidence. In convicting a young person, the court shall always consider the age of the person as of the time of commission of the offence.

A court inquiring into the charge against a child should sit either in a different court building or court room as against the ordinary court room where adult cases usually take place.[75] In furtherance with the attendant of child offender in court, Sections 417–440 of the Criminal

[71] Aguda, T. A., and Okagbue, I., *Principles of Criminal Liability in Nigerian Law* (Ibadan: Heinemann Educational Books, 1990), 323–329; See also Osinbajo and Kalu, Law Development and Administration in Nigeria, pp. 168–169.

[72] See Section 30 of the Criminal Code Act cap C38 Laws of the Federation of Nigeria, 2004.

[73] (1919)83 J.P. 136. See also the following cases of *T vs. D.P.P.* (1989) Crim. L.R. 498, *McC vs. Runecles* (1984) Crim. L.R. 499, *C vs. DPP* (1994) Crim. L.R. 801 and *W (An Infant) and Another vs. Simpson* (1967) Crim. L.R. 360.

[74] *State vs. Nwabueze* (1980)1 NCR 41.

[75] See Section 415 of CPA.

Procedure Act prohibit the court from allowing the child to associate with an adult charged with any offence. In addition to this, only the members of the child charged with an offence, officers of the court, parties to the case, legal practitioners and other persons directly concerned in the case will have the rights to attend proceedings unless the leave of the court is sought and obtained. These procedures are meant to protect the child offender from public stigmatisation.

The relevance of age in dealing with the child can also be gleaned from the position of the Criminal Procedure Act which prohibits the use of the words "conviction and sentence"[76] when punishing a child or young person. Similarly, the court is enjoined to order where ever practicable an alternative means of punishment like probation, fine, corporal punishment rather than imprisonment of a child or young offender; whenever impracticably, the child should be detained in legal or suitable custody and not be associated with adult detainees or prisoners; and where the offence is capital in nature and the offender has not attained the age of seventeen years, the court is enjoyed to invoke Section 368(3) of the Act.[77] The foregoing provisions also spell out various methods of dealing with the child found guilty of an offence by the court ranging from dismissal to supervision, institutionalisation, imprisonment,[78] and ordering of fine or damages by the child, parent or guardian.

More so, Chapter 9 of the Criminal Procedure Act provides for the treatment of juvenile offenders and imposition of probation by empowering the court to adopt the provisions of the Children and Young Persons Act when dealing with a child or young person.[79]

[76] See Section 414 of CPA.

[77] This provision provides thus: "Where an offender who in the opinion of the court had not attained the age of seventeen years at the time the offence was committed is found guilty of a capital offence sentence of death shall not be pronounced or recorded but in lieu thereof the court shall order such person to be detained during the pleasure of the President and if so ordered he shall be detained in accordance with the provisions of Part 44 of this Act notwithstanding anything to the contrary in any written law".

[78] It has to be noted that by the effects of the provisions of Section 432 of the Criminal Procedure Act, a child below the age of nine or above nine but below fourteen years of age shall not be sentenced to imprisonment or committed to prison in default of a fine or damages unless if the court is satisfied that the child is unruly of a character that cannot be detained in government institutions.

[79] See Section 413 of CPA.

6 The Penal Code and Criminal Procedure Code

Nigeria operates a dual legal system; this accounts for the existing two codes (Criminal and Penal Codes) regulating crime in Nigeria. Like the Criminal Code, some sections of the Penal Code deal with issues of child justice system in Nigeria. A relevant starting point is the section that provides for penal responsibility thus:

> No act is an offence which is done by a child under seven years of age; or by a child above seven years of age but less than twelve years of age who has not attained sufficient maturity of understanding to judge the nature and consequence of such act.[80]

The above section offers protection to children because it is presumed that children have limited control over their actions due to their minority. Thus, even when a child has committed an offence, for instance, with an adult or a murder,[81] such a child can be detained till the pleasure of the President. This provisions of the law though, it is argued, an exception to Section 50 Penal Code; it may create room for child abuse because presidential pleasure is discretionary in nature. It thus allows for unlimited detention of the child.

In the spectrum of corrective measures of punishment, this study contends that the section of the Penal Code[82] which provides for physical corrective measure is discriminative of children or child offenders and contrary to international standard as contained in the UNCRC.[83] An example of physical corrective measure against child offender is whipping and imposition of corporal punishment.[84]

In the context of international law, physical corrective measure ought to be the last resort when other available means of correcting the child

[80] Section 50 of the Penal Code.

[81] Section 319(2) CPC.

[82] Section 55 Penal Code Act.

[83] See Article 19 of the UNCRC which provides thus: "The State shall protect the child from all forms of maltreatment by parents or others responsible for the care of the child and establish appropriate social programmes for the prevention of abuse and the treatment of victims".

[84] See generally Section 223, Nigerian CRA on methods of dealing with child offender particularly Subsection (2). See also Section 18 CC, see also Sections 302(1) & (2) and 427 CPA, Section 295 CC.

offender had been employed but failed. This is what the Child Rights Act of Nigeria had proposed which, if properly implemented, would have met the stipulations of the international standards of treatment of juvenile offenders. For example, the Nigerian CRA which is *mutatis mutandis* with UNCRC provides that a child shall not be placed in any government institution like prison or Borstal unless it is being employed as measure of last resort and it should not even be ordered unless there is no other way of dealing with the child.

It is pertinent to note that some provisions of the Nigerian laws dealing with crime, criminal justice and child justice give more priority and emphasis to punishment (imprisonment, execution, fine or corporal punishment) for offenders either adult or child. These measures are not in compliance with international standards particularly in respect of child, where much emphasis on punishment is to achieve rehabilitation, social readjustment or even deterrent as against retributive objective that can only be achieved through punishment like imprisonment or fine etc. This argument is supported by the provision of the Nigerian Child Rights Act which is more in line with international standard where it states: "No child be ordered to be imprisoned or subjected to corporal punishment or subjected to death penalty or have the death penalty recorded against him".[85]

7 The Shari'ah Penal Code and Criminal Procedure Code

The Nigerian legal system as noted earlier in this chapter is dual in nature as evidenced in the recognition of Islamic law in Nigeria. This makes the examination of the Islamic perception of child justice system relevant to this study. It must be noted that Islamic law or Shari'ah legal system has been a part of the main sources of the Nigerian legal system until 1999 when its application was extended to criminal matters and the Shari'ah courts were vested with criminal jurisdiction in some northern states of Nigeria.[86]

[85] See Section 221(1) Nigerian CRA, 2003.

[86] One of the States that adopted Shari'ah Law is Zamfara State. Shari'ah Courts Law of 1999 (Zamfara 1-1999) and Zamfara Penal Code were adopted in January 2000.

In general terms, Shari'ah does not provide any special treatment for juvenile offenders in term of punishments. Thus, *Hudud*[87] offences such as sexual offences (adultery and Fornication) have their punishments fixed under the Shari'ah without any distinction or special treatment for the adult or child offender.[88]

The unique feature of the Zamfara Shari'ah Penal Code that safeguards the rights of children is the stipulation in the code[89] that "No sentence of *hudud* or *qisas*[90] shall be imposed on a person who is under the age of *taklif*[91] and that when court is of the view that a person was under the age of *taklif* when he committed an offence, the court shall deal with him/her in accordance with Section 11 of the Children and Young Persons Law (CYPL) and Section 95 of the Shari'ah Penal Code".[92]

This unique feature of child justice is underscored from Section 95 of the Shari'ah Penal Code of both Zamfara and Yobe States, to the extent that when an accused person who has completed his/her 7th year but not completed his/her 18th year of age is convicted by a court of any offence, the court may instead of passing the sentence prescribed under this code subject the accused to confinement in a reformatory home for a period not exceeding one year; or twenty strokes of the cane, or with fine or with both.

An important weakness of the Shari'ah Penal Codes of Zamfara laws adopted in 2000 and of Yobe relating to administration of criminal justice is that there is no adequate provision for the protection of children navigating the court system. A good example is that the law does not create any special court for children.[93] This is because Section 5(b) of Zamfara Shari'ah Courts Criminal Procedure Law provides that "the Courts shall have jurisdiction in criminal proceedings under Islamic law

[87] *Hudud* means offences or punishments that is fixed under the Shari'ah and includes offences or punishments which include sexual offences like *Zina* (Fornication). See Sections 126 to 141 of the Shari'ah Penal Code.

[88] See Quran 4.

[89] Section 71 of the Zamfara Penal Code. See also, Zamfara State Shari'ah Criminal Procedure Code law of 2000, No. 1, Vol. 4.

[90] *Qisa* means punishments inflicted upon the offenders by way of retaliation for causing death of or injuries to person.

[91] *Taklif* means the age of puberty.

[92] See similar provision in Section 238(1) of the Zamfara State Shari'ah Criminal Procedure Code Law 2000, No. 1, Vol. 4.

[93] See Section 5(b) Shari'ah Penal Code.

involving or relating to any offence, penalty or forfeiture, punishment or other liability in respect of an offence committed by any person". But some of the provisions relating to children will be reiterated below as an exception to these general provisions.[94]

Instructively, children under the Islamic law are not strictly liable for certain offences but are punished under *Ta'zir*.[95] For example, the gravity of offence, the demeanour, age and conduct of child are considered before sentence is passed. Where the offence is a simple one, the child may be given some strokes of the cane or he/she is sent to attend a counselling session from a religious priest especially where the child looks remorseful.[96]

[94]The implication of this provision is that, age of criminal responsibility as being defined by the law to be either puberty or 18 years means once a child has reached puberty and commits any offence under the Law, he will be prosecuted and punished like adults and by implication, where children reach puberty earlier than 18 years, no distinction is made between juvenile and adults in dispensing Shari'ah punishment under this general provision. See Integrated Regional Information Networks (IRIN), Nigeria: Focus on the Administration of Juvenile Justice, 26 August 2002. Available at http://www.irinnews.org/report.asp?ReportID=29531 (accessed on 7 February 2010). Similarly, by Section 7(1) of the Shari'ah Law, the applicable laws and rules of procedures for hearing and determination of all civil and criminal proceedings before Shari'ah Courts shall be as prescribed under Islamic Law. The implication of this provision is that juvenile offenders are not protected under the general provisions. The notion of this law is that the juvenile offender will be tried before Shari'ah Courts instead of juvenile Courts and in essence he or she will be punished or sanctioned by flogging or amputation as an adult who has committed the offence that warrants flogging or amputation. This, of course, violates Article 37 of the United Nations Convention on the Rights of the Child which stipulates that "No child shall be subjected to torture, cruel treatment or punishment, unlawful arrest, or deprivation of liberty. Both capital punishment and life imprisonment without the possibility for release are prohibited for offences committed by persons below 18 years. Any child deprived of liberty shall be separated from adults unless it is considered in the child's best interest not to do so. A child who is detained shall have legal and other assistance as well as contact with the family". At the same time, the Shari'ah Court Law allows discrimination against girls in determining age of criminal responsibility because girls often achieve puberty earlier than boys as the menstruation is often considered as the achievement of 'maturity' or 'puberty' even though the onset of menstruation is not the same for all. See Okoli, B., Nigeria: The Constitution and Child Rights, October 19, 2007, available at http://allafrica.com/stories200710190453.html (accessed on 15 December 2009).

[95] *Ta'zir* relates to stipulation of punishment according to the discretion of the Shari'ah Court judges, Grand Kadis or Magistrates.

[96]See the UNICEF report on the Profile of Existing Diversion Programmes in Nigeria. Available at http://www.unicef.org/nigeria/ng_publications_diversionpdf-similar (accessed on 28 May 2011), p. 30.

8 Administration of Criminal Justice Act 2015 (ACJA)

The Criminal Procedure Act and Criminal Procedure Code have been repealed by the Administration of Criminal Justice Act (ACJA) which came into force in 2015 in respect of matter pertaining to courts in the Federal Capital Territory and other Federal High Courts in Nigeria and for related matters.[97]

ACJA was enacted to govern criminal proceedings pertaining to Federal courts[98]; in other words, as a result of the enactment of the ACJA in 2015, Nigeria now has a unique and integrated law applicable in all Federal courts and with respect to offences contained in Federal Legislations. By the provisions of the ACJA 2015, innovative provisions aimed at ensuring efficiency in the Nigerian criminal justice were included such as the compulsory notification of the relatives of the arrestee,[99] proper treatment of suspects including the rights of arrestees,[100] police central criminal record registry at both the Federal and State levels,[101] institution of criminal proceedings at the magistrate court within the prescribed time limit,[102] criminal justice monitoring committee,[103] among others. Meanwhile, by the provision of Section 86 of the ACJA 2015, the provisions of Parts 8 to 30 of the Act shall apply to all criminal trials and proceedings unless express provisions are made in respect to any particular court or form of trial or proceedings. Also, the provisions of the Act are not applicable to a court martial.

The scope of the ACJA is wider than the Criminal Procedure Act and the Criminal Procedure Code; the reason been that the scope of the ACJA goes beyond criminal procedure, it includes the entire criminal justice process from arrest, investigation, trial, custodial matters and sentencing guidelines.[104] Hence, the ACJA by merging and preserving the major provisions of the two principal criminal justice legislations in

[97] See the preamble to the ACJA 2015.

[98] Section 2 Administration of Criminal Justice Act 2015.

[99] Section 6 Administration of Criminal Justice Act 2015.

[100] Section 8, ibid.

[101] Section 15, ibid.

[102] Section 110, ibid.

[103] Section 269, ibid.

[104] Available at https://lawpavilion.com/blog/the-administration-of-criminal-justice-act-2015-acja/ (Accessed on 25 April 2018).

Nigeria, that is Criminal Procedure Act and Criminal Procedure Code, and introducing new provisions has provided a unified and advanced legislation for the administration of criminal justice in Nigeria.

More importantly, the recent enactment of the Administration of Criminal Justice Act, 2015, has emphatically allowed CRA to be applied in all procedures for trying child offenders in Nigeria when it provides under Section 452(1) thus: "Where a child is alleged to have committed an offence, the provisions of the Child Rights Act shall apply".

The purpose of ACJA is contained in Section 1 of the Act which provides as follows;

> to ensure that the system of administration of criminal justice in Nigeria promotes efficient management of criminal justice institutions, speedy dispensation of justice, protection of the society from crime and protection of the rights and interests of the suspect, the defendant and the victim.

ACJA introduces innovative provisions in furtherance of its purpose. Some of these innovations include the introduction of plea bargain,[105] suspended sentence and community service,[106] remand time limit,[107] electronic recording of confessional statements[108] and day-to-day trial.[109]

The provisions of ACJA indicate a paradigm shift from retributive criminal justice system to restorative criminal justice system particularly because it pays serious attention to the needs of the society, the victims, vulnerable persons and human dignity generally.[110] However, in spite of the innovations and objectives of ACJA, there has been little to no improvement in the administration of criminal justice system in Nigeria since its enactment.[111]

[105] Section 270 Administration of Criminal Justice Act, 2015.

[106] Section 460, ibid.

[107] Section 296, ibid.

[108] Section 15, Subsection 4, ibid.

[109] Section 396, ibid.

[110] See the provisions of Sections 8(1), Section 460(1), Section 460(2), Section 468, Section 314, Administration of Criminal Justice Act, 2015, among others.

[111] See Akeem Nafiu and Tunde Oyesina, "ACJA 2015: So Far, Not Too Good", available at https://newtelegraphonline.com/2017/12/acja-2015-far-not-good/ (accessed on 25 April 2018).

Regrettably, most of these efforts have failed to yield the needed results either because they were poorly conceived or implemented or as a result of the fact that they largely ignore the need for innovative reforms. This is evident from the challenges that hinder the effectiveness of ACJA which is the non-domestication of ACJA in some of the States in the Federation. It was observed in this book that currently in Nigeria, only 14 out of the 36 States have domesticated the ACJA. Therefore, the 22 other States have not domesticated ACJA.

9 Institutional Framework for Child Justice Administration in Nigeria

This section of the chapter examines the custodial institutions for child justice administration in Nigeria.

9.1 The Police Force

The Nigeria Police Force is an important institution worth considering for child justice administration in Nigeria especially at the entry point. The Nigeria Police was established in 1930 by merging the Northern Nigeria Police Force and the Southern Nigeria Police Force.[112] The institution has survived to the present day Nigeria, and all Nigerian Constitutions from 1963, 1979, and 1999 (as amended)[113] recognise the establishment of the police for the maintenance of peace and order in the country.

The general philosophy behind the establishment and existence of the Police is to prevent crime, apprehend criminals and prosecute the offender irrespective of whether the offender is an adult or juvenile.[114] However, in the realm of child justice the law provides for the establishment of a special unit within the police for children offenders.[115] The reason behind the creation of such special children's unit in the police

[112] See Ahire, P. T., 'Native Authority Police in Northern Nigeria: End of an Era?' in T. N. Tamuno, I. L. Bashir, E. E. O. Alemika, and A. O. Akano (eds.), *Policing Nigeria: Past, Present and Future* (Lagos: Malthouse Press Ltd., 1993).

[113] Sections 105–110 of 1963, Section 194–196 of the 1979 Constitution and Sections 214–216 1999 Constitution of Nigeria.

[114] Section 4 Police Act.

[115] See generally Section 207–212 of the CRA 2003.

is to ensure that the child's first contact is well managed in such a way as to respect his/her legal status, promote the well-being of the child and avoid harm to him or her with due regard to the circumstances of the case.[116] For instance, the police are enjoined under the children's law to consider the detention of the child offender as a last resort, meaning that Police detention should only be employed in the absence of other approved children's centres established for child offenders.[117]

The significance of the law regulating child justice demands that the police are required to provide care, protection and individual assistance to child offenders including social, educational, vocational, physical, medical and psychological assistance having regard to his/her age, sex and personality. This is because any action taken by the police officer and any other police officers involved in the handling of a juvenile case has the potential to change the child's life in a positive direction. This will only be possible when there are special units within the Police, and there are officials especially skilled in handling juveniles as contemplated by the CRA.[118]

However, despite the enactment of the CRA, the creation of special unit within the Police has not been complied with nor has there been any sufficient training and retention in paradigm of children justice throughout Nigeria. More so the Police Force is in fact indifferent towards the laws on child justice system. This is evident from the views of the majority of the respondents in an administered questionnaire by the author where 1170 (93%) respondents lamented that "Police officers often falsify the ages of juvenile offenders to pass them off in courts as adults in order to avoid adhering to the legal requirements for their treatment".[119]

The argument of the author is further affirmed in an administered questionnaire where 849 (71%) of the respondents hold the views that "there were no special cells for children in police stations in Nigeria, as such, child offenders are held together with women in the juvenile and women centre (JWC) of the police force in Nigeria".[120] To complement

[116] See also Section 211 of the Child Rights Act.

[117] See Section 209 CRA 2003.

[118] See Ahire, P. T. 'Native Authority Police in Northern Nigeria: End of an Era?', in T. N. Tamuno, I. L. Bashir, E. E. O. Alemika, and A. O. Akano (eds.), *Policing Nigeria: Past, Present and Future.*

[119] Author's field survey at Lagos, Kaduna, Port Harcourt, Enugu, Bauchi and Ilorin in 2014.

[120] Ibid.

the above finding is an interview conducted by the author in Bauchi State Police Headquarter, Nigeria where one of the respondents has this to say: "we do not have separate police cells for child offenders; we do put them behind the counter or in an empty adult cell".[121] There seems to be no variation in the views expressed by the respondents above with the comments of some respondents in an interview when they said that: "the police force in Nigeria neither possesses the specialised skills and facilities for the treatment of child offenders nor do they possesses the necessary skills for diverting child offenders from the criminal justice system".[122] This corresponds with the responses of the majority of the respondents representing 897 (71.3%) out of the total population of 1258 respondents that the "laws and policies on the rights of the child in Nigeria are inadequate to address the role of police in the administration of child justice".[123] This is further confirmed by one of the respondents interviewed that "the effectiveness of Police force in the administration of child justice in Nigeria is poor".[124] These findings confirm with the studies of Alemika and Chukwuma,[125] Tamuno, Bashir, Alemika, and Akano[126] that, "the existing laws and policies dealing with the personnel, funding and structures of Police institution in Nigeria are inadequate". This assertion is in tandem with another finding in an administered questionnaire where majority of the respondents representing 88% (1103), 84% (1051) at different intervals strongly disagree and disagree that "there is enough commitment by government on Police institution to anchor the administration of child justice in Nigeria".[127] This is so because the Police force is not adequately funded.

[121] Interview conducted by the author in Bauchi State Police Headquarters dated 12 February 2014.

[122] Ibid.

[123] Author's field survey at Lagos, Kaduna, Port Harcourt, Enugu, Bauchi, and Ilorin in 2014.

[124] Interview conducted by the author in Kaduna State dated 14 February 2014.

[125] Alemika, E. E. O., and Chukwuma, I. C., *Juvenile Justice Administration in Nigeria: Philosophy and Practice* (Lagos: Centre for Law Enforcement Education, 2001).

[126] Tamuno, T. N., Bashir, I. L., Alemika, E. E. O., and Akano, A. O. (eds.), *Policing Nigeria: Past, Present and Future* (Lagos: Malthouse Press Ltd., 1993).

[127] Author's field survey at Lagos, Kaduna, Port Harcourt, Enugu, Bauchi and Ilorin in 2014.

9.2 The Juvenile/Family Court

This part of the chapter examines the juvenile/family court as one of the institutions of child justice administration in Nigeria. As rightly observed in Chapter three, the first children's court identified was the one established by the United States of America in 1899 in Chicago and the second juvenile/family court was established in Colorado in 1903 and as from 1908, juvenile courts were established in England, Canada and Hungary.[128] As noted earlier in Chapter 3 of this book, Nigerian juvenile court was modelled after the British style of juvenile court with the enactment of the Children and Young Persons Act. The law was enacted for the establishment of juvenile courts.

The reason behind the establishment of special courts for children is to achieve a practical way of ensuring that children are protected during the trial process. It is, therefore, not misplaced when the Act provides for the establishment of "Family Court" under Section 149 for the purpose of hearing and determining matters relating to children' in Nigeria. The Act empowered the court to hear both civil and criminal cases involving children in Nigeria.[129] However, the author argues that the unlimited jurisdiction of the family court under the Child Rights Act may lead to a congestion of children's cases and create an unnecessary delay in the administration of child justice which at the long run conflict with Section 215(3) which expects the court to "handle each case brought before it expeditiously without unnecessary delay". Another adverse effect follows that a single magistrate will be presiding over cases involving both children and adults, as the Child Rights Act has not made provision for separate courts although, in practice, the same magistrate adjudicates on both children in conflict with the law and those in need of care and protection, but in different in judge's chambers or at different sittings.[130] Author's further argument is the question which begs for answer as to the issue of whether the establishment of a court for each State of the Nigerian federation as a family court[131] referred to

[128] See Schafer, S., *The Victim and His Criminal: A Study of Functional Responsibility* (New York: Random House, 1978) cited by Chinwe R. Nwanna and Naomi E. N. Akpan, Research Findings of Juvenile Justice Administration in Nigeria.

[129] See Section 151 CRA.

[130] This represents the view of the respondent in an interview conducted by the author in Kwara State, Nigeria dated 18 February 2014

[131] See Sections 149 and 150 of the Child Rights Act, 2003.

in the CRA should be read as meaning "all the High Courts or all the Magistrate's Courts in each of the states in the federation", or "any High Court or any Magistrate's court of the State". The literal meaning of the provision of the Act affirms the last-mentioned interpretation, which is "any High Court or any Magistrate's Court in the State". However in practice, this could lead to a very unsatisfactory situation, considering the doctrine of "*forum convenience*", as the location of the "State Family Court could make children's matters very problematic", particularly those of "children in rural areas across the vast geographical area that each Nigerian State occupies".[132] For instance, findings from the field survey by the author[133] revealed that

> Kwara State, Nigeria has domesticated the Child Rights Act,[134] and has 16 local government areas and more than 30 Magistrate's Courts, with only one Magistrate's Court in the city designated as the Family Court. The unfortunate situation is that each local government in Kwara State, Nigeria has a Magistrate's Court, but this Court cannot hear and determine the case of a child offender unless it is taken to the city where the Family Court is situated. This poses a challenge to the rights to a fair hearing of children in conflict with the law or in need of care and protection in local government areas that are far from the city as provided in section 35(4) and (5) of the Constitution of the Federal Republic of Nigeria, 1999 (as amended) thus: "a person arrested or detained should be taken to court within a reasonable time, and this means within a radius of 40 kilometres or a day or two days or longer period, as the court may consider reasonable in the circumstances.

Another challenge worthy to note from the author's field survey is non-uniform in the style of children's courts (i.e. family court) in most States in Nigeria. The findings from the survey revealed that "different States of the Federation have adopted two approaches to the establishment and operations of Juvenile/Family Courts".

[132] See, Abdulraheem-Mustapha, M. A., 'Child Justice Administration in the Nigerian Child Rights Act: Lessons from South Africa' (2016), *African Human Rights Law Journal* 16(1), 435–457. Published by Faculty of Law, University of Pretoria, South Africa.

[133] Author's field survey and interview conducted at Ilorin, Kwara State, 2014.

[134] Kwara State, Nigeria domesticated the Child Rights Act into Law in 2006. See Kwara State of Nigeria, Gazette 7, Vol. 41, 2007.

> In the first style/approach, separate and permanent structures or buildings with personnel are established for administration of child justice while in the second approach, the regular court structures (i.e. Magistrate or High Court Building) are temporarily used for the administration of child justice. Therefore, in some States in Nigeria (especially Lagos State), a visible structure akin to the first approach is dedicated for the administration of child justice. Whereas, in most States of the Federation; such structures are not usually put in place. Thus, instead of a permanent juvenile/family court, Magistrates hear cases involving child offenders outside the normal courtrooms or outside normal court sessions either in the courtrooms or in their chambers.[135]

The style of family court practice is to protect the privacy of the child offender and also to protect him or her from the effects of stigmatisation that may result from public trial.[136] However, the Act "prohibits the publication of the identity of young offenders" and the publication must have been considered a serious offence to warrant "fine of fifty thousand Naira or imprisonment".[137]

While the idea of family court for administration of child justice by the Act is laudable, it is argued that "children's right may not be properly protected where the same judge who sit over adult cases in regular courts are

[135] Author's field survey at Lagos, Kaduna, Port Harcourt, Enugu, Bauchi and Ilorin in 2014.

[136] See Sections 6(2), 6(4) and 12(3) CYPA which provide that a court when hearing charges against children or young persons shall, unless the child or young person is charged jointly with any person not being a child or young person, sit either in a different building or room from that in which the ordinary sittings of the court are held, or on different days or at different times from those at which the ordinary sittings are held. The rationale is ostensibly to prevent contamination of juveniles by adult offenders and possibly also ensuring that a juvenile Court maintains its peculiar character and tenor. See Osibanjo, Y., Juvenile Justice Administration in Nigeria, p. 67. This is clear from additional provisions in Section 6(5) (6), which state that: (5) In a juvenile court no person other than the members and officers of the court and the parties to the case, their solicitors and counsel, and other persons directly concerned shall, except by leave of such court, be allowed to attend: provided that such bona fide representative of a newspaper or news agency shall not be excluded, except by special order of the court. (6) No person shall publish the name, address, school, photograph or do anything likely to lead to the identification of the child or young person before a juvenile court, save with the permission of such court or in so far as required by the provisions of this Ordinance. Any person who acts in contravention of the provisions of this subsection shall be liable to a fine of fifty pounds.

[137] See Section 157(2) of the Child Rights Act.

saddled with the responsibility of hearing children's cases". This has been pointed out by Owasanoye[138] that "there is no separation or demarcation of the Court by specialised Juvenile/Family Courts or Judges". The fact remains that the provisions[139] that allow magistrates who sit at regular courts to be designed as children's judges jeopardise the requirement of specially trained personnel and also affect the judgment of the courts as there is the strong likelihood that when the judges are appointed as family court judges, they tend to focus "more on the crime and less on the status of the offender and are unable to distinguish between the adult and the child offender".[140] This style shows that "a judge who frequently switches between trials of adult offenders and child delinquents in a punitive legal system as in Nigeria cannot possess the right attitude and mood for humane treatment of young offenders". Author's field survey has confirmed this position where 774 (63%) of the respondents out of 1258 respondents hold the views that "the rights of child offenders to separate court and to the exclusion of public during trials are not adequately protected under the Nigerian Child Justice System".[141]

It is this author's argument that the use of existing court structures for trial of child offenders derogates from the international standards and exposes the child offenders to the formal criminal process. This diminishes the right of the child to separate legal treatment in accordance with international standards which stipulate the separation of child offenders from adult criminals at all stages of the process. In addition, since the juvenile/family courts are located within the regular court premises, it defeats the objective of the CRC and international standards of preventing mingling of juvenile with adult criminals.[142] The author's argument

[138] Ibid.

[139] Section 6 CYPA.

[140] Ibid. See also Stephenie J. Mill, 'The Age of Criminal Responsibility in an Era of Violence: Has Britain set a Vandabult' (1995), *Journal of Transnational Law* 28(2), Vandabult University Nashville p. 300, who argued that the British system also operates a similar system where the juvenile Courts are not separate tribunals but simply a special sitting of the magistrates' Court to hear only juvenile matters. The only difference is that there are more advanced policies to protect the juvenile.

[141] Author's field survey at Lagos, Kaduna, Port Harcourt, Enugu, Bauchi and Ilorin in 2014.

[142] Report of the Seventh United Nations Congress on the Prevention of Crime and Treatment of Offenders: CA/Conf.121/22/Rev., 1.

gains support from the views expressed by 70% (881) of the respondents that "establishment of juvenile/family court outside the conventional court's environment will prevent mingling of child delinquents with adult criminals".[143]

Therefore, it is worthy of note to emphasise that juvenile/family courts administration, unlike the adult courts, is supposed to always aim at providing the child/juvenile with about the same care and protection that the child would have been given by the child's parents under the doctrine of "*parens patriae*" (the natural responsibility of parents to take care of their child). Accordingly, this author suggests that juvenile/family court judges should have special training in child development and must be acquainted with contemporary social problems, especially as they affect children and young persons. Lack of special training and skills in child development by the juvenile/family courts judges will have an adverse effect on the reformation and reintegration of the child offender into the society as law-law-abiding citizens. The author's argument gains support of the respondents representing 744 (59%) where they hold the views that "presumption of innocence as one of the constitutional rights of the child offender is not adequately considered in the trial of child offenders in Juvenile/ Family Court in Nigeria".[144] This view is in tandem with the responses of some of the respondents in an interview conducted by the author at Borstal institutions at Ilorin[145] and Kaduna,[146] Nigeria that "one of the reasons for congestion in the Borstal institutions is that; the courts do not presume child offenders to be innocent since many of them were taken to court by their parents and adjudged to be beyond parental control". It is therefore submitted that the family court judges must be emotionally stable with a high sense of integrity, patience, possess a willingness to learn new ways of protecting children and young persons from delinquencies, be of a matured age of at least thirty years and must have a family.

[143] Author's field survey at Lagos, Kaduna, Port Harcourt, Enugu, Bauchi and Ilorin in 2014.

[144] Ibid.

[145] Interview conducted by the author at Ilorin, Kwara State, Nigeria dated 18 February 2014.

[146] Interview conducted by the author at Kaduna State, Nigeria dated 12 February 2014.

9.3 The Approved Institutions or Schools

According to Milner, approved school unlike Borstal is a place where children, and young persons are committed for vocational and educational training with no or less emphasis on physical training.[147] Beyond a general political rhetoric and declarations in government publications about the correction, reformation and rehabilitation of the child offender, there has not been adequate implementation of and commitment by government to the realisation of these goals. This ranges from inadequate funding and budgetary allocations, inadequate of the existing laws and policies on juvenile's custodial institutions among others. To support this argument is the views of 813 (64.6%) of the respondents in an administered questionnaire that "juvenile institutions are not adequately funded".[148]

To give proper exposition on child institution in Nigeria, it is important to state that Nigerian's first experience of reformatory home was 1903, but, it did not provide any separation between adult and child offenders. This experience continued till 1933 when[149] the first reformatory and industrial schools were established in Enugu and since then there has been concerted efforts by the Nigerian government at providing special institutions for juvenile offenders.[150]

According to Ogbolumani,[151] the law establishing approved schools demands that every inmate shall receive education according to his/her

[147] Milner, A., *The Nigerian Penal System* (London: Sweet and Maxwell, 1972), cited in Abdul-Mumin Sa'ad, 'Juvenile Justice in Nigeria', A Paper Presented at the Conference Session of the Research Committee on Deviant Behaviour (RC 29) During the XVI International Sociological Association (ISA) World Congress of Sociology (Durban, South Africa, 2006).

[148] Author's field survey at Lagos, Kaduna, Port Harcourt, Enugu, Bauchi and Ilorin in 2014.

[149] This institution sprang from the early nineteenth-century schools of industry in Britain, chiefly directed to the suppression of child begging. See Ferguson, T., *The Young Delinquent in His Social Setting* (London: Oxford University Press, 1952) cited Abdul-Mumin Sa'ad, 'Juvenile Justice in Nigeria'.

[150] Igbo, E. U. M., *Introduction to Criminology* (Nsukka: Afro-Orbis Publishing Co. Ltd., 1999) cited by Chinwe R. Nwanna and Naomi E. N. Akpan, Research Findings of Juvenile Justice Administration in Nigeria. 84.

[151] Ogbolumani, B. O. I., 'Institutional Treatment of Juveniles', in T. O. Elias (ed.), *The Magistrate and the Offender* (Lagos: University Press, 1972), p. 119. Cited by Chinwe R. Nwanna and Naomi E. N. Akpan, Research Findings of Juvenile Justice Administration in Nigeria, p. 37. See also Rule 10 of the Approved Institutions Regulations made under the CYPA.

age and development and such education shall be at least the equivalent of that which he/she would receive in his/her own special circumstances where he/she attending school in the usual way of education. Those who cannot cope with educational training have the option to get into various other vocational trades such as welding, tailoring, signwriting and carpentry. The girls are taught domestic science subjects such as dress-making, cookery and bakery. Corporal punishment is discouraged in order to avoid giving the wrong message to the inmates that they are in school for punishment instead of treatment. Similarly, recreational facilities such as football, netball and table tennis as well as facilities for moral and religious trainings are provided to make inmates feel at home as much as possible. However, the questions have always been whether or not the institutions are adequate and whether they have been achieving the reformative objective of establishing the institution? The answer is in the negative from the findings of the author in her fieldwork survey where 517 (41%) of the respondents ranked "government approved schools" as 3rd in the effectiveness of custodial institutions in the administration of child justice in Nigeria. The respondents hold the views thus:

> Borstal home was ranked 1st in the juvenile justice administration with 663 representing (53%). With 554 (44%) respondents, Remand Home was ranked 2nd in the Juvenile justice administration. With 517 (41%) respondents, Government Approved School was ranked 3rd in juvenile justice administration. This was followed by Prison with 501 (39.8%) and lastly the Police Cell with 457 (36%).[152]

9.4 *The Remand Home*

The remand home is established by the Borstal Institutions and Remand Centre Act.[153] Also, Section 15 of CYPA empowers native or local authority and local government councils to establish remand homes. Remand homes are established to cater for child offenders whose offences would attract imprisonment if they were adults. Remand homes are for short periods only and are for serious offences committed. Remand home shares most of the characteristics of prisons and serve as a

[152]Author's field survey at Lagos, Kaduna, Port Harcourt, Enugu, Bauchi and Ilorin in 2014.

[153]Borstal Institutions and Remand Centre Act No. 32 1960 now cap B38 Laws of the Federation of Nigeria 2004.

place where children facing trial in a juvenile/family court are sent pending the final determination of their cases. Children who are thought to be beyond parental control or in need of care and protection are sent to remand homes until suitable foster homes are found for them. According to Igbo, children in remand homes are usually there on transit.[154]

Remand homes in Nigeria are meant for the following:

(i) The detention of children on trial for the purpose of "conducting a special scrutiny of the children with a view to obtaining information about the child offenders which may assist the court in disposing of the child offender's case"[155];
(ii) Custody of endangered children; and
(iii) Committal of child offenders for short sentences (a maximum of six months), although the Minister can extend the mandate.[156]

In Nigeria, remand homes are also being used as approved or Borstal institutions. In fact, remand homes are being used as substitutes for approved schools where the latter do not exist. The deficiency in the provision of remand homes is that it does not specifically require vocational or literacy education for the inmate. This makes remand homes appear to be more like a custodial home rather than reformative centres for child offenders.[157] Study has shown that remand homes, approved schools and Borstal centres are not equipped to serve their statutory functions.[158] This corresponds with the views of the majority of the respondents in an administered questionnaire by the author where 1121 (89%) of the total population 1258 respondents strongly agreed that "there are inadequate functional programmes in the Nigerian remand homes/custodial institutions". In another interval, findings from the author's fieldwork survey revealed that "juvenile custodial institution-remand home in particular is not performing

[154] Igbo, E. U. M., *Introduction to Criminology*, pp. 86–87.

[155] See Milner, A., The Nigerian Penal System, p. 357.

[156] See Sections 4, 7, 9, and 26 of the Children and Young Persons Act.

[157] Okagbue, I., the Treatment of Juvenile Offenders and the Rights of the Child in the Rights of the Child in Nigeria, p. 243.

[158] See UNICEF, report on the Profile of Existing Diversion Programmes in Nigeria. http://www.unicef.org/nigeria/ng_publications_diversionpdf-similar (last visited 28 May 2011).

creditably well".[159] This position was further supported by 655 (52.1%) of the respondents[160] in another interval. However, it can be viewed from the respondents' views in Sect. 9.3 of this chapter where remand home was ranked second in hierarchy in the effectiveness of custodial institutions in Nigeria. It is, therefore, submitted that commitment by the Nigerian government in terms of funding and training of personnel in the custodial institutions will have positive impact on the reformation and rehabilitation of child offenders. This submission gains credence from the views of 1107 (88%) of respondents in a fieldwork survey by the author that "the use of children remand homes would provide corrective measure to reduce child delinquency"[161] and 1158 (92%) of the respondents in another interval further buttressed this position when they expressed that "adequate funding of child justice institutions would have positive impact on the administration of child justice in Nigeria".[162]

9.5 The Prison and the Borstal Training Institution

The prison system is not a new institution in Nigeria; it was firmly established and practised by most traditional communities before the advent of colonialism.[163] In fact, the idea of prisons and imprisonment was known to the Tiv, Yoruba, Edo and the Fulani nations long before colonialism was established.[164] Old empires such as Oyo, Benin and Kanem–Bornu (to mention but a few) were known to have kept prisoners[165] and since they all predate colonialism, the point must be taken as established that prisons and imprisonment were in existence no matter how rudimentary they might have been. The modern prison system, however, was introduced by

[159] Author's field survey at Lagos, Kaduna, Port Harcourt, Enugu, Bauchi, and Ilorin in 2014.

[160] Ibid.

[161] Ibid.

[162] Ibid.

[163] Lord Lugard as Governor of Nigeria and the apostle of Indirect Rule encouraged Native Authorities to establish prisons to enable the authorities exert coercive control over their subjects or opposition to governmental policies. Awe, B., 'The History of The Prison System in Nigeria', in T. O. Elias (ed.), *The Nigerian Prison System* (University of Lagos, 1968), 1.

[164] Ibid. See also Egu, M. A., *History of the Nigerian Prison Service: An Insider Account* (Abuja: Garkida Press Ltd., 1990), 1.

[165] Crowder, M., *The Story of Nigeria* (London: Faber and Faber, 1978), 36–47.

the colonialists, and the first to be established in Nigeria was the Broad Street Prison, Lagos, 1872, with a capacity of 300 inmates.[166]

The Nigerian prisons had right from the beginning no identifiable objectives and/or philosophy. The various laws promulgated so far do not even have a section on objectives. For the avoidance of doubt, the Prisons Act[167] has 20 sections and 2 schedules, none of which clearly declares the objectives and or philosophy of imprisonment. It would appear that the objectives and/or philosophy of the Nigeria Prisons Service are fluid and dependent on those at the helms of affairs. It has to be noted that the Nigerian Prisons Service has no separate prisons for women, girls, those in need of special care and young offenders who are in conflict with the law. 658 (52.3%) of the respondents in a fieldwork survey carried out by the author lamented that child delinquents in prison custody were not separated from adult prisoners that the delinquent children were only "incarcerated in a wing but still within the prison premises".[168] Apart from Kirikiri Maximum Prison that has a special wing for women and girls, women and girls are hardly considered a place in the construction of prisons.[169] All that is done is to allocate a section within the general prisons for women and girls irrespective of their special needs whether as pregnant or nursing mothers.[170]

Instructively, Borstal institution was later established to cater for young offenders that are incarcerated in prisons. Recourse need to be made to the historical antecedence of Borstal institution in Nigeria, and this can be traced to "a town in England near Chatham" where in 1902, "an attempt was made to separate young prisoners from associating with older offenders by grouping them apart in a wing of the convict prison at Borstal".[171] The establishment of the institution was also premised on confining the youths to solitary confinement in order to stimulate

[166] E.g. Prisons Ordinance 1916; Laws of Nigeria 1948; 1958; Prisons Decree No 9 of 1972; Federal Government White paper released in 1971. See Awe, B. O., 'History of the Prison System in Nigeria', in T. O. Elias (ed.), *The Prison System in Nigeria*.

[167] Prison Act, Cap P.29, Laws of the Federation of Nigeria, 2004.

[168] Author's field survey at Lagos, Kaduna, Port Harcourt, Enugu, Bauchi and Ilorin in 2014.

[169] Ehonwa, O. L., *Prisoners in the Shadows* (Lagos: Civil Liberties Organization, 1993), 20.

[170] Ibid.

[171] Ogbolumani, B. O. I., 'Institutional Treatment of Juveniles', in T. O. Elias (ed.), *The Magistrate and the Offender*, p. 122.

young offender to his/her best through large workshops by a system of marks and privileges. Thus, the Borstal system of institution seeks to turn around the youths mostly from "ages sixteen to twenty-one" by

> instilling in them habits of industry, self-respect, and self-control through the technique of manual labour, games, physical training, mental education, the incentive of useful and interesting trade and carefully planned series of rewards.[172]

Basically, in the delivery of criminal justice system in Nigeria, the corrective institution was fashioned after the English model. In history, the first known attempt at establishing Borstal institution in Nigeria was at "a wing of the Port Harcourt Prison".[173] However, this establishment did not produce the expected results. It was not until 1960 that the first law on Borstal institution in Nigeria was enacted.[174] Instructively, the purpose of this enactment is to "bring to bear upon the inmates every good influence which may establish in them the will to lead a good and useful life on release and to fit into do so by fullest development of his character, capacities, and sense of personal responsibilities".[175]

Like the 1960 Act, it defines a Borstal as "any building or place or any part thereof declared to be a Borstal institution under Section 3 of this Act".[176] Section 3 referred to authorises the Minister to declare any building or place a Borstal institution where "offenders who were not less than sixteen but fewer than twenty-one years of age on the day of conviction may be detained and given such training and instructions as will conduce to their reformation and the prevention of crime".[177] Furthermore, the Borstal Institution and Remand Centre

[172] Ibid.

[173] Ibid.

[174] Presently, the applicable law is the Borstal Institutions and Remand Centre Act Cap B38 Laws of the Federation of Nigeria, 2004, which is a replication of the 1960 Act.

[175] The Government of the Federal Republic of Nigeria publication on the Crime and the quality of life in Nigeria in Lagos on August 1980 postulated that the establishment of Borstal institutions is aimed at effecting reform by inculcating habits of industry, self-respect and self-control through manual labour, games, physical training and mental education.

[176] Ibid., Section 2.

[177] The law also declares Borstal Remand Center as "a place for the detention of persons not less than sixteen but under twenty-one years of age who are remanded or committed in custody for trial or sentence".

Act specify a maximum of three years of institutionalisation in the Borstal institution, and with a possible additional one year of aftercare supervision.[178]

Study has shown that "Borstal institution has two major functions".[179]

> The first is the "encouragement of a personal relationship between the Borstal staff and inmates through which the inmates will be given 'progressive trust-demanding personal decision, responsibility and self-control'", and secondly; the placement of emphasis on "regular educational and vocational training regimen with a demanding physical training content".

To buttress the findings in the above study is the author's fieldwork survey which shows that the "provision for educational and vocational trainings in the Borstal institutions" makes the respondents in the field survey "to rank the Borstal institution first in the hierarchy of the effectiveness of custodial institutions in Nigeria".[180]

Interestingly, Borstal training institutions are established with the following objective:

> Avoiding criminalising and penalising of a young person for behaviour that does not cause serious damage to the development of the person or harm to others.[181]

[178] See Ogbolumani, B. O. I., 'Institutional Treatment of Juveniles', in T. O. Elias (ed.), *The Magistrate and the Offender*, p. 122. See also, Igbo, E. U. M., Introduction to Criminology, 85–86. See also, Alemika, E. E. O., and Chukwuma, I. C., Juvenile Justice Administration in Nigeria: Philosophy and Practice, 52–53. See also Crime and the Quality of Life in Nigeria. Government of the Federal Republic of Nigeria Publication, Lagos, August 1980, p. 35.

[179] Milner, A., *The Nigerian Penal System* (London: Sweet and Maxwell, 1972).

[180] See Section 7.3 of this chapter for detailed analysis of the ranking of custodial institution in the administration of child justice in Nigeria.

[181] See Ogbolumani, B. O. I., 'Institutional Treatment of Juveniles', in T. O. Elias (ed.), *The Magistrate and the Offender*, p. 122. See also, Igbo, E. U. M., Introduction to Criminology, 85–86. See also, Alemika, E. E. O., and Chukwuma, I. C., Juvenile Justice Administration in Nigeria: Philosophy and Practice, 52–53. See also Crime and the Quality of Life in Nigeria. Government of the Federal Republic of Nigeria Publication, Lagos, August 1980, p. 35.

The policy thrust and measures that are put in place for the effective performance of Borstal institutions are[182]:

a. Provision of opportunities, in particular educational and vocational opportunities to meet the diverse needs of young persons, as well as provide a supporting direction for safeguarding the development of all young persons, especially those who are not able to pass through the process of formal educational institutions and those in need of special care and protection.
b. The programme of the centre is designed in such a way that members of the society and the families of persons on admission at the centre work hand in hand with the institution's personnel to ensure that young persons are routed to acceptable behavioural standards and norms.
c. The overall interest of the young person is the main reason for any official intervention in the well-being of young persons. The individual takes part in deciding any programme that will help him to make positive adjustments.
d. The rights and the interests of the young person are given premium in the efforts to safeguard his/her well-being and development.
e. The awareness that labelling a young person as "deviant" or delinquent often times leads the person to internalising such behavioural pattern. This knowledge guides handlers to ensure that such an impression is not formed.

However, Borstal institutions in Nigeria are basically for boys and provide facility for only male delinquents without any provision or facility for female delinquents.[183] Thus, girls that have been alleged to have committed offence experience the system differently from boys. The differences place a particular obligation on authorities to ensure that service delivery does not discriminate against the female minority and that the particular needs of girls should not be overlooked. However, it is not clear to what extent these differences derive from more lenient treatment, from a lack of facilities available for female offenders in custodial

[182] See generally Sections 4, 19, 47, 50, 52, 54 and 123 of the Borstal Institutions and Remand Centres Act.

[183] See generally the Borstal Institutions and Remand Centre Act, Cap B38 Laws of the Federation of Nigeria, 2004.

institution, Borstal institution in particular.[184] More importantly, inadequate female personnel at the custodial institutions present a peculiar problem since it is not viable for most prison officers to provide specific services for girls.[185] Therefore, this book argued that the law that provides for preventive mechanisms must reflect, and build on, the fact that boys and girls appear to make the transition to adulthood at different rates and with different degrees of success, thus, there is need for developing gender-specific interventions for girls who are subject to forms of statutory supervisions. Unfortunately, Nigeria's custodial institution such as Borstal institution has no programme that addresses the unique needs of girls in the institution. The need to respond appropriately to their situation cannot be overemphasised. For instance, Section 236(3) Child Rights Act provides that: 'a female child offender' placed in an institution shall- "be treated fairly; receive no less care, protection, assistance, treatment and training than a male child; and be given special attention as to her personal needs and problems".

The foregoing provisions provide for the need and protection of female child in custodial institutions without addressing the adjudication of the female offender. This book voices a concern for the establishment of girls' custodial institutions or the amendment of the Borstal Institution and Remand Centre Act to cater for the protection of female/girls delinquents in order to have a crime-free society.

Similarly, the Borstal Institution and Remand Centre Act are also silent as to what happens to child delinquents below the age of sixteen years. This book, therefore, argues that the Act limits the operation of the CRA which defines a child as "any person below the age of eighteen years".[186] This also negates the primary objective of reformation and reintegration of child delinquents who may be either male or female. In addition, there are

[184] See "Navigating the Juvenile Justice System: A Handbook for Families". Developed by the Maryland Coalition of Families for Children's Mental Health. Available at http://www.mdcoalition.org/documents/jjhandbook06.pdf (accessed on 26 February 2013).

[185] As aptly summed up by a British NGO, The Howard League, that "Prisons are ill equipped to deal with young women who are damaged and who display extremely challenging and difficult behaviour. The numbers of juvenile girls within the system are small and as a result they are simply tacked onto the rest of the system with little recognition that their needs are different and separate from older women. It also means that they attract fewer resources...".

[186] See Child Rights Act, 2003, Section 278.

only three Borstal institutions in Nigeria located at Abeokuta, Ilorin and Kaduna.[187] These three are expectedly too few and too far apart to cater for the teeming youths now languishing in adult prisons[188] under inhuman and deplorable conditions. Majority of the respondents representing 808 (64%) raised their voices up that "in no circumstances should prison be used as a substitute for custody of child offenders in any State of the federation where there is no Borstal institution".[189] This appears to be in support of the views earlier expressed in this book that "keeping the child offenders in prison will only increase their criminal inclination because they will be mixed up with adults inmates". Although, the Borstal facilities that make provisions for "vocational training in tailoring, photography, welding, building (masonry or bricklaying), electrical installation, etc., as well as formal educational instruction, up to General Certificate of Education" (ordinary level) were fairly managed in the 1970s.[190] However, by the 1980s, facilities and training in these institutions had deteriorated[191] and were virtually non-existent in the 1990s.[192] The problem of the institutions is more compounded with the personnel deployed into the institutions. For instance, the staff of Borstal institutions is drawn from prison staff.[193] This is seen as a serious handicap to the reformation and rehabilitative ideals of Borstal training for child offenders.[194] This is in view of the fact that prison staff is trained to handle adult criminals.[195] The views of 820 (66%) of the respondents in an administered

[187]Kaduna, Abeokuta, and Ilorin. See Aduba, J. N, 'From Punishment to Treatment: Humane Approach to the Sentencing of Young Offenders', in *Women and Children Under the Nigerian Law* 6, (1989). See also Ogbolumani *supra* note 58 at 117–130.

[188]This can be confirmed from the report gathered from The Vanguard Newspaper of 5 September 2008 at p. 10 that "No fewer than 200 juveniles are currently languishing in Port Harcourt Prison as they have been put behind bars amongst over 2,400 inmates, in (sic) which over 1,800 of the adults and children are awaiting trial".

[189]Author's field survey at Lagos, Kaduna, Port Harcourt, Enugu, Bauchi and Ilorin in 2014.

[190]Alemika, E. E. O., A Study of Socio-Cultural and Economic Factors in Delinquency Among Kaduna Borstal Inmates, 1978.

[191]Ahire, P. T., 'Juvenile Delinquency and the Handling of Young Prisoners in Nigerian Borstal Institutions', in *The Nigerian Prisons Service and the Public* 23, (1987).

[192]Human Rights Monitor, Administration of Juvenile Justice: the Example of the Borstal Training Institution Kaduna 10, (1997).

[193]See the Nigerian Prisons Service Annual Report for 1986, p. 46.

[194]See Section 236 of the Child Rights Act, 2003.

[195]Chinwe, R. N., and Naomi, E. N. A., *Research Findings of Juvenile Justice Administration in Nigeria* (Lagos: Constitutional Right Project [CRP], 2003).

questionnaire by the author are in support of this assertion when they hold that "laws and policies on the role and functions of Nigeria prison service as relate to the custodial of child offenders under the administration of child justice are not well spelt out to engender the protection of the rights of child offenders in prison custody".[196] Hence, the staff is not used to the "large-hearted approach required in the case of child offenders who should be handled as if they are in their own homes".[197] This book, therefore, argues for the implementation of Sections 233, 234, and 235 of the Child Rights Act which specifically provides for non-institutional treatment as a strategy to reduce juvenile recidivism in Nigeria. Further, studies have shown that the laudable goals of the institution are not realised due to the lack of proper policies and legal and institutional frameworks for child offender correction and child delinquency prevention.[198] This position was confirmed by 716 (57%) respondents in a fieldwork survey conducted by the author that "the existing laws and policies on custodial institutions under child justice administration are not adequate".[199]

Furthermore, the author's field survey corresponds with the study of Alemika and Chukwuma which revealed that

> the objectives of the institution are compromised by lack of proper planning and implementation; gross under funding; inadequate staff-in qualitative and quantitative terms; and lack of necessary training facilities in the workshops and educational programmes.[200]

In another interval, the challenges of Borstal institution have also been captured by the respondents from the author's fieldwork where 813 (64.6%) of them strongly agreed that "juvenile institutions are poorly funded in Nigeria" and some respondents representing 710 (56.4%) expressed that "there is no enough commitment by the government on custodial institution in Nigeria".[201] It is interesting to listen to the

[196] Author's field survey at Lagos, Kaduna, Port Harcourt, Enugu, Bauchi and Ilorin in 2014.

[197] Chinwe, R. N., and Naomi, E. N. A., *Research Findings of Juvenile Justice Administration in Nigeria* (Lagos: Constitutional Right Project [CRP], 2003).

[198] Alemika, E. E. O., and Chukwuma, I. C., *Juvenile Justice Administration in Nigeria: Philosophy and Practice* (Lagos: Centre for Law Enforcement Education, 2001).

[199] Author's field survey at Lagos, Kaduna, Port Harcourt, Enugu, Bauchi and Ilorin in 2014.

[200] Ibid.

[201] Ibid.

concurrent statements made by some respondents about government commitment to child justice administration. A police and prison officers in an interview said "the government is not committed to juvenile justice administration in Nigeria and this can be seen from inadequate funding and personnel in the institutions of juvenile justice".[202] This was confirmed further by Alemika and Chukwuma[203] in their field survey that:

> less than half of the population sampled representing 180 (48.3%) of the child offenders had access to education and vocational training.[204] Apart from counselling which was reported on a positive note, educational and vocational facilities were inadequate or non-existent.

Conversely, an effective rehabilitation programme must include measures such as: "education"; "vocational training"; "individual and group counseling", "psychiatrist and psychological treatment",[205] "Students' Personnel Services",[206] "Student Welfare Services",[207] "Student Social Recreational Services",[208] "Student Library Services",[209] and "Health Services".[210] Apparently from the findings of the fieldwork conducted by the author, the rehabilitation objective was not fulfilled.[211]

[202] Interview conducted by the author at Port Harcourt and Enugu, Nigeria dated 27 February and 13 March 2014.

[203] Ibid.

[204] Ibid.

[205] Holland, Paul, and Mlyniec, Wallace J., *Whatever Happened to the Right to Treatment? The Modern Quest for a Historical Promise* 68, (1995), 1791–1836.

[206] Yusuf, S., 'Students' Personnel Services and Academic Performance in Ilorin- South Local Government Area Secondary School. Kwara State', 2011.

[207] Ibid.

[208] Edem, D. A, Introduction to Educational Administration in Nigeria 10, (1998). See also Ojo F., Human Resource Management: Theories and Issues 15 (1988).

[209] Adeleke, A. A., 'Use of Library Resources by Academic Staff if the Nigerian Polytechnics' (2005), *Journal of library science* 12(2), 15–24.

[210] Olaitan, G. I., (2003). Relationship Between Provision, Utilization of Students' Services and Academic Achievement in Secondary Schools in Ilorin Metropolis.

[211] Author's field survey at Lagos, Kaduna, Port Harcourt, Enugu, Bauchi and Ilorin in 2014.

10 Conclusion

The chapter demonstrates the progress made in Nigeria towards supporting and sustaining national responses to enable children to realise their rights. This chapter further establishes the efforts consistently directed through legislative synergy at various point in the history of Nigeria on the treatment and protection of children alleged for infringing penal law or children in need of care and protection. The chapter examines the influence of international legal instruments which Nigeria is signatory to, on the protection of children and young persons'. This chapter established that until 2003, Nigeria has been applying various legislations for the treatment and protection of children alleged as, or accused of, having infringed penal law. It traced the enactments of the instruments and links them to the promulgation of the Child Rights Act in Nigeria. This ranges from the provisions of the Children and Young Persons Act, Criminal Procedure Act, Criminal Procedure Code, Criminal Code, Penal Code and the Constitution of the Federal Republic of Nigeria, 1999. From the exposition in this chapter, it can be deduced that appropriate implementation and compliance with CRA and other international conventions on matters of children can serve as guidance for the three stages of the process of child administration. The three stages are: first, the application of social policies to prevent and protect young persons from offending; second, the establishment of a progressive justice system for young persons in conflict with the law; and finally, the safeguarding of the fundamental rights of children and young persons' through the establishment of measures to ensure the dignity and welfare of children and young persons' deprived of their liberty, whether in prison or other institutions.

The chapter also contends that some progress has been achieved in Nigeria towards supporting and sustaining national responses to enable children to realise their rights. However, despite all the legal instruments and institutions, child offenders are still suffering from the administrational system. The chapter contends that since the Child Rights Act seems to have incorporated all provisions dealing with child offenders in the Criminal Code, Penal Code, Criminal Procedure Code, Criminal Procedure Act and the Children and Young Persons Act, there is need for harmonisation of the existing legislation in the form of amendments to evolve a child justice system that is humane and responsive in line with what is obtainable in most developed countries.

The chapter has also analysed the conceptual custodial institutions in Nigeria. Though the Child Rights Act provided for same, some of these institutions derogate from the international standards and expose children to formal criminal process by mingling them with adult criminals as against what is obtainable in South Africa under the Child Justice and Children's Acts.[212] Therefore, this chapter contends that where these concepts of custodial institutions are combined with community-based programmes that are obtainable in South Africa, particularly involving families of offenders will ensure the child offenders' proper rehabilitation and they will avoid repeat offences.

References

Abrifor et al., 'Differences, Trend and Pattern Recidivism Among Inmates in Selected Nigerian Prisons' (2010), *European Scientific Journal.*

Adeleke, A. A., 'Use of Library Resources by Academic Staff if the Nigerian Olytechnics' (2005) *Journal of Library Science* 12(2), 15–24.

Aduba, J. N., 'From Punishment to Treatment: Humane Approach to the Sentencing of Young Offenders', in *Women and Children under the Nigerian Law* (Vol. 6, Federal Ministry of Justice Publication, 1989).

Aguda, T. A., and Okagbue, I., *Principles of Criminal Liability in Nigerian Law* (Ibadan: Heinemann Educational Books, 1990).

Ahire, P. T., 'Juvenile Delinquency and the Handling of Young Prisoners in Nigerian Borstal Institutions', in *The Nigerian Prisons Service and the Public* (Abuja: Nigerian Prisons Service, 1987).

Ahire, P. T. 'Native Authority Police in Northern Nigeria: End of an era?', in T. N. Tamuno, I. L. Bashir, E. E. O. Alemika, and A. O. Akano (eds.), *Policing Nigeria: Past, Present and Future* (Lagos: Malthouse Press Ltd., 1993).

Alemika, E. E. O., *A Study of Socio-Cultural and Economic Factors in Delinquency Among Kaduna Borstal Inmates*, Unpublished (B.Sc. Sociology Original Essay, University of Ibadan, Ibadan Nigeria, 1978).

Alemika, E. E. O., and Chukwuma, I. C., *Juvenile Justice Administration in Nigeria: Philosophy and Practice* (Lagos: Centre for Law Enforcement Education, 2001).

Awe, B. O., 'The History of the Prison System in Nigeria', in T. O. Elias (ed.), *The Nigerian Prison System* (University of Lagos, 1968).

Chinwe, R. N., and Naomi, E. N. A., *Research Findings of Juvenile Justice Administration in Nigeria* (Lagos: Constitutional Right Project [CRP], 2003).

[212] See Chapter 6 of this book for detail examination of the South African perspectives.

Crowder, M., *The Story of Nigeria* (London: Faber and Faber, 1978).

Edem, D. A., Introduction to Educational Administration in Nigeria 10, (1998).

Egu, M. A., *History of the Nigerian Prison Service: an Insider Account* (Abuja: Garkida Press Ltd., 1990).

Ehonwa, O. L., *Prisoners in the Shadows* (Lagos: Civil Liberties Organisation, 1993).

Falobi, F., (2009), Empowering Prison Inmates, http://www.independentngonline.com/.

Ferguson, T., *The Young Delinquent in His Social Setting* (London: Oxford University Press, 1952).

Holland, Paul, and Mlyniec, Wallace J., *Whatever Happened to the Right to Treatment? The Modern Quest for a Historical Promise* 68, (1995).

Idyotough, Alamveabee E., *Operational Research Report on Challenges of Borstal Institutions, Remand Homes, Reformatories and Approved Schools in Nigeria* (Abuja Nigeria: Federal Department of Social Welfare, Federal Ministry of Women Affairs and Social Development, 2013).

Igbo, E. U. M., *Introduction to Criminology* (Nsukka: Afro-Orbis Publishing Co. Ltd., 1999).

Mill, Stephenie J., 'The Age of Criminal Responsibility in an Era of Violence: Has Britain set a Vandabult' (1995), *Journal of Transnational Law Vandabult University Nashville*, 28(2).

Milner, A., *The Nigerian Penal System* (London: Sweet and Maxwell 1972).

Nafiu, Akeem, and Oyesina, Tunde, "ACJA 2015: So Far, Not Too Good", available at https://newtelegraphonline.com/2017/12/acja-2015-far-not-good/.

Ogbolumami, B. O., 'Institutional Treatment of Juveniles', in T. O. Elias (ed.), *The Nigerian Magistrate and the Offender* (Benin City: Ethiope Publishing Corporation, 1970).

Ojo, F., Human Resource Management: Theories and Issues 15, (1988).

Okagbue, I., 'The Treatment of Juvenile Offenders and the Rights of the Child', in I. A. Ayua and I. E. Okagbue (eds.), *The Rights of the Child in Nigeria* (Nigerian Institute of Advance Legal Studies, 1996).

Okoli, B., Nigeria: The Constitution and Child Rights, October 19, 2007, available at http://allafrica.com/stories200710190453.html.

Olaitan, G. I., (2003). Relationship Between Provision, Utilisation of Students' Services and Academic Achievement in Secondary Schools in Ilorin Metropolis, 2003.

Osinbajo and Kalu, *Law Development and Administration in Nigeria* (Lagos: Federal Ministry of Justice, 1990).

Owasanoye, B., and Wenham, M., *Street Children and Juvenile Justice System in Lagos State of Nigeria* (Human Development Initiative, 2004).

Sa'ad, Abdul-Mumin, 'Juvenile Justice in Nigeria', A Paper Presented at the Conference Session of the Research Committee on Deviant Behaviour (RC

29) During the XVI International Sociological Association (ISA) World Congress of Sociology, (Durban, South Africa, 2006).

Schafer, S., *The Victim and His Criminal: A Study of Functional Responsibility* (New York: Random House, 1978) cited by Chinwe R. Nwanna and Naomi E. N. Akpan, Research Findings of Juvenile Justice Administration in Nigeria.

Soyombo, O., Sociology and Crime Control: That We May Live in Peace, (2009).

Tamuno, T. N., Bashir, I. L., Alemika, E. E. O., and Akano, A. O. (eds.), *Policing Nigeria: Past, Present and Future* (Lagos: Malthouse Press Ltd., 1993).

Ugwuoke, C. U., Criminology: Explaining Crime in the Nigerian Context 23.

Wilson, H., (2009), Curbing Recidivism in Our Society, Available at http://www.pioneerng.com/article.php?title=Curbing_Recidivism_In_Our_Societyandid=2765.

Yusuf, S., 'Students' Personnel Services and Academic Performance in Ilorin-South Local Government Area Secondary School. Kwar State' (2011).

CHAPTER 6

Legal and Institutional Frameworks on Child Justice Administration in South Africa

1 Introduction

As noted earlier in Chapter 3 of this book, the development of child justice administration in South Africa was influenced by various developments and reforms. These developments include the enactment of the Care of Neglected Children's Act 24 of 1895, the Child Protection Act 38 of 1901, the Children's Care and Protection Act 25 of 1913, which was replaced by the Children's Act 31 of 1937 and later repealed to become the Children's Act 33 of 1960. This Act of 1960 was also replaced with the Child Care Act 74 of 1983.

However, the South African constitutional development in 1993 and 1996 with the ratification and domestication of the UN Convention on the Rights of the Child, the Hague Conventions on Abduction and Adoption ushered in a comprehensive legislation on the protection of the rights of the children in conflict with the law and those children who are in need of care and protection who are the subject matter of this book. With the Constitution as the *grund norm* which gives legitimacy to the protection of children, two new sets of legislation were enacted to complement the constitutional protection with other policies put in place for the welfare of children in South Africa.

These new legislations are the Children's Act No. 38 of 2005 and Child Justice Act No. 75 of 2008. These legislations have harmonised all the existing laws on the administration of child justice in South

© The Author(s) 2020

M. A. Abdulraheem-Mustapha,
Child Justice Administration in Africa,
https://doi.org/10.1007/978-3-030-19015-6_6

Africa which shall be examined in this chapter. However, the aspects of the South Africa Constitution, 1996 which serves as the *grund norm* together with the South Africa Criminal Procedure Act that address issues relating to children in crisis situation such as children in conflict with the law and those children that are in need of care and protection were analysed. The chapter further analyses the structures of children's custodial institutions in the achievement of the primary objective of reintegration of child offender into the society. The chapter interrogates the establishment of partial care facility, a drop-in centre, boarding schools, etc., as applicable in South Africa.

2 The Constitution of the Republic of South Africa, 1996

After various reforms to the South African legal regime on the administration of child justice, the important is the Republic of South Africa Constitution, 1996 which serves as the *grund norm* where other laws derive their status and legitimacy.[1] The first point of reference in the Constitution that specifically deals with child justice administration is the provisions which accord a child offender the right to fair hearing and due process. These rights are enshrined in Chapter 2 of the Constitution as "Bills of Rights".[2] In particular, Section 28(3) defines a child as "a person under the age of 18 years" and by Section 28(1)(g) of the Constitution, a child is enjoyed "not to be detained except as a measure of last resort" and "may be detained only for the shortest appropriate period of time". By Section 28(1)(g) the Constitution thereof, its (g)(i) and g(ii) emphasises that "a child who is detained must be kept separately from detained persons over the age of 18 years" and the child must be "treated in a manner, and kept in conditions, that take account

[1] By Section 1 of the South Africa Constitution, 1996, "Republic of South Africa is one, sovereign, democratic state founded on the following values" to wit: Section 1(c) that states: "supremacy of the Constitution and the rule of law". By Section 2 of the Constitution further provides that "this Constitution is the supreme law of the Republic; law or conduct inconsistent with it is invalid, and the obligations imposed by it must be fulfilled".

[2] By Section 7(1)(2) of the Constitution, "this Bill of Rights is a cornerstone of democracy in South Africa". "It enshrines the rights of all people in 'South Africa' and affirms the democratic values of human dignity, equality and freedom". Therefore, "the state must respect, protect, promote and fulfil the rights in the Bill of Rights". Although, these rights "are subject to the limitations contained or referred to in section 35, or elsewhere in the Bill of Rights". See Section 7(3) of the Constitution.

of the child's age". Section 28(2) of the Constitution provides for the application of "a child's best interest to be of paramount importance in every matter concerning the child". Importantly, by Section 34 of the Constitution, everyone including children has "right to court" such as "right to remain silent",[3] "right to be informed promptly",[4] "right not be compelled to make confession or admission that could be used in evidence against him/her",[5] "right to be brought before a court as soon as possible"[6] and "right to have a legal representative"[7] of his own choice or "right to be assigned a legal practitioner by the state and at the state expense, if substantial injustice would otherwise result"[8] among all other rights provided in Section 34 thereof. Particularly, this Constitution emphasises the presumption of innocence of all the accused person.[9]

Some rights were also captured in the Bill of Rights to include—"right to life",[10] and "right to freedom of movement and residence".[11] Section 12 under the Bill of Rights also deals generally with "rights to freedom and security of the person" including children[12] also, there is also right to privacy,[13] of all people of South Africa including children. Section 35 of the Constitution deals generally with persons arrested and detained in South Africa. However, the Rights of Bill is subject to limitations provided in Section 36(1) of the Constitution. Other significant constitutional provisions dealing with the rights of children like adult are "right to human dignity",[14] "rights not to be subjected

[3] See Section 34(1)(a) of the 1996 Constitution.

[4] See Section 34(1)(b) of the Constitution, ibid.

[5] See Section 34(1)(c) of the Constitution, ibid.

[6] See Section 34(1)(d) of the Constitution, ibid.

[7] See Section 34(2)(b) of the Constitution, ibid.

[8] See Section 34(1)(c) of the Constitution, ibid.

[9] Section 35(3)(h) and the section further gives general detail provisions of rights to fair trial of every accused person.

[10] See Section 11 of the 1996 Constitution.

[11] See Section 21 of the Constitution, ibid.

[12] It should be noted that Section 12 of the Constitution needs to be read together with Section 9 especially Subsection 3 which provides that "the state may not unfairly discriminate directly or indirectly against anyone on one or more grounds, including race, gender, sex, colour, age", etc.

[13] See Section 14 of the Constitution, ibid.

[14] See Section 10 of the Constitution, ibid.

to slavery, servitude or forced labour",[15] "right to education",[16] and "rights to health care, food, water and social security".[17] Unlike in the Nigerian perspectives[18] where socio-economic rights are not enforceable, socio-economic rights are guaranteed in the South African Constitution as all rights are interdependent and interrelated and they are enforceable in the South African courts.

Significantly, most of the provisions in the Bill of Rights under the Constitution deals with issues relating to the treatment of a child for the purpose of adjudicating a child alleged to be in conflict with the law or child in need of care and protection. It is interesting to note that these provisions conform to the relevant UN Conventions on the Rights of the Child, the UN Rules and Guidelines on treatment of offenders inclusive of children and the African Charter on the Rights and Welfare of the Child examined under Chapter 4 of this book.

3 Criminal Procedure Act 51 of 1977 (As Amended)

The discussion of Criminal Procedure Act in the administration of child justice in South Africa cannot be over-emphasised. It is an adjectival law that prescribes the practical method of enforcing rights or obtaining redress for their invasions. It should be noted from onset that the provisions of the Criminal Procedure Act relating to navigation of children under the criminal justice system have been embedded in the Child Justice Act 75 of 2008. The provisions range from "methods of securing the attendance"[19] of a child in court to "modes and procedures of arrest, summons and written notice"[20]; "procedures for bail"[21];

[15] See Section 13 of the Constitution, ibid.

[16] See Section 29 of the Constitution, ibid.

[17] See Section 27 of the Constitution, ibid.

[18] All these rights were not classified as they are enshrined under the Bill of Rights. Socio-economic rights such as "rights to education" and "security of the people" are enshrined under Chapter II of the Constitution of the Federal Republic of Nigeria, 1999 (as amended) and as such they are not enforceable.

[19] See Chapter 4 of the Criminal Procedure Act 51 of 1977.

[20] Chapter 5, ibid.

[21] Chapter 9, ibid.

"rights of assistance"[22]; "plea"[23]; "preparatory examination and trial"[24] proper; "criminal proceedings"[25]; "sentencing"[26] procedures; "reviews and appeals"[27] were all incorporated into the provisions of the Child Justice Act.[28] However, for emphasising an appraisal of the Act, some aspects dealing with children will be briefly examined. Of much importance is the provision of the Act dealing with the determination of the age of the accused person. The Criminal Procedure Act set down the procedure to be taken whenever the age of any person is an issue in order to determine whether the person is a child for his or her matter to be heard in either the child justice or children's courts.[29] This is important just like in Nigerian perspectives that determination of an accused's age to be a child is more favourable to such person under the South Africa criminal justice system. More importantly that the accused's youthful age at the time of the commission of the offence may be used to mitigate his sentence[30] and also for the purpose of incarceration[31] in order to satisfy the provision of Section 28(1)(g)(i) of the Constitution, 1996 which requires that "all minors be kept separately from detained persons who are over 18 years of age". For instance, Section 337 of the Act mandated the presiding judge or judicial officer in addition to the provisions of Sections 14–16 of the Child Justice Act to "estimate the age of such person by his or her appearance or from any information which may be available which estimated age will be deemed to be the correct age of such person" unless if there is "any subsequent proof that the estimated age was incorrect".[32]

[22] Chapter 11, ibid.

[23] Chapters 15, 17, and 18, ibid.

[24] Chapter 21, ibid.

[25] Chapter 22, ibid.

[26] Chapter 28, ibid.

[27] Chapters 30 and 3, ibid.

[28] See detail examination of Child Justice Act in the next section of this chapter.

[29] See generally the case of *S v. Gani NO* 2012 (2) SACR 468 (GSJ).

[30] See *S v. Thonga* 1993 (1) SACR 365 (V).

[31] See *S v. Z en vier ander sake* 1999 (1) SACR 427 (E). See also, *Mpofu v. Minister for Justice and Constitutional Development & Others* 2013 (2) SACR 407 (CC).

[32] Although, the provision of Section 337 of the Criminal Procedure Act has been substituted by Section 99(1) of the Child Justice Act. See generally the case of *R v. Matipa & Others* 1959 (2) SA 396 (T).

The case of *S v. Kamfer*[33] practically set down the appropriate procedures to reaffirm the provision of the Act when the court held that:

> There are two steps in the process of ascertaining the age of an accused:
> (a) first, the judicial officer must enquire as to whether evidence on the accused's age is available or not;
> (b) if there is insufficient or no evidence, then recourse must be had to Section 337 and an estimate must be made.

In 1988, the two-prolonged process in the above decision was further reaffirmed in the case of *S v. Mavhungu*[34] to be "a last resort and extraordinary solution that can only be invoked if evidence relating to age was sought and all sources available to the State or defence were exhausted". The application of the provision of Section 337 of the Act was used by the reviewing court in the case of *S v. Dial*[35] to "criticised the trial court for not having done enough to determine the true age of the accused". In that case, the social worker failed "to obtain the accused's birth certificate and the accused was not referred to the nearest district surgeon or State hospital for a medical examination to determine his or her age". It is however observed in this chapter that "mere observation" of the appearance of the accused person in the determination of his age in the case of *S v. Mavhungu (supra)* is not enough, and it is regarded by the author as an "ill-advised" approach which can only be utilised in cases where the age of the accused is not really an issue even though his or her age is not known. The author's reason being that the physique of the appearance of such person may be influenced by the environment, physical deprivation, and even the abuse of substances of the person,[36]

[33] 1969 (4) SA 250 (C).

[34] 1988 (3) SA 67 (V). See also *S v. Naude* 1978 (1) SA 566 (T).

[35] 2006 (1) SACR 395 (E) at 4–10. At page 13 of the judgement, Plasker J. and Pickering J. emphasised that "the consequences of estimating age can be significant; an estimation of 19 years instead of 17 years can, for example, deprive an accused person of the special protection afforded by section 28 of the Constitution as well as the provisions of Child Justice Act 75 of 2008". See also, *S v. R* 1991 (2) SACR 287 (T); *S v. Gumede* (unreported, ECG Case No. CA&R181/2011, 17 November 2011); *Mpofu v. Minister for Justice and Constitutional Development* 2013 (2) SACR 407 (CC); *S v. Swato* 1977 (3) SA 992 (O); *R v. Machambere & Another* 1950 (1) SA 315 (SR); *R v. Botha & Another* 1947 (2) SA 1281 (C); *S v. M* 1967 (1) SA 70 (N).

[36] See the case of *S v. Dial (supra)*. See also *S v. Dumba* 2011 (2) SACR 5 (NCK) at 4.

thus, the appearance of the accused in the determination of his or her age should be the very last consideration in estimating age as appearance will provide little or no reliable evidence.[37] Therefore, it should only "be resorted to as an emergency method". In support of the above position, the reviewing court dismissed the inference made by the magistrate in the case of *S v. M (supra)* when the trial magistrate observed that "it was apparent from the victim's build that her breasts had not yet developed and that the girl had only menstruated a week before the case was tried" for the purpose of determining the age that the girl "was at the age of puberty and had thus not attained the age of 16 years".

It should be noted that the findings, grounds for the findings and method by which the age of the accused was determined by the court must be carefully noted on the record of proceedings,[38] and it must further be noted that the estimation of the age of the accuse is "case specific" and cannot be regarded as the accused's correct age for the purpose of other subsequent cases.[39] More importantly, the appearance of the accused at the time of trial must be differentiated from his appearance at the time of the commission of the offence.[40] It should be further noted that the limitations under Section 112(1)(b) procedure of the Criminal Procedure Act can neither be used nor the provision of Section 220 of the Act relating to a formal admission by the accused in order to prove his age could be used in the determination of the age of the accused.[41] In essence, these limitations under Sections 112(1)(b) and 220 together with the consideration from the provision of Section 337 of the Act and case laws must be read together with the provisions and

[37] See the case of *S v. Naude (supra)* and *S v. Dial (supra)*.

[38] See the following cases: *S v. Nyathi* 1978 (2) SA 20 (B); *R v. Hadebe & Another* 1960 (1) SA 488 (T); *R v. Hlongwane* 1960 (1) SA 309 (T); *R v. Fana* 1960 (4) SA 277 (T); *S v. Sibiya* 1964 (2) SA 379 (N); *S v. Butelezi* 1964 (3) SA 519 (N); *S v. Manyololo* 1969 (4) SA 356 (E); *S v. Tango* 1969 (2) SA 648 (C); *S v. Mavundla & Another; S v. Sibisi* 1976 (2) SA 162 (N); *S v. Mavhungu* 1988 (2) SA 67 (V); *S v. Gumede* (unreported, ECG Case No. CA&R181/2011, 17 November 2011; *Mpofuv. Minister for Justice and Constitutional Development & Others* 2013 (2) SACR 407 (CC); *S v. Kumalo* 1991 (2) SACR 694 (W); *S v. Dumba* 2011 (2) SACR 5 (NCK); and *S v. Ngoma* 1984 (3) SA 666 (A).

[39] See the following case: *S v. Thomas* 1961 (4) SA 850 (C); *S v. Skenjane* 1965 (2) SA 86 (O).

[40] See case of *R v. Ndhlovu* 1948 (1) SA 289 (O) and *R v. Kuwuseb* 1949 (1) SA 651 (SWA).

[41] See the following cases: *S v. Chiloane*; *S v. Masango*; *S v. Mabusa* 1977 (4) SA 69 (T); *R v. Kaplan* 1942 OPD 232; *R v. C* 1955 (1) SA 380 (C).

procedures in Sections 13, 14, 15, and 16 of the Child Justice Act 75 of 2008.[42]

Under the general provisions in Chapter 33 of the Criminal Procedure Act, its Section 335A(2) makes it an offence punishable with fine or imprisonment for a period not exceeding five years or both if any person publish any information prohibited under Section 335A(1) of the Act of which the identity of a person under the age of 18 years has been revealed. Directives for Public Prosecutions[43] have been embedded in the schedule to the South Africa Criminal Procedure Act which, in all intents and purposes aligned with the provision of Section 97(4) of the Child Justice Act. These directives were given detailed procedures on the handling of children that are in conflict with the law and those children in need of care and protection by the prosecuting authority. For instance, the directives distilled the procedures for determining the age of criminal responsibility and at what age could a child alleged to have committed an offence could be arrested and prosecuted by the prosecuting authority.[44] In particular, the prosecutor is empowered to release a child alleged to have committed an offence under Schedule 1 of the Child Justice Act on bail[45] based on Section 59A of the Criminal Procedure Act.[46] South Africa Criminal Procedure Act has been used in many ways before the advent of the Child Justice Act 78 of 2008.

These directives further give the prosecuting authority the discretion after due application of the law whether to divert the child at the earlier stage and refer the matter to a probation officer who will thereafter take the child to children's court for necessary diversion options or

[42] See the case of *S v. Mbelo* 2003 (1) SACR 84 (NC).

[43] The "Directives (Public Prosecutions), 2010 which is in terms of section 97(4) of the Child Justice Act 75 of 2008" was published under "GN R252 in GG 33067 of 31 March, 2010". These directives were "issued by the National Director of Public Prosecutions in consultation with the Cabinet member responsible for the administration of justice".

[44] See Directives D, E, G, I, J, K, L, M, N, O, P, Q, R, and S of the Schedule to the Criminal Procedure Act.

[45] See Directive O of the Schedule to the Criminal Procedure Act.

[46] Section 59A of the Criminal Procedure Act provides that "Prosecutor may in respect of the offences referred to in Schedule 1 of the Child Justice Act and in consultation with the police officer charged with the investigation authorise the release of the child on bail".

decide to prosecute the child after a preliminary inquiry has been concluded.[47] It should be noted that by the provision of directive "T" of the Schedule, "a disciplinary steps will be taken against a prosecutor who fail to comply with the directives or the duty imposed on him under the Child Justice Act". The application of some of the provisions of the Act has caused adverse effects to the rehabilitation and reintegration of child offenders into the society. One of the notable effects is double jeopardy in the application of the Act. For instance, before Child Justice Act, the provisions of Act that permits the National Prosecution Authority to have discretion either to prosecute or to reinstate the prosecution of a child accused after he or she had successfully completed a diversion programme were overturned by the reviewing court in the case of *S v. EA*[48] where the court set aside the conviction and found that "the reinstatement of the prosecution was not fair to the accused, because the prosecutor had created an expectation that the accused would not be prosecuted if he completed the diversion programme successfully".[49] By provision of Section 30 of the Criminal Procedure Act, all children cases are subject to automatic review in terms of the Child Justice Act where a child was:

> under the age of 16 years at the time of his or her commission of the offence, irrespective of the sentence;
> the child is 16 years or older, but under the age of 18 years, and has been sentenced to any form of imprisonment that was not wholly suspended or any sentence of compulsory residence in a Child and Youth Care Centre providing a programme provided for in section 191(2)(j) of the Children's Act;
> the child is sentenced to a period of imprisonment after a suspended sentence had been put into operation in terms of section 297(9)(a)(ii) of the Criminal Procedure Act;
> this would be irrespective:
> of the duration of the sentence and the length of time a judicial officer has held the substantive rank of Magistrate; or
> if the child were legally represented; represented; or
> if the child had been sentenced by a regional court

[47] See Directive O of the Schedule to the Criminal Procedure Act.

[48] 2014 (1) SACR 183 (NCK) at 13–14, 16, 19.

[49] See also the case of *National Directorate of Public Prosecution v. Puma* 2009 (1) SACR 361 (SCA) at 39, 80.

The Review Court decision in the case of *S v. Fortuin*[50] is apposite to this position when the court held that:

> The provisions of section 302 of the Criminal Procedure Act are not applicable to any child who was under the age of 16 years when he or she committed the offence. And,
> The provisions of section 85(1)(b) of the Child Justice Act are not applicable to a child who, at the time when the offence was committed, was 16 years or older, but not older than 18 years, and on whom a sentence other than that contemplated in section 85(1)(b) is imposed, which includes a fine and a suspended sentence.[51]

The rationale for the automatic review of children cases who are either represented by legal practitioner or not is due to compulsory provision of legal representation of children under Sections 82 and 83 of the Child Justice Act and argued to better promote the object set out in Section 2(c) of the Child Justice Act and promote the spirit, purport and objects of the Bill of Rights.[52] In the same vein, Section 309(1) of the Criminal Procedure Amendment Act 42 of 2003 has reaffirmed this position by specifically identifying the conviction and sentence of a child to be as of right in all matters without leave of court to appeal against the judgement to the High Court.[53] This is to give muscle to the provision of Section 84 of the Child Justice Act. In another similar case of

[50] Unreported NCK Case No. 38/2011, at 13 particularly at 64.

[51] See also the case of *S v. FM* 2013 (1) SACR 57 (GNP) where the court held that "sentences imposed on children who were legally represented were not for that reason alone excluded from automatic review". Further, see *S v. CS* 2012 (1) SACR 595 (ECP) at 13 and 26.

[52] See *S v. LM (Faculty of Law, University of the Western Cape: Children Rights Project of the Community Law Centre & Others as Amici Curiae)* 2013 (1) SACR 188 (WCC). In *S v. Sekoere* 2013 (2) SACR 426 (FB) at 28.2, 30, Daffue J. Hold that "all matters falling within the provisions of Section 85(1) of the Child Justice Act must be referred to the High Court for automatic review in accordance with that section, whether or not the children concerned wee represented by legal representatives". The judge hold in another paragraph that "to hold that Section 85(1) applies to unrepresented minor accused only, will make a mockery of the constitutional rights of minors and the introduction of a new criminal justice option for children".

[53] See also Section 390(1) of the Criminal procedure Amendment Act 42 of 2003 as amended by Section 10 of the Judicial Matters Amendment Act 42 of 2013.

S v. Z & 23 Similar Cases,[54] the court "intervened to protect the constitutional rights of juveniles who were sentenced to reform school but were detained elsewhere for unreasonably long periods".

Similarly, in line with Section 35(3)(d) of the Constitution, 1996 which emphasises that "every accused person has a right to a fair trial, which includes the right-to have their trial begin and conclude without unreasonable delay", Section 342A of the Criminal Procedure Act lay down the procedure to be taken by the court in investigating any trial of the accused including children that are unreasonably delayed.[55] The purpose of this procedure is to provide court with a "statutory mechanism to avoid unreasonable delays in the finalisation of criminal proceedings" and the rendering of judgement within a reasonable time.[56] In support of the provision of the Act is the pronouncement made by Mynhardt J. in *S v. Maredi*[57] who ordered that "the authorities should investigate the conduct of the prosecutor and magistrate concerned as the accused's fundamental right to speedy trial had been violated". In the same vein, the concurrent pronouncements by Griesel and Motala J.J. were reiterated by Moosa J. in *S v. Jackson & Others*[58] that "three basic forms of prejudice can be caused by unreasonable delays which are: loss of personal liberty; impairment of personal security; and trial-related prejudice such as witnesses becoming unavailable".[59] It should be noted that the provision of Section 89(1) of the Magistrate' Courts Act 32 of

[54] 2004 (1) 400 (E) 1 at 403f–h.

[55] See Van Zyl, 'Pre-trial Detention in South Africa: Trial and Error', in Van Kempen (ed.), *Pre-trial Detention: Human Rights, Criminal Procedural Law and Penitentiary Law, Comparative Law* (2012), 661 at 672.

[56] See *S v. Myaka & Others* (unreported, GSJ Case No. A5040/2011, 215/2005, 21 September 2012) at 4; *New Clicks South Africa (Pty) Ltd. v. Minister of Health & Another* 2005 (3) SA 238 (SCA) at 4–6.

[57] 2000 (1) SACR 611 (T).

[58] 2008 (2) SACR 274 (C). In *Sanderson v. Attorney-General, Eastern Cape* 1998 (1) SACR 227 (CC), 1997 (12) BCLR 1075 (CC), the Constitutional Court pointed three factors to be consider in the investigation of unreasonable delay of trial to be—"the nature of the prejudice suffered by the accused; the nature of the case; and the systemic delay". See also, *Barker v. Wingo* 407 US 514 (1972).

[59] See also *S v. Ndibe* (unreported, WCC Case No. 14/544/2010, 14 December 2013) at 6; *Director of Public Prosecutions North Gauteng v. Makhubela* (unreported, GNP Case No. A91/2014, 6 August 2014) at 19.

1944 which deals with "lack of jurisdiction" does not preclude a district court from invoking Section 342A above in investigating the unreasonable delay of trials.[60]

Summarily, it is the submission of the author that incorporating the provisions of the Criminal Procedure Act into the Child Justice Act shows the commitment of the South African government to the protection of children alleged to have been in conflict with the law or in need of care and protection. It also shows a special procedure laid down for speedy dispensation of justice and special treatment of child offenders in the administration of criminal justice system.

4 Child Justice Act 75 of 2008 (As Amended)

It is instructive to note that South Africa became one of the countries that have a comprehensive legislation on the protection of children who are in conflict with the law after her ratification of the UN Convention on the Rights of the Child in 1995 and the African Charter on the Rights and Welfare of the Child in 2000 with domestication of same in her Child Justice Act 75 of 2008 (as amended). Although, the Act introduces certain reforms in the criminal justice system in order to ensure that children in conflict with the law are treated in a manner that takes into account their age, vulnerability and special needs, the provisions of the Constitution particularly under the Bill of Rights in Chapter 2 and the Criminal Procedure Act with the Common Law of South Africa were not altered by the Child Justice Act.[61] In support of this position is the provision of Section 63(4) of the Act which provides that "a Child Justice Court must, during the proceedings of the child, ensure that the best interests of the child are upheld".[62] The case of *S v. Ndwandwe*[63] is apposite when the Appeal Court emphasised that "the primacy of the rights of children prevails irrespective of whether the child witness is a complainant or an accused" and thus, "the Child Justice Court had failed to comply with section 63 of the Child Justice Act by not

[60] See *S v. Khalema and Five Similar Cases* 2008 (1) SACR 165 (C) at 26–30. See also, *S v. Thenga* 2012 (2) SACR 628 (NCK).

[61] See *S v. Mahlangu & Another* GSJ Case No. CC70/2010, 22 May 2012 (unreported).

[62] See section 28(2) of the South Africa Constitution, 1996 discussed above.

[63] KZP Case R 99/12, 6 August 2012 (unreported).

promoting the best interest of the child". The Act has "100 sections" with "5 schedules" and "57 regulations relating to child justice" with "15 Forms", "directives in terms of section 97(4) of the Act" and "three schedules" depending on the severity of the offence.

For criminal responsibility, the Child Justice Act creates three distinct categories of children and young persons. First, children under 10 years old at the time of the offence are not criminally liable. A child under the age of 10 years cannot be arrested. This means that a child under 10 years does not have criminal capacity and cannot be charged or arrested for an offence. It should be noted that the children under this category will be "handed over to a probation officer to be dealt with in accordance with section 9" of the Act.[64] It is the responsibility of the probation officer to assess the child in accordance with Section 9 thereof, and in such a case the child will be referred to the children's court.[65] Children over 10 years old but younger than 18 years at the time of "arrest"[66] or when the "summons"[67] or "written notice"[68] was served on them are the primary focus of the Act.[69] The probation officer after assessment[70] and after serving either the summon, written notice or warrant of arrest on the child proceed either to "release the child on written notice of parent or guardian or detain the child"[71] or proceed for preliminary inquiry[72] before an inquiry magistrate who will determine whether to divert[73] the matter or to refer the matter to child justice or children's court for appropriate adjudication. The Act equally protects persons between the ages of 18 and 21 who committed the offence when they were less than 18 years of age.[74] This section recognises that 18–21

[64] See Sections 5, 17, and 29 of the Child Justice Act 75, 2008.

[65] See Sections 9 and 10 of the Child Justice Act 75, 2008.

[66] see Section 20 of the Act, ibid.

[67] See Section 19 of the Act, ibid.

[68] See Section 18 of the Act, ibid.

[69] See Section 10 of the Child Justice Act, ibid.

[70] See generally Chapter 5 of the Act, ibid.

[71] See generally Chapter 4 of the Act, ibid.

[72] See generally Chapter 7 of the Act, ibid.

[73] See generally Chapters 6 and 8 of the Act, ibid.

[74] See Sections 12–16 of the Act, ibid.

years old are still young and can benefit from the procedures in the Act. However, in 2016, the minimum age of criminal liability has been increased from 10 to 12 years[75] and this is in line with Sections 8 and 96 of the Act which allows the review of the minimum age of criminal capacity. The consolidated annual report from the Department: Justice and Constitutional Development Republic of South Africa confirms the review of the minimum age of criminal capacity when the report[76] states that "94% of the convictions between 2015 and 2016 were in respect of children between the ages of 15 and 18 years and there is no convictions registered against children between ages of 10 to 12 years".

It is of interest to note that, in enhancing the provisions of the Constitution, 1996, the Child Justice Act makes provisions for "presumption of innocence",[77] "right to privacy" and that "no person may be present at any sitting of a Child Justice Court unless that person's presence is necessary and granted by the court",[78] "right to remain silent",[79] "proof beyond reasonable doubt"[80] by the prosecution, "right to legal representation".[81] It is compulsory for a child who has been alleged to have committed an offence to be represented and in no circumstance shall the child offender "waive" this right of representation[82] as the "presiding officer may direct that the child offender be represented by legal aid".[83]

[75] The South African cabinet met on 17 February 2016 and approved the report on upward review of the minimum age for criminal responsibility to 12 years with some special protection measures in place for 13- and 14-year-old children. See South African Press Report dated 22 February 2016.

[76] The implementation of Child Justice Act consolidated annual report by the Department: Justice and Constitutional Development Republic of South Africa from 1 April 2015 to 31 March 2016. Available at http://www.justice.gov.za.cja-anr-2015-2016. Accessed 24 December 2018.

[77] See Section 63 of the Act, ibid.

[78] Ibid.

[79] Ibid.

[80] See Section 11 of the Act, ibid. See also, *S v. Mgcina* 2007 (1) SACR 82 (T).

[81] See generally Sections 80–83 of the Act, ibid.

[82] See Section 83 of the Act, ibid.

[83] See Section 24(1) of the Legal Aid South Africa Act, 2014. See also Section 25(1) of the Child Justice Act 39 of 2014; *S v. Bekisi* 1992 (1) SACR 39 N (C); *S v. Manuel & Others* 1997 (2) SACR 505 (C).

Again, the Act creates a child justice system for children accused of crime separate from the main criminal justice system which ordinarily applies to adults. Thus, the trial of children is conducted at the Child Justice Court ranging from diversion[84] of children's matters to the appropriate court in minor offences[85] in order to meet the child's basic needs to the general sentencing options[86] available to children adjudged to be in conflict with the law in order to promote the "best interest of the child".[87] The Act seeks to keep children out of detention and away from the formal criminal justice system, mainly through diversion. Author's interview[88] at Grahamstown, South Africa confirms this position when one of the respondents said that "since the inception in 2010, the Act promotes the imposition of non-custodial sentences against children convicted of criminal offences". This corresponds with the diversion follow-up study[89] conducted in the nine provinces of South Africa by Maepa where "93.3% of the participants did not re-offend within the first 12 months following completion of the diversion option". And in another follow-up study[90] by Maepa, it was founded that "84% of programme participants did not re-offend within a three-year period". The study of Steyn[91] further attests to this position when he opined that "with the introduction of the Child Justice Act 75 of 2008 in April 2010, a more regulated and structured legal response was provided for children in conflict with the law". These findings show that the

[84] See generally Chapter 8 of the Child Justice Act.

[85] Section 64 of the Act provides to the effect that "if it appears to a presiding officer at the Child Justice Court during the course of proceedings that a child is in need of care and protection, the presiding officer must act in accordance with this Act and refer such child to the children's court as contemplated under section 50 of this Act".

[86] See generally Chapter 10 of the Act ibid. The sentencing options range from "community-based sentences"; "restorative justice sentences"; "correctional supervision"; "postponement or suspension of passing of sentences"; "fine or alternative to fine"; "sentence of imprisonment" and "compulsory residence in a child and youth care centre".

[87] See generally Chapters 9 and 10 of the Act, ibid.

[88] Interview conducted by the author at Grahamstown, South Africa, 2015.

[89] Maepa, T., 'Magistrates' and Prosecutors' Views of Restorative Justice' (ISS Monograph, 2007). Available at http://www.iss.co.za/pubs/monograph/no111.htm. Accessed 23 June 2013.

[90] Ibid.

[91] Steyn, F., *Approaches to Diversion of Child Offenders in South Africa: A Comparative Analysis of Programme Theories* (Pretoria: University of the Free State, 2010).

diversionary measures provided in the Act have enhanced the effective rehabilitation of the child offenders. The Act also regulates the establishments of child and youth care centres[92] that are suitable for children in conflict with the law and "One-stop child justice centre"[93] for the administration of child justice. Also, the Act amends the minimum age of criminal capacity and provides for a new justice system for children that are in compliance with international and constitutional obligations placed upon South Africa.[94]

Aside from the provisions in the Criminal Procedure Act which have emphasised the application of this Act when it comes to matters relating to children, this Act appears to have extends its scope to accommodate most of the Criminal Procedure Act provisions. For instance, this Act provided for procedure for "determining the age of criminal responsibility",[95] "taking of plea in Child Justice Court"[96]; "those that may be present at the proceedings"[97]; "publication of information relating to the child"[98]; "appeals and automatic review of certain convictions and sentences"[99]; and "expunging of records of certain convictions and diversion orders".[100] Interestingly, the Act empowers the Child Justice Court to "postpone the proceedings" and await the compliance of the "diversion order" made against the child offender which can eventually "stop criminal proceedings" in its entirety after receipt of the "report from the probation officer of the child offender's compliance with the order".[101] The Child Justice Act entrenches important provisions in relation to parliamentary oversight. Section 96(3) of the Act provides that:

[92] See Section 76 of the Child Justice Act.

[93] See Section 89 of the Child Justice Act.

[94] Terblanche, S. S., 'The Child Justice Act: A Detailed Consideration of Section 68 as a Point of Departure with Respect to the Sentencing of Young Offenders' (2012), *Potchefstroom Electronic Law Journal*, 15(5). Available at http://www.scielo.org.za/scielo.php?script=sci_arttext&pid=S1727-37812012000500014#top4.

[95] See Chapter 2 of the Act, ibid.

[96] See generally Chapter 9 of the Act, ibid.

[97] Section 63(5) of the Act, ibid.

[98] See Section 63(6) of the Act, ibid.

[99] See generally Chapter 12 of the Act, ibid.

[100] See generally Chapter 13 of the Act, ibid.

[101] See Section 67 of the Act, ibid.

> The Cabinet member responsible for the administration of justice must, after consultation with the Cabinet members responsible for safety and security, correctional services, social development and health –
>
> (a) within one year after the commencement of this Act, submit reports to; Parliament, by each Department or institution referred to in section 94(2), on the implementation of this Act; and
> (b) every year thereafter submit those reports to Parliament.

Instructively, despite the commendable efforts on the Act, inadequate budgetary allocation has hindered its full implementation. In support of this assertion is the annual report by the Department: Justice and Constitutional Development Republic of South Africa on the implementation of Child Justice Act revealed that as at 2016, there is "no possibility of securing the necessary budget to construct more 'one stop child justice centres' for the administration of child justice".[102] This confirms the response of some of the respondents interviewed[103] by the author that "due to budgetary constraint, some Child Justice Courts are situated at the conventional courts' premises". Another challenge is in respect of shortage of expert personnel in the administration of child justice. For example, study has shown that as at 2012, only 30% of the children alleged to have committed an offence were assessed by the probation officer leaving 70% of them without enjoying the benefits of early intervention programmes.[104]

5 Children's Act 38 of 2005 (As Amended)

As noted earlier in Chapter 3 of this book, the Children's Act came in as a result of inadequate protection of the Black and street children under the Child Care Act 74 of 1983.[105] The Children's Act became

[102]The implementation of Child Justice Act consolidated annual report by the Department: Justice and Constitutional Development Republic of South Africa from 1 April 2015 to 31 March 2016. Available at http://www.justice.gov.za.cja-anr-2015-2016. Accessed 24 December 2018.

[103]Interviews conducted by the author at Cape Town and Grahamstown, 2015.

[104]See South Africa (Republic). National Prosecuting Authority, 2012. Annual Report 2011/2012. Available at http://www.npa.gov.za. Accessed 20 February 2013. See also, Badenhorst, C., "Second Year of the Child Justice Act's Implementation: Dwindling Numbers". Child Justice Alliance Research Report. The Child Justice Alliance, c/o The Children's Rights Project, Community Law Centre (University of the Western Cape).

[105]See Dawes, A., 'The South African Children's Act' (2009), *Journal of Child and Adolescent Health*, 30(10), iv–vi.

the comprehensive piece of legislation after South African's signatories and ratifications of the international and regional legal instruments especially the Convention on the Rights of the Child and the African Charter on the Rights and Welfare of the Child. It came in with the purpose of "affording children the necessary care, protection and assistance to ensure that they can develop to their full potential".[106] However, the enactment of this Act did not supersede the provisions of the 1996 Constitution particularly the "Bill of Rights", instead, the Act derives its status and legitimacy from the Constitution being the ***grund norm*** and "any right which the child has in terms of this Act supplement the right which a child has in terms of the 'Bill of Rights'".[107] The Act explicates the Constitution in its Chapter 1 that "Bill of Rights" "means the 'Bill of Rights' contained in Chapter 2 of the Constitution" and "child" "means a person under the age of 18 years".

The Act has 315 sections with 4 schedules and one of its cardinal objectives as "giving effect to the constitutional rights of the children such as 'the best interests'[108] of the child as paramount importance[109] in every matter'".[110] *Van Deiji v. Van Deiji*[111] gave credence to this position when the court in deciding on the best interests of the child has this to say:

> The interests of the minor means the welfare of the minor and the term welfare must be taken in its widest sense to include economic, social, moral and religious considerations. Emotional needs and the ties of affection must also be taken into account and in the case of older children their wishes in the matter cannot be ignored.

[106] See Department of Social Development: Consolidated Regulations Pertaining to the Children's Act, 2005. Government Gazette 33076, Government Printer, Pretoria (2010).

[107] See Section 8 of the Children's Act 35, 2005 (as amended).

[108] See Section 9 of the Children's Act, ibid.

[109] The Constitutional Court emphasised in *S v. M (Centre for Child Law as Amicus Curiae)* 2008 (3) SA 232 (CC) para. 25 at 249D that "the correct approach is to apply the 'paramountcy' principle in a meaningful way without unduly obliterating other valuable and constitutionally protected interests".

[110] See Section 2(b)(iv) of the Children's Act 35, 2005 (as amended).

[111] 1966 (4) SA 260 (R) at 261H. See also, *French v. French* 1971 (4) SA 298 (W) 298H; *Martens v. Martens* 1991 (4) SA 287 (T); *McCall v. MacCall* 1994 (3) SA 201(C) 205 B-G.

To supplement further, the provision of the Constitution under Section 34 is the provision of Section 14 when it echoes that "every child has the right to bring and to be assisted in bringing a matter to a court, provided that matter falls within the jurisdiction of that court". Although, the provision of Section 14(1) of the Act has taken the child's right a bit far by allowing the child to be "assisted".[112] The Act further gives details to the court as referred to when it provides in Section 42 that:

> ...every magistrate's court, as defined in the Magistrates' Court Act, 1994 (Act No. 32 of 1944), shall be a children's court and shall have jurisdiction on any matter arising from the application of this Act for the area of its jurisdiction.

This is a commendable provision which gives any matter relating to a child its importance and to be dealt with without any delay. "Every magistrate court" indicates "the court of the area in which the child involved in the matter is ordinarily resident[113]; or if more than one child is involved, it means the court of the area which any of those children is ordinarily resident".[114] In *Phillip v. Commissioner of Child Welfare, Bellville*[115] and *Gold v. Commissioner of Child Welfare, Durban*,[116] the court in construing the provision of Section 13(1) of the Child Care Act 74 of 1983 which is *pair material* with Section 44(1) of Children's Act defined "resident" to mean "the place where the child eats, drinks or sleeps or where his family eats, drinks or sleeps". This provision brings justice to the doorstep of any child in compares with what is obtainable in Nigeria where in most States of the federation of Nigeria, only one magistrate court situated at the city is designated to hear and determine the issue relating to children.[117]

[112] See Boezaat, T., and De Bruin, D. W., 'Section 14 of the Children's Act 38 of 2005 and the Child's Capacity to Litigate' (2011), *De Jure*, 416–438. See also, Boezaat, T., '*Law of Persons*' (2010), 87; and Boezaat, and De Bruin (2011), *De Jure*, 418–419, 422; *Legal Aid Board in re Four Children* (unreported, 512/10 [2011] ZASCA 39, 29 March 2011), para. 11.

[113] See Section 44(1)(a) of the Children's Act.

[114] See Section 44(1)(b) of the Children's Act.

[115] 1956 (2) SA 330 (C).

[116] 1978 (2) SA 301 (N).

[117] See Chapter 5 of this book for typical example.

The Act in essence makes special provision for the proceedings of children's court to be conducted in an informal atmosphere and as such, the court must under Section 42(8)(c) of the Act sit in "a room which as far as practicable: (c) not ordinarily used for the adjudication of criminal trials..."[118] It is the submission of the author that the underline emphasises if strictly adhered to in practice will protect the child from brutalisation and traumatisation that a child may be subjected to in court proceedings. This warrants the establishment of "one-stop child justice centres" under Section 89 of the Child Justice Act 75 of 2008 (as amended). However, the author observed that in all the nine provinces of South Africa, there are only three centres designated which cannot meet the full implementation of Section 42(8) stated thereof. This confirms the responses of some respondents in an interview that "some children's courts/child justice courts are situated within the conventional courts' premises".[119] It is undoubted that lack of adequate budgetary allocation[120] hinders the establishment of more centres for the adjudication of children's matter in a special room. The children's court serves as the civil jurisdiction for children's matters in South Africa. Basically, the Act deals with children in need of care and protection.[121] However, the provisions of Section 1(4) and 45(3) of the Act limit the jurisdiction of the children's court in respect of;

> any proceedings arising out of applications in terms of the Administration Amendment Act, 1929; the Divorce Act; the Maintenance Act; the Domestic Violence Act, 1998; the Recognition of Customary Marriages Act, 1998.
>
> Section 45(3)-
>
> Pending the establishment of family courts by an Act of Parliament, the High Courts and Divorce Courts have exclusive jurisdiction over the following matters contemplated in this Act:

[118]The underline is author's emphasis.

[119]Interviews conducted by the author at Cape Town and Grahamstown, 2015.

[120]The implementation of Child Justice Act consolidated annual report by the Department: Justice and Constitutional Development Republic of South Africa from 1 April 2015 to 31 March 2016. Available at http://www.justice.gov.za.cja-anr-2015-2016. Accessed 24 December 2018.

[121]See Section 45 and generally Chapter 9 of the Children's Act 38, 2005 (as amended).

(a) The guardianship of the child;
(b) the assignment, exercise, extension, restriction, suspension or termination of guardianship in respect of a child;
(c) artificial fertilisation;
(d) the departure, removal or abduction of a child from the Republic;
(e) application requiring the return of a child to the Republic from abroad;
(f) the age of majority or the contractual or legal capacity of a child;
(g) the safeguarding of a child's interest in property; and
(h) surrogate motherhood.

The above provisions show that the jurisdiction to hear and determine those matters fall within the exclusive jurisdiction of the High Courts.[122] Similarly, the author observes that the ordinary interpretation of the word "and" as construed under Section 150(1)(a) of the Act may conflict with the provisions of Sections 45 and 46 to show that all the three requirements under Section 150(1)(a) must be present before a child can be regarded to be in need of care and protection. For instance, this interpretation may hinder a child abandoned by his or her parents and who is placed in the care of his or her grandparent not to be regarded as a child in need of care and protection. However, whatever the case may be, the author argues in line with the decision of the South Gauteng High Court in the case of *SS v. Presiding Officer of the Children's Court, Krugersdrop and Another*[123] that in deciding whether or not a child is in need of care and protection, recourse must be made to the process stipulated in Part 2 of Chapter 9 of the Act and makes order to that effect.

Aside from the orders that children's court can make under Section 46 of the Act, it is also empowered under Sections 47 and 48 to make "referral of children for investigation when it appears that the child involved or affected is in need of care and protection" and also "order the social workers to investigate the child's matter". Additional powers under Section 48 include "interdicts and auxiliary relief". Interestingly, a children's court is enjoyed to "order a lay-forum hearing before it decides

[122] See Section 45(4) of the Children's Act. See also, *AD and Another v. DW and Others (Centre for Child Las as Amicus Curiae; Department for Social Development as Intervening Party)* 2008 (3) SA 183 (CC); *De Gree and Another v. Webb and Others (Centre for Child Law, University of Pretoria as Amicus Curiae)* 2006 (6) SA 51 (W); and *De Gree and Another v. Webb and Others (Centre for Child Law, University of Pretoria as Amicus Curiae)* 2007 (5) SA 185 (SCA).

[123] Unreported GSJ Case No. A3056/11, 29 August 2012, para. 19.

a matter"[124] to see if there will be an amicable settlement between the parties. The processes may be through "pre-hearing conferences", "family group conferences"; or other lay forum and settling of matters out of court' as provided under Sections 69–73 of the Act. The rationale for these provisions is to empower the court to take a constructive role in encouraging the parties to "engage with each other in a proactive and honest endeavour to find mutually acceptable solutions" and by engaging on this, it demonstrates the court's support for a "restorative approach to resolving disputes between parties".[125] However, the author observes that the renewal or extension of "the administration of foster grants" beyond two years through an application to the children's court for an order instead of dealing with the renewal/extension administratively as provided for under the earlier provision of Section 16(2) of the Child Care Act will create delay and systematic failure of the administration of child justice.[126] Surprisingly, the decision of the North Gauteng High Court in *Centre for Child Law v. Minister for Social Development and Others (supra)* has overturned the provision of the Act by allowing the extension to be made administratively. Therefore, this decision calls for amendment of the Children's Act to reflect the changes.

Instructively, the Act makes room for "rules of court",[127] compulsory "legal representation"[128] of the child, and those that may be in "attendance" at the child proceedings[129] and the mode of publication of information relating to the proceedings.[130] A child is enjoyed to adduce "evidence and cross-examine any witness"[131] which, is in line

[124] See Section 49 of the Children's Act.

[125] See *Elizabeth Municipality v. Various Occupiers* 2005 (1) SA 217 (CC); *S v. M (Centre for Child Law as Amicus Curiae)* 2008 (3) SA 232 (CC); *Dikko v. Mokhatla* 2006 (6) SA 235 (CC); *Le Roux and Others v. Dey (Freedom of Expression Institute and Restorative Justice Centre as Amici Curiae)* 2011 (3) SA 274 (CC); Sloth-Nielsen, J., and Gallinetti, J., 'Just Say Sorry? Ubuntu, Africanisation and the Child Justice System in the Child Justice Act 75 of 2008' (2011), *Potchefstroom Electronic Law Journal*, 14(4), 63.

[126] Case of *Centre for Child Law v. Minister for Social Development and Others* (unreported, GNP Case No. 21726/11) is apposite.

[127] See Section 52 of the Children's Act.

[128] Sections 54 and 55 of the Act, ibid.

[129] Sections 56 and 57 of the Act, ibid.

[130] Section 74 of the Act, ibid. See also, *Johncom Media Investments Ltd. v. M and Others (Media Monitoring Project as Amicus Curiae)* 2009 (4)(CC).

[131] Sections 58 and 59 of the Act, ibid.

with the principle of fair hearing enshrined under the "Bills of Rights". In essence, the conduct of the court proceedings is informal, and it is inquisitorial in nature[132] which avoids any technicality to be used if it will be inappropriately damaging the best interest of the child. The Act provides for "partial care",[133] "alternative care", "foster care",[134] "child and youth care centres"[135] and "drop-in centres"[136] which shall be examined in the next section of this chapter as the custodial institutions for the treatment of children.

6 Institutional Framework for Child Justice Administration in South Africa

It is pertinent to note that South African legislation on the rights of children equally makes substantial provisions for children's homes in contemplation of the best interest of the child principle. The rationale behind these provisions is the welfare of a child who because of his or her age might not have been capable of committing crime or if such a child is in need of care and protection. Such institutions include "Child Justice Court", "Children's Court"; "Child and Youth Care Centres"; "One-Stop Child Justice Centres"; "Drop-in Centres" and "Prison".

As noted in the previous sections of this chapter, Section 89 of the Child Justice Act provides for the establishment of "One-Stop Child Justice Centres" by "the Cabinet member responsible for the administration of justice in consultation with the Cabinet members responsible for social development, safety and security and correctional services". It is pertinent to note that this centre if established must with all intent and purposes contain "Child Justice Court", "Children's Court"; "Office of Probation officers"; "Office of Police Service" "Temporary facility to accommodate children pending conclusion of preliminary inquiry"; "Office for child's legal representative"; "Office for diversion and prevention services"; "Office for correctional services", etc.[137]

[132] Section 60 of the Act, ibid.

[133] See generally Chapter 5 of the Act, ibid.

[134] See generally Chapter 12 of the Act, ibid.

[135] See generally Chapter 13 of the Act, ibid.

[136] See generally Chapter 14 of the Act, ibid.

[137] See Section 89(4) of the Child Justice Act 75, 2008 (as amended).

The rationale is to attend to children's matters timeously without unnecessary delay and for the purpose of handling children's matters outside the conventional court premises in order to prevent the child from mingling with adults. Also, as noted earlier, "Child Justice Court" is specifically designed for children coming in contact with crime and it has criminal jurisdiction.[138] While "Children's Court" is specifically designated for children in need of care and protection and it has civil jurisdiction.[139] However, it has been shown in the previous section in this chapter that in all the nine provinces in South Africa, only three One-Stop Child Justice Centres have been established. They are situated at Nerna, Port Elizabeth in Eastern Cape, Mangaung in Free State and Matlosana, Klerksdorp in North West.[140] Nerina One-Stop Child Justice Centre was the first in history, and it has rooms for police, legal aid services, probation officer, two court rooms (one for preliminary inquiries and the other room for Child Justice Court), it also has a room for temporary detention.[141] In between 2015 and 2016, the centre recorded 693 preliminary inquiries. Two of the matters were transferred to children's court, 73 of the matters were diverted, 349 matters were transferred to the Child Justice Court, 60 matters were later withdrawn after completion of the children's diversion, and 209 were struck off the roll. In between 2015 and 2016, 285 matters were recorded of which 103 children matters were withdrawn, 3 were referred to the children's court, 100 were diverted and 80 were struck off the roll.[142] "The Mangaung One-Stop Child Justice Centre" is the second in the history, and it is situated at Bloemfontein in Free State. It was formally a "secure care centre" before converting it to One-Stop Child Justice Centre in 2010.

[138] See Preamble to the Child Justice Act, ibid.

[139] See Preamble to the Children's Act, ibid.

[140] The implementation of Child Justice Act consolidated annual report by the Department: Justice and Constitutional Development Republic of South Africa from 1 April 2015 to 31 March 2016. Available at http://www.justice.gov.za.cja-anr-2015-2016. Accessed 24 December 2018.

[141] Ibid.

[142] See the Nerina One-Stop Child Justice Centre, 2013/2014–2015/2016 reported in the implementation of Child Justice Act consolidated annual report from the Department: Justice and Constitutional Development Republic of South Africa from 1 April 2015 to 31 March 2016. Available at http://www.justice.gov.za.cja-anr-2015-2016. Accessed 24 December 2018.

The centre was the first in history to have a "Regional Court" which commenced its sitting in January 2016.[143]

Between 2015 and 2016, 629 preliminary inquiries were recorded. Children's court handled 5 matters while 453 children's matters were diverted and 176 matters were transferred to Child Justice Court, 436 matters were withdrawn after the children have successfully completed their diversion.[144] It is submitted that the withdrawal of the matter after successful completion of the diversion is in tandem with the provision of Section 67(2) of the Child Justice Act. Between the years 2015 and 2016, 176 matters were recorded of which 29 were guilty, 12 children were discharged and acquitted while 74 children's matters were withdrawn and 24 matters were stuck out the roll and 32 matters were diverted.[145] Matlosana is the third One-Stop Child Justice Centre which was established in 2013.[146] The building formerly belonged to the Department of Social Development before its conversion. It recorded 231 matters under preliminary inquiries of which 60 children were diverted and 109 children were transferred to the Child Justice Court between 2015 and 2016.[147] Further, 172 matters were recorded out of which 1 was postponed, 14 children were found guilty and 3 were discharged and acquitted. From the report, 34 matters were withdrawn, 2 were diverted and 10 were struck out the roll.[148]

[143] The implementation of Child Justice Act consolidated annual report by the Department: Justice and Constitutional Development Republic of South Africa from 1 April 2015 to 31 March 2016. Available at http://www.justice.gov.za.cja-anr-2015-2016. Accessed 24 December 2018.

[144] Ibid.

[145] See the Mangaung One-Stop Child Justice Centre, 2013/2014–2015/2016 reported in the implementation of Child Justice Act consolidated annual report from the Department: Justice and Constitutional Development Republic of South Africa from 1 April 2015 to 31 March 2016. Available at http://www.justice.gov.za.cja-anr-2015-2016. Accessed 24 December 2018.

[146] The implementation of Child Justice Act consolidated annual report by the Department: Justice and Constitutional Development Republic of South Africa from 1 April 2015 to 31 March 2016. Available at http://www.justice.gov.za.cja-anr-2015-2016. Accessed 24 December 2018.

[147] Ibid.

[148] See the Matlosana One-Stop Child Justice Centre, 2013/2014–2015/2016 reported in the implementation of Child Justice Act consolidated annual report from the Department: Justice and Constitutional Development Republic of South Africa from 1 April 2015 to 31 March 2016. Available at http://www.justice.gov.za.cja-anr-2015-2016. Accessed 24 December 2018.

Furthermore, Section 191 of the Children's Act established the "Child and Youth Care Centre". It is a residential facility established to care for children outside the child's facility. The minimum children must not be less than six children at the Child and Youth Care Centre. The centre is funded from the office of the "provincial department of social development"[149] for governmental and non-governmental Child and Youth Care Centre.[150] By Section 191(2) of the Children's Act, the centre "must offer a therapeutic programme designed for the residential care of the children". The centre is established purposely for child welfare such as children home, place of safety, secure care facility, school of industry and reform school. The centre must be managed and maintained in line with the Act, the environment must be safe, easily accessible to children and children properly registered for accountability.[151] It should be noted that this centre may be closed for violation of any provision of the Act or consequent upon cancellation of registration.[152]

Another custodial institution is "Foster Care"[153] which has the sole objective of protecting and nurturing a child, promote, and planning for unification of the child with his or her family.[154] According to South African Law Commission, "foster care" is "considered to be the preferred forms of substitute care for children who cannot remain with their biological families and who are not available for adoption". The placement of the child could be with a person who is either a "non-family member" or "a family member who is not the parent or guardian of the child" or "a cluster foster care scheme".

Another custodial institution is the "Drop-in Centres" provided under Chapter 14 of the Children's Act. It is a centre that manages children living on the street for the purpose of accessing food, healthcare services and recreational or educational programmes.[155] It is an open

[149] Section 193 of the Children's Act.

[150] See the South African Development Planning Evaluation and Research *Study into the funding of government subsidised children's homes* in South Africa (2004) Pretoria.

[151] See generally Chapter 13 of the Children's Act.

[152] Ibid.

[153] See generally Chapter 12 of the Act, ibid.

[154] Ibid.

[155] See Skelton, A. M., and Proudlock, P., 'Interpretation, Objects, Application and Implementation of the Children's Act', in C. J. Davel and A. M. Skelton (eds.), *Commentary on the Children's Act* (2014), 74. Available at http://www.jutalaw.co.za. Accessed 20 February 2015.

day facility, and it does not require the order of the court.[156] Prison is another custodial institution established under the Correctional Services Act No. 111 of 1998. Prison service was renamed as correctional services after the prison reforms in 1990.[157] By Section 5(1) of the Correction Services Act, the "minister is empower by notice in the Gazette to establish prisons for the detention and treatment of offenders in accordance with this Act". However, under the note 11.2.3 of the White Paper on Corrections, a child under the age of 14 years has no place in the correctional centres. This shows that the alternative sentencing measure put in place under the Child Justice Act and Children's Act must be complied with and in essence, it shows that the White Paper has encouraged the application of diversionary measures contemplated under the Child Justice Act and Children's Act. It is important to note that the cumulative effects of Chapter VI and Section 7(1)(c) of the Correctional Services Act indicate that children adjudged to be in conflict with the law must be placed under the "community corrections" wherever practicable but under the supervision of "correctional officer". If at all, they need to be in prison, the children "must be kept separate from adult prisoners and in accommodation appropriate to their age". This is in line with the provision of Section 28 in the Bill of Rights enshrined in the Constitution. It is, therefore, the author's submission that, to avoid prison being used as custodial institution for child offenders in South Africa, more alternative care facilities must be put in place by the South African government.

7 Conclusion

This chapter of the book examined the legislative efforts on the protection and promotion of children's rights before and after the promulgation of Child Justice Act and Children's Act. The chapter also analyses the structures of children's custodial institutions in the achievement of the primary objective of reintegration of child offender into the society. The chapter further appraises and interrogates the establishment of partial care facility, One-Stop Child Justice Centre, A drop-in

[156] Ibid.

[157] See White Paper on Corrections in South Africa (2005). Available at https://www.acjr.or.za. Accessed 10 November 2018.

Centre, Foster care centre, etc., as applicable in South Africa. From this exposition, the chapter observes that the objectives of the institutions are compromised by inadequate budgetary allocations.

References

Badenhorst, C., 'Second Year of the Child Justice Act's Implementation: Dwindling Numbers'. Child Justice Alliance Research Report. The Child Justice Alliance, c/o The Children's Rights Project, Community Law Centre (University of the Western Cape).

Boezaat, T., and De Bruin, D. W., 'Section 14 of the Children's Act 38 of 2005 and the Child's Capacity to Litigate' (2011a), *De Jure*, 416–438.

Boezaat, T., and De Bruin, D. W. (2011b), *De Jure*, 418–419.

Dawes, A., 'The South African Children's Act' (2009), *Journal of Child and Adolescent Health*, 30(10), iv–vi.

Maepa, T., 'Magistrates' and Prosecutors' Views of Restorative Justice' (ISS Monograph, 2007). Available at http://www.iss.co.za/pubs/monograph/no111.htm.

Skelton, A. M., and Proudlock, P., 'Interpretation, Objects, Application and Implementation of the Children's Act', in C. J. Davel and A. M. Skelton (eds.), *Commentary on the Children's Act* (2014), 74. Available at http://www.jutalaw.co.za.

Sloth-Nielsen, J., and Gallinetti, J., 'Just Say Sorry? Ubuntu, Africanisation and the Child Justice System in the Child Justice Act 75 of 2008' (2011), *Potchefstroom Electronic Law Journal*, 14(4), 63.

Steyn, F., *Approaches to Diversion of Child Offenders in South Africa: A Comparative Analysis of Programme Theories* (Pretoria: University of the Free State, 2010).

Terblanche, S. S., 'The Child Justice Act: A Detailed Consideration of Section 68 as a Point of Departure with Respect to the Sentencing of Young Offenders' (2012), *Potchefstroom Electronic Law Journal*, 15(5). Available at http://www.scielo.org.za/scielo.php?script=sci_arttext&pid=S1727-378120120005 00014#top4.

Van Zyl, 'Pre-trial Detention in South Africa: Trial and Error', in Van Kempen (ed.), *Pre-trial Detention: Human Rights, Criminal Procedural Law and Penitentiary Law, Comparative Law* (2012), 661.

CHAPTER 7

Reforming Child Justice Administration in Africa: Comparative Perspectives, Conclusion and the Way Forward

1 Introduction

The previous chapters have analysed the concept of child justice administration, the international legal regime of child justice administration and the legal framework for child justice administration in Nigeria and South Africa. It was shown that while Africa has a system of child justice administration in place, the same may not be adequate for the protection of the rights of African children. There are of course instructive laws in this area but the extents to which these laws have been stood up to the twenty-first-century challenges in child justice administration remain doubtful. Specifically, while there are established legal frameworks on child justice administration in African countries, there are still critical areas that need to be addressed to ensure a more cohesive child justice system which takes the interest of the child as paramount. Indeed, as stated in Chapter 1 of this book, "child justice is a critical aspect in the administration of criminal justice of any country".

From the foregoing, this chapter has two main objectives. First, an analysis has been carried out on the challenges of child justice system in Africa in general. In this regard, key challenges have been identified which cut across most countries in Africa however with Nigeria and South Africa as key focal points. The second objective of this chapter investigated the key reforms that can be carried out to enhance the child

© The Author(s) 2020
M. A. Abdulraheem-Mustapha,
Child Justice Administration in Africa,
https://doi.org/10.1007/978-3-030-19015-6_7

justice system in African countries. Certain themes were identified for reform and suggestions were made from a comparative perspective.

2 Challenges of Child Justice Administration in Africa

While most countries in Africa have one form of legal regime or another on child justice, the adequacy of the existing legal regime still remains questionable. There are many perspectives from which the legal framework issue can be a challenge to child justice. First, it has been observed that most African countries have child justice framework that is substantially influenced by colonialism. Most of these laws were adopted during the colonial era and continue to be applicable till today. For instance, as discussed in Chapter 5 of the book, Nigeria has two legislations on child justice system, and the first legislation has been in existence since the colonial era. This has some significant impact on the child justice system. This old colonial legislation has been observed to have laid more emphasis on confinement of child offenders in custodial institutions without any community-based options as against the international best practices.

Secondly, many African countries having signed and ratified the relevant international treaties quickly domesticate such treaties. However, most of these countries did not take any initiative to conduct a feasibility study on the full implementation of such treaties. For example, African countries, Nigeria and South Africa as case studies lack preventive mechanisms for child delinquency as Chapters 5 and 6 of this book have demonstrated the continuous increase in the rate of crimes committed by children in both countries. In addition, Chapters 3, 5 and 6 of this book show that there is no standardised child justice system procedures in Nigeria and South Africa as the author's fieldwork revealed non-uniformity in the implementation of the extant laws especially by the presiding officers. The chapters also demonstrated how family/juvenile/child justice/children's courts arbitrarily used the provisions of the Acts, and this can be seen from the sittings of these courts which are still sited within the conventional court premises. As Nigeria and South Africa adopted and domesticated Convention on the Rights of the Child and African Charter on the Rights and Welfare of the Child by the enactments of the Childs' Rights Act, 2003, Children's Act 35 of 2005 and Child Justice Act 78 of 2008, the author observes a disturbing trend on the application of the provisions of the Child Rights Act in Nigeria compare to South

Africa where her child justice regime is of universal application. Chapter 5 of this book has demonstrated this challenge when it was observed that not all States in Nigeria have adopted the Child Rights Act and this hampers the uniformity in the treatment of children generally. This challenge is further complicated by the fact that issue of children is culturally relative and therefore on the Concurrent Legislative List of the Nigerian Constitution. The Concurrent Legislative List contains matters which can only be legislated by the Federal and State government.[1] Thus, thirteen Nigerian States are yet to domesticate the Act and continue to use relevant provisions in the Criminal Code, Penal Code, Criminal Procedure Code, Criminal Procedure Act and the Children and Young Persons laws. Some of the laudable provisions of the Child Rights Act were not implemented in these States due to their refusal to domesticate the Act and those States that have domesticated the Act are yet to fully implement the provisions of the Act. Surprisingly, even if the Child Rights Act has been domesticated in all the States of the Federation, studies have shown that the Act is still inadequate to engender efficient child justice administration in Nigeria. For instance, the Act makes no provision for the expunging of criminal records of children adjudged to have committed an offence compare to South Africa child justice regime which has a laudable provision and laid down procedures to be followed under Section 87 of the Child Justice Act. In particular, Chapter 5 of this book has shown many situations where presumption of innocence of child offenders was not considered before the family courts and children were not legally represented especially in status offences, and most of the child offenders waived their right to be represented. More importantly, non-universal application of the Act allows for arbitrariness in its implementation from all the stakeholders. The prosecution and police arbitrarily assigned age to suspects in order to facilitate their prosecution. The implementation of the Act is further complicated by the fact that children are not specifically protected in the Constitution of the Federal Republic of Nigeria, 1999 which is the *grund norm* compare to the South African Constitution, 1996. Some of

[1] By Section 318 of the Constitution of the Federal Republic of Nigeria, 1999 (as amended), "Concurrent Legislative List" means "the list of matters set out in the first column in part II of the Second Schedule to this Constitution with respect to which the National Assembly and a House of Assembly may make laws to the extent prescribed, respectively, opposite thereto in the second column thereof". See first column in part II of the Second Schedule.

the provisions of the Act dealing with the rights of children such as "right to education" are not guaranteed and, thus, remain unenforceable in the law court due to its inclusion under Chapter II of the 1999 Constitution instead of Chapter IV of the Constitution. Notwithstanding the protection of the children's rights in the Child Rights Act, enforcement of such rights cannot solely be effectively achieved under the Act because in the hierarchy of Nigerian legislations, the Constitution is supreme[2] to any Act of the National Assembly. The author's argument is that, irrespective of the protection of children's rights under the Act, their enforceability can be enhanced if they are expressly provided in the Constitution. The author therefore calls for harmonisation of the existing legislation in the form of amendments to evolve a child justice system, humane and responsive and in line with what is obtainable in South Africa child justice regime. The author also calls for practical measures towards the implementation of the reform and that Nigeria should move beyond mere enactment of the law.

Thirdly, there are inconsistencies in the age of criminal responsibility in the various provisions on child justice in Africa as indicated in Appendix A of this book. Minimum age of criminal responsibility starts from 7 years, and only South Africa appears to have reviewed its minimum age of criminal responsibility to meet up with international standard of 12 years. The application of different laws in Nigeria makes it difficult to adopt a unified minimum age of criminal responsibility. Chapter 5 has demonstrated this position by analysing various provisions relating to criminal culpability under the Criminal and Penal Codes, Children and Young Persons Act/ Law and Child Rights Act. Surprisingly, the Child Rights Act which seems to have incorporated all existing legislation on issue of children generally has no minimum age and yardstick for determining the age of criminal culpability compare with South Africa child justice regime which has more elaborate systemic models and procedures for assessing the cognitive, moral, emotional, psychological and social development of a child in the determination of criminal culpability. It is the argument of the author that the South African procedures could influence the Nigerian response to child justice. The author observes another challenge of clear precision of what should be "the best interest of the child" as contemplated in the

[2]To give credence to the supremacy of the Constitution, Section 1(3) of the Constitution of the Federal Republic of Nigeria, 1999 (as amended) provides that "If any law is inconsistent with the provisions of this Constitution, this Constitution shall prevail, and that other law shall to the extent of the inconsistency be void".

Child Rights Act. There is lack of clear definition of "best interest of the child" unlike in South Africa child justice regime where "preliminary inquiry" is condition precedence in the determination of any case against the child. This challenge in Nigeria brings about different views expressed by many scholars where some places the burden of culpability for committed crimes on child offenders themselves, regardless of their age at the time of commission while some are of the view that parents should be held responsible for crimes committed by their children. In essence, the Act does not provide for a definitive concept of parental responsibility, and this challenge brings about different and conflicting interest on the determination of issues relating to children in Nigeria. Lack of clear definitive concept of "the best interest of the child" in the Act allows for non-applicability of diversionary measures in the determination of cases on children, and this challenge increases the number of children in custodial institutions. This challenge is further complicated with the fact that there is no adequate provisions for separate custodial facilities for children and young persons and the existing provisions of the Act were not implemented. Chapter 5 has shown the failure to create special police unit for children at the police force despite the enactment of the Child Rights Act and the adverse effect of mingling child suspect with adult or women in most of the Nigerian police stations. The chapter also demonstrated that the roles of custodial personnel were not well spelt out in the Act and as such child offenders are incarcerated in squalid prison yards as against international best practices. In like manner, for most African countries including Nigeria and South Africa, vulnerable children are more susceptible to poverty, stigmatisation and discrimination. These are probable causes of child delinquency as examined in Chapter 2 of this book.

Additionally, there is the problem of insufficient number of specially trained personnel in most of the child custodial institutions in Africa. Even in South Africa that has been argued to possess the best practice of child justice administration in the world, there is shortage of personnel in both the child justice and children's courts. For instance, in an interview by the author in Grahamstown in South Africa,[3] despite having two different courts, most of time, "Magistrate sitting at Child Justice Court is also saddled with the responsibility of sitting at Children's Court". Similarly in Nigeria, magistrate judges are saddled with the responsibility of sitting as

[3]Interview conducted in 2015.

magistrate for adult and children cases. More so, as discussed in Chapter 5 of this book, this challenge gets more complicated with limited numbers of family/juvenile courts and the fusion of their jurisdiction to hear and determine both civil and criminal cases compare with what is obtainable under the South Africa child justice regime where children's court is saddled with civil jurisdiction and child justice court hears criminal matters. Further discussion in Chapter 5 of this book shows that personnel at the Borstal institutions in Nigeria are drawn from pool of prison officers who are trained to deal with adult inmates, and in the similar manner, personnel of the police force are not skilled for diverting child offenders from formal criminal justice system. Also, most of the social workers at the social welfare department are not specialised in psychology or sociology as envisaged by the Child Rights Act. Attitudinal problem of social workers is a challenge not only for Nigeria but also for South Africa as discussed in Chapter 3 of this book. This situation gets more complicated due to the weakness of the child justice system as there is lack of comprehensive legal solutions for implementation of the laws, and this hinders the effective performance of the social workers. Most of the African countries with the exception of South Africa alone have not put in place diversionary measure as contemplated by the Convention on the Rights of the Child.

Further still, there is inadequate budgetary allocation by the government on the administration of child justice in Nigeria and South Africa. Examples can be found from series of unreasonable delays of trials which calls for investigation by reviewing courts in South Africa. For instance, reports from the Department of Correctional Services and the Department of Justice in *S v. Motsasi*[4] and *S v. Motsasi en andere*[5] revealed that the departments concerned "did not have the financial resources to address, in the proper manner, the matters in the earlier judgment". As discussed and shown by relevant statistics in Chapter 5 of this book, Nigeria child justice administration is also bedeviled with inadequate budgetary allocation which hinders effective performance of the relevant institutions in the administration of child justice. More importantly is the lack of facility for girls in the custodial institutions. For instance, Borstal institution which has been effectively ranked first in the hierarchy of custodial institutions is limited in numbers and basically for boys and also has no facility for children below the age of sixteen years.

[4] 1998 (2) SACR 35 (W).

[5] 2000 (1) SACR 574 (W).

3 Prospects for Reforms of Child Justice Administration in Africa

Child justice is a unique system of justice. It involves having not only specialist in handling children but also special system. All these mean that sufficient attention must be devoted to this unique system. It must be taken as an issue of priority by the government to make for a successful regime. Prioritising child justice system will involve the setting aside of resources to make the system work. More importantly, there is need for constitutional recognition of the special system for child justice administration. The South African example in this connection is quite commendable. This is because the Constitution of South Africa, 1996 makes eloquent provisions on the child justice system in its Bill of Rights under Chapter 2 as analysed in Chapter 6 of this book. The implication of this is that child justice administration in South Africa has a constitutional status. Some other African countries, such as Ghana, Kenya, Rwanda, Uganda, etc., also contain provisions in their Bill of Rights on child justice administration. It is suggested that other African countries such as Nigeria that has no such specific provisions in their Constitutions should make child justice administration a constitutional matter. As matter of urgency, there is need for mandatory legal representation in all matters relating to children in Nigeria be it capital or minor offence.

In addition to the above, there is need for the amendment of some African countries' child justice legislation to conform to international standards. In the first instance, the minimum age for criminal liability should be reviewed to 12 years as contemplated by the Convention on the Rights of the Child. South Africa stands out in this respect, and it is recommended that other African countries such as Nigeria should follow this example. Secondly, the diversionary measures provided in almost all African legislations have not been implemented in countries such as Nigeria. The exception is South Africa which has put in place community services as informal custodial measures especially for children in need of care and protection. Another laudable provision in the South African Child Justice Act is that for expunging the record of children who have been convicted from the central criminal record. This constitutes a good example for countries such as Nigeria that have no similar provision.

As noted above, all African countries lack sufficient budgetary allocation for child justice administration. For example, as analysed in Chapter 5 of this book, there is no special police unit as provided for in the Nigerian Child Rights Act in Nigeria. Family/juvenile courts are still sited within the conventional court premises. Out of the 36 States of the Nigerian Federation, only Lagos State has more than one designated magistrate court for children matters. Again, out of 16 local government areas in Kwara State, only one magistrate court is designated as family court in the State capital of Ilorin. Similarly, the Borstal institutions that have been ranked first in the effectiveness of custodial institutions in Nigeria are limited in number and purposefully cater for children that are boys only as against what is obtainable in South Africa. However, as analysed in Chapter 6 of this book, even in South Africa, most of the children's and child justice courts are sited within the conventional courts. This situation needs to change because the special nature of child justice administration as variously noted in this book requires a departure from the conventional styled courts.

4 Conclusion

This book examined child justice administration in Africa while using Nigeria and South Africa as case studies. The book began with the general background and conceptualisation of childhood and how the concept evolved in Africa. The book observed that different definitions were ascribed to the meaning of the term "child" and the minimum age at which a child can be alleged to be in conflict with the law or in need of care and protection. In particular, Nigeria and South Africa as case studies respectively of developing and transitioning countries in Africa have no uniform definition of a child and when the status of child terminates. The book makes suggestions on how to determine the status of a child that is alleged to have been in conflict with the law or in need of care and protection. The historical analysis of child justice administration in Africa as well as the various theoretical positions and approaches indicates to have been adopted in the explanation of child delinquency in this book.

The findings in this book show that child delinquency in majority of African countries such Nigeria and South Africa sprang from sociological theory. The theoretical approaches adopted therefore suggested that child delinquency is better explained in the context of failure of the child justice administration in Africa. Recourse was made to some African countries in order to determine the strength and weakness of the reforms made after the countries' ratifications of the international and regional legal instruments.

The findings show that there are substantial provisions of law on child justice administration in Africa especially in the Constitutions of some African countries. However, their implementation continues to be problematic due to many challenges identified in the course of the author's field survey such as inadequate budgetary allocations, lack of awareness and lack of well-trained personnel in the administration of child justice to mention but a few. In investigating the implications of the non-implementation of the existing laws on child justice system, particularly in Nigeria and South Africa, the main question for this book was whether the legal and institutional frameworks on child justice system adequately safeguard the rights of the child offenders in Africa? And if not, how can the rights of the children that have been alleged to have committed offences are adequately protected? From the findings, South Africa appears to be more proactive in its implementations in comparison to Nigeria. Thus, the book drew some insights from the South African legal regime to be used in Nigeria as well as in some of the African countries that require some fast tracks in their implementation processes.

The aim and objectives of the book have been achieved through:

i. The examination of the various relevant legal and institutional frameworks; the NGOs research reports; the Nigerian and South African Constitutions; international legal instruments and conventions; government publications and reports; courts pronouncements and decided cases; and some statutory provisions and regulations in respect of the rights of child offenders within the child justice administration in Nigeria and South Africa.
ii. Questionnaires and interviews with the police, probation officers, social workers/welfare officers, prisons/correctional officers, judiciary, remand homes, legislatures, legal practitioners, parents, non-governmental organisations and community leaders in the cities of Bauchi, Enugu, Ilorin, Kaduna, Lagos and Port Harcourt (Nigeria), and Grahamstown, Cape Town, and Pretoria (South Africa) containing information on the child justice administration in Nigeria and South Africa. The data gathered were critically examined, reviewed and analysed.

From the analysis of the foregoing legal and institutional frameworks on the rights of the child, it is imperative to stress that every child alleged as, or accused of, having infringed the penal law has the rights guaranteed under those provisions. It can be concluded from the challenges associated with the stages of child justice administration that the system of child proceedings in Nigeria has not been aligned with the Child Rights Act, which accords special treatment for the child. The book noted the achievements as well as key gaps in the enforcement of child protection laws and contends that lack of enforceability of the laws make vulnerable children to be more susceptible to stigmatisation and discrimination. In view of the analysis of the development in the international instruments on the rights of the child, the book made some recommendations by way of reforms in this chapter towards maintaining the rights of the child beyond what was currently obtainable in Nigeria and South Africa in order to evolve a child justice system regime that will be humane and responsive in future.

5 Way Forward

There is the need for further empirical research to understand the court and the legal practitioners' perspectives on why child offenders have not been represented in the family courts in Nigeria for status offences. This book analysed the legal and institutional frameworks for child justice administration in Nigeria and South Africa by administering questionnaire and conducting interviews with some stakeholders. It would be desirable if future studies to interview children in the custodial institutions in Nigeria and South Africa. More importantly, if the children at the alternative care facilities in South Africa are interviewed in order to ascertain the level of performance of those facilities in the rehabilitation and reintegration of those children into the society. In so doing, Nigeria could have leverage on the South African models on the diversionary measures adopted. In this book, findings have shown that Nigeria is yet to implement the diversionary measures indicated in the Child Rights Act.

Finally, a more comprehensive process of legislative reform is required in Nigeria to ensure that vulnerable children's rights are systematically addressed in national laws and policies for a coherent consolidated children's legislation. This process has been initiated in some States in the Federation, but in some other States, it is either very slow or yet to begin. Where there is adequate legislation and policy in place like what is obtainable in South Africa, there remains a clear gap between this and implementation on the ground such as inadequate budgetary allocation.

Appendix A

Below is a table which shows the official age of criminal responsibility ranging from eight to eighteen years in countries round the world.

© The Editor(s) (if applicable) and The Author(s), under exclusive license to Springer Nature Switzerland AG 2020

M. A. Abdulraheem-Mustapha,
Child Justice Administration in Africa,
https://doi.org/10.1007/978-3-030-19015-6

8	9	10	11	12	13	14	15	16	17	18
Australia	Australia	Ethiopia	Australia: Most States	Turkey	Canada	Algeria	Armenia	Czech Republic	Argentina	Colombia
Tasmania	ACT	Iraq	Fiji		Dominican Republic	Benin	Austria	Denmark	Andorra	Ecuador
Bangladesh	Kenya	Malta	Nepal			Bosnia and Herzegovina	Azerbaijan	Finland	Belarus	Guinea
Barbados	Saint Kitts and Nevis	Oman	New Zealand		Greece	Burkina	Bulgaria	Lao PDR	Belgium	Venezuela
Belize	Saint Vincent and the Grenadines	Philippines	Saudi Arabia		Guatemala	Faso	DPR of Korea	Norway	Bolivia	
Egypt	Sri Lanka		Sierra Leone		Honduras	Burundi	Georgia	Peru	Cape Verde	
Gambia	UK:		Suriname		Israel	Central African Rep.	Germany	Slovakia	Chile	
Ghana	Scotland		UK (Isle of Man)		Jamaica		Hungary	Sudan	Cuba	
Grenada			UK (O.T.)		Morocco	Chad	Japan	Sweden	DR of the Congo	
India			Vanuatu		Netherlands	Comoros	Kyrgyzstan		Guinea-Bissau	
Ireland					Netherlands	Djibouti	Latvia		Micronesia - Fed States	
Jordan					Antilles	Gabon	Liechtenstein		Mozambique	
Kuwait					Peru	Croatia	Lithuania		Portugal	
Lebanon					Spain	Italy	Mauritius		Portugal	
Lesotho					Uganda	Mali	Paraguay			
Libyan Arab Jamahiriva						Monaco	Rep. of Moldova			

8	9	10	11	12	13	14	15	16	17	18
Malawi						Nicaragua	Russian Federation			
Maldives						Niger	Rwanda			
Myanmar						Romania	Slovenia			
Namibia						Serbia and Monten.	Viet Nam			
Nigeria						Slovenia	FYR Macedonia			
Qatar						Togo				
Pakistan						Tunisia				
South Africa						Uzbekistan				
Sudan										
Switzerland										
Syria										
Thailand										
Trinidad and Tobago										
Uganda										
United Arab Emirates										
Yemen										
Zimbabwe										

Countries with no stated minimum age include: Bahrain, Cambodia, Luxembourg, Mauritania, Mexico, Poland and Togo

Sources UNICEF and Melchiorre 2002 in 'Juvenile Justice: Modern Concepts of Working with Children in Conflict with the Law' (Save the Children UK). Available at www.crin.org/docs/savejjmodern_concepts.pdf-similar. Accessed on 20 December 2010

Appendix B

Department of Public Law,
Faculty of Law,
University of Ilorin,
Ilorin, Kwara State

Dear Respondent,

Questionnaire

This questionnaire is designed to elicit information on "**Child Justice Administration in Africa**". However, your responses must be limited to your area of residence (e.g. Bauchi, Enugu, Ilorin, Kaduna, Lagos or Port Harcourt).

Please note that information given shall be treated as confidential. Your cooperation is highly solicited in filling the questionnaire. In order to maintain anonymity and confidentiality, personal identification is not required in the questionnaire. Kindly supply the information as accurately as possible.

Thank you for your anticipated cooperation.

Yours faithfully,

Abdulraheem-Mustapha, Mariam A. (Ph.D.)

© The Editor(s) (if applicable) and The Author(s), under exclusive license to Springer Nature Switzerland AG 2020

M. A. Abdulraheem-Mustapha,
Child Justice Administration in Africa,
https://doi.org/10.1007/978-3-030-19015-6

INSTRUCTIONS

(1) Where you come across boxes tick (√) the appropriate one.
(2) Carefully read before responding to the questions.
(3) Categories of the respondents are: Police, Judiciary, Delinquent Home officer Legal Practitioners/Legislatures and others.
(4) Please ignore Type B if you are not within the category of respondents in paragraph 4(a-e) of the questionnaire.

GENERAL INFORMATION

Socio-Demographic Characteristics

1. Sex:
a. Male ( ) b. Female ( )

2. Age:
a. 18-45 years ( ) b. 46-65 years ( ) c. 66 years and above ( )

3. Marital Status
a. Married ( ) b. Single ( ) c. Others Specify............

4. Occupation/Profession
a. Police ( ) b. Prison officer ( )
c. Delinquent Home officer ( ) d. Judiciary ( )
e. Legal Practitioners/Legislatures f. Others Specify...............................

5. Educational Qualification(s)
a. No formal education ( ) b. Primary School ( )
c. Post Primary Education (Secondary) ( ) d. Tertiary Education ( )

6. Religious Affiliation
a. Christianity ( ) b. Islam ( ) c. Traditional Religion ( )
d. Others ( )

7. State of Origin..

8. In which city are you residing presently?
a. Bauchi ( ) b. Enugu ( ) c. Ilorin ( )
d. Kaduna ( ) e. Lagos ( ) f. Port Harcourt ( )

9. For how long have you been residing in the city?..................

Type A

Juvenile Justice Administration in Nigeria

S/No.	Items	Good	Poor	Undecided
1	How would you rate the effectiveness of the police in juvenile justice administration in Nigeria?			
2	How would you rate the effectiveness of the Nigerian judiciary in administration juvenile justice?			
3	How would you rate the effectiveness of the juvenile custodial institutions in juvenile justice administration in Nigeria?			
4	In your assessment, rate the effectiveness of the following institutions in the juvenile justice administration in Nigeria. (a) Remand Home (b) Borstal Institution (c) Government Approved Schools (d) Police cell (e) Prison			

Tick (✓) the column in the options provided. Strongly Agree (SA), Agree (A), Strongly Disagree (SD), Disagree (D) and Undecided (UD).

S/No.	Items	SA	A	SD	D	UD
5	Do you agree that prison should be used as a substitute for custody of juvenile in places where there is no Borstal institution in Nigeria?					
6	Do you agree that juvenile custodial institutions in Nigeria achieve the desire objectives of correctional measures in the performance of their mandate, such as rehabilitation and reformation of juvenile offenders?					
7	Do you agree that there is enough commitment by government in respect of juvenile justice administration in Nigeria such as provision of adequate funding and personnel?					

S/No.	Items	SA	A	SD	D	UD
8	Are juveniles protected against maltreatment under the Nigerian Juvenile Justice Administration?					
9	Are there adequate educational and vocational programmes in Nigerian custodial institutions?					
10	Are the juveniles who are in conflict with the law in Nigeria subjected to long detention without trial?					
11	Are the juveniles in detention separated from adult prisoners?					

Causes of Juvenile Delinquency in Nigeria

S/No.	Items	SA	A	SD	D	UD
12	Inferiority complex make some children to engage in juvenile delinquency					
13	The exposition of children to different types of foreign films and other materials with immoral and violent contents aggravates criminal tendency among children					
14	Poor socio-economic background may lead children to commit delinquency					
15	Laxity on the part of parents/guardian in child upbringing may leads to development of criminal tendencies among youths (e.g. poor parenting)					
16	Lack of equal opportunities for social and emotional adjustments may leads to juvenile delinquency					
17	Peer group influence contributes to the involvement of children/youths in juvenile delinquency					
18	Drug addiction and abuse have the tendency for children involvement in juvenile delinquency					
19	Child abuse may make children vulnerable to juvenile delinquency					
20	Children from single parenthood are prone to juvenile delinquency					
21	Domestic violence may leads to delinquency					

Control of Juvenile Delinquency

S/No.	Items	SA	A	SD	D	UD
22	Enactment of relevant laws and policy regulations would control the excesses of youth involvement in juvenile delinquency					
23	Appropriate control and censorship of mass media and illegal contents would reduce youth exposure to juvenile delinquency					
24	National orientation on ethical standard of behaviour would help the youth not to be involved juvenile delinquency					
25	The use of children remand homes would provide corrective measures to control juvenile delinquency					
26	Crime control through policing and tracking of delinquent youth would help to instil discipline on the youth					
27	Exposure of youth to discipline in rehabilitation centres would curb juvenile delinquency					
28	Establishment of juvenile court outside the conventional courts environment would prevent the mingling of youth offenders with adult criminals					
29	Enlightenment programmes for youth and children on the benefits of good behaviour would reduce juvenile delinquency					
30	Coordinated efforts by parents and schools in instilling discipline would minimize juvenile delinquency					
31	Adequate funding of the of juvenile justice institutions would have positive impact on juvenile justice administration in Nigeria					
32	Family and society most often accept juvenile after discharge from sentence, detention or committal					

Type B

Specific Professional Information on Juvenile Justice Administration in Nigeria

S/No.	Items	Good	Poor	Undecided
1	How would you rate juvenile justice administration in Nigeria?			

Tick (✓) the column in the options provided. Strongly Agree (SA), Agree (A), Strongly Disagree (SD), Disagree (D) and Undecided (UD).

S/No.	Items	SA	A	SD	D	UD
2	Do you agree that the enactment of Child Right Act is adequate for juvenile justice administration in Nigeria?					
3	Do you agree that Child Right Act adequately provide for effective juvenile justice administration in Nigeria?					
4	Do you agree that the refusal to enact Child Right Law by some states in Nigeria will adversely affect juvenile justice administration in those states?					
5	Do you agree that the enactment and implementation of Child Right Law by some states will improve juvenile justice administration in Nigeria?					
6	Do you agree that the existing legal measures to regulate juvenile justice administration in Nigeria are adequate?					
7	Do you agree that juvenile justice administration in Nigeria respect the rights of the child offender to fair trial in Nigeria?					
8	Do you agree that the existing laws and policies deal with the personnel, funding and structures of the Nigerian juvenile custodial institutions are adequate?					
9	Are the rights of child offenders to separate court and to the exclusion of the public during trials is adequately protected under the Nigerian juvenile justice system?					

S/No.	Items	SA	A	SD	D	UD
10	Is the constitutional presumption of innocence considered by Nigerian courts in the trial of juvenile offenders?					
11	Are juveniles protected against involuntary confession during plea taking?					
12	Are the juvenile institutions adequately funded?					
13	Are there children cells in police station in Nigeria?					
14	Do juveniles in correctional homes and prisons entitled to parents/family visitation?					

Laws and Policies on the Rights of the Child in Nigeria

S/No.	Items	SA	A	SD	D	UD
15.	Are laws and policies on the rights of the child in Nigeria adequate to address juvenile offences?					
16.	Are laws and policies on the rights of the child adequate to address the role of police in juvenile justice administration?					
17.	Are roles and functions of the Nigerian Prison service well spelled out in the laws and policies in juvenile justice administration?					
18.	Are the responsibilities of rehabilitation/correctional homes are fully provided in the Laws and policies on the rights of the child?					
19	Are there sufficient budgetary allocations for the juvenile justice administration in Nigeria?					
20.	Is observance of the rights of the child likely to control juvenile delinquency?					
21.	Are laws and policies on the rights of the child curb the excesses of juvenile offences?					
22.	Are the laws and the policies provide for mass media reporting of juvenile offences?					

Note The interview in Nigeria and South Africa was drawn and reframed from the questionnaire in Appendix B.

Index

© The Editor(s) (if applicable) and The Author(s), under exclusive license to Springer Nature Switzerland AG 2020

M. A. Abdulraheem-Mustapha,
Child Justice Administration in Africa,
https://doi.org/10.1007/978-3-030-19015-6

FSC
www.fsc.org
MIX
Papier | Fördert gute Waldnutzung
FSC® C083411

Kolibri 360 GmbH
Ferdinand-Jühlke-Straße 7
99095 Erfurt, Deutschland
produktsicherheit@kolibri360.de